Analysing Women's Imprisonment

Analysing Women's Imprisonment

Pat Carlen and Anne Worrall

WILLAN
PUBLISHING

Published by

Willan Publishing
Culmcott House
Mill Street, Uffculme
Cullompton, Devon
EX15 3AT, UK
Tel: +44(0)1884 840337
Fax: +44(0)1884 840251
e-mail: info@willanpublishing.co.uk

Published simultaneously in the USA and Canada by

Willan Publishing
c/o ISBS, 5824 N.E. Hassalo St,
Portland, Oregon 97213-3644, USA
Tel: +001(0)503 287 3093
Fax: +001(0)503 280 8832

First published 2004

ISBN 1-84392-069-7 (paperback)
ISBN 1-84392-070-0 (hardback)

British Library Cataloguing-in-Publication Data

A catalogue record for this book is available from the British Library.

Project management by Deer Park Productions, Tavistock, Devon
Typeset by GCS, Leighton Buzzard, Beds.
Printed and bound by T.J. International Ltd., Padstow, Cornwall

Contents

Introduction

I did not stir, I stood waiting in the middle of the cell, I listened, my ears were filled with the shutting of the cell door: I shall never forget it. I took another step and was up against the cell wall … then I set about measuring the distance between the other two walls, I went back again to the middle of the cell, then to the left up to the wall … this was the cell, they had assigned it to me, and I was busy taking possession of it, taking possession of it.

(Bienek 1950, in Davies 1990: 61)

Once you get into prison you have to become an automaton, ultimately, in order to survive. Have you ever read *Lord of the Rings*? In it there's something called the Land of Mordor, the Dark Lord. And there's a magic ring, and whoever has the magic ring on can vanish physically, but those who are in the domain of the Dark Lord, the Vaders, can see you. That's what the prison system is. You actually have to obliterate your own self in order to preserve it. But they can see you.

(Claire, aged 37, England 1997, in Carlen 1998)

I thought how unpleasant it is to be locked out; and I thought how it is worse perhaps to be locked in.

(Virginia Woolf 1929)

Relatively few women commit crime. Even fewer go to prison. Why, then, a separate text on women's imprisonment? Three main reasons: first, because the rapid increases in women's prison populations which have occurred in England and Wales and jurisdictions around the world from the beginning of the 1990s have occasioned an acceleration of interest in women's crimes and the social control of women; second, because research indicates that women's experience of the criminal courts, as well as of imprisonment itself, is very different to men's; and third, because an understanding of women's imprisonment can significantly inform understanding of prison issues in general and the historical and contemporary politics of gender and penal justice in particular.

What are women's prisons for? What are they like? Why are lone mothers, ethnic minority and very poor women disproportionately represented in women's prison populations? Should babies be sent to prison with their mothers? Why have recent attempts to reduce the numbers of women in custody repeatedly failed? Can knowledge of women's imprisonment be better informed by the various theories, research studies, philosophies of punishment and cultural analyses which demonstrate the decisive impact on penal affairs of economic and political change? Do feminists have anything important to say on these issues? Who cares?

This introductory text has been written to guide students of penology – lay, undergraduate and postgraduate – carefully through the main historical and contemporary discourses on women's imprisonment. Each chapter, with its clear themes, 'concepts to know', recommendations for further reading, topics for discussion and essay questions, has also been designed to help students prepare confidently for seminars, course assignments, examinations and project work. The extensive and up-to-date References and Further reading section at the end, together with lists of the postal and web addresses of all the main statutory agencies and voluntary organisations with which the researcher on women's imprisonment will need to be familiar, is designed to relieve some of the burdens of busy undergraduate and postgraduate supervisors, while the 'topics' for discussion likewise aim to provide immediate questions for debate in student discussion groups and seminars.

Chapter 1 examines the various histories of women's imprisonment, indicating their continuities, silences and contradictions, and showing how they have been shaped within ever-changing ideologies of gender and punishment. Chapter 2 then presents the contemporary facts about women's imprisonment, as presented in official statistics and official and unofficial reports. In this chapter readers will find out which women go to prison and for what offences, and, equally important, what happens to them as they proceed through the criminal justice and penal systems. Chapter 3 discusses the main contemporary issues raised by women's penal incarceration, while Chapters 4, 5 and 6 are the book's main theoretical chapters, outlining and discussing both mainstream and feminist approaches to women's imprisonment and theorizing the non-custodial alternatives. Finally, in Chapter 7, the authors speak very directly to readers as they outline and discuss, on the basis of their own experiences over many years, some of the main practical and ethical issues likely to confront new researchers in the area.

We should at the outset declare the domain assumptions and values of the authors. Basically, we both believe that imprisonment should be used much less frequently as a punishment for lawbreaking and, given the types of crimes which women in prison have most frequently committed, we believe that a reduction in the women's prison population would be especially appropriate. However, we also believe that, while prisons exist, the more that can be understood about what goes on behind the walls, and why women's imprisonment takes the form it does, the more will be understood about social relationships and how they impact on state punishment.

Chapter 1

Histories of women's imprisonment

Introduction

There are as many histories of women's imprisonment as there have been women in prison and no single textbook can claim to do justice to any one of them. Yet even within the composite story of women's imprisonment in England which we choose to give in this chapter, there are glimpses of several different histories. To attempt an understanding of women's imprisonment as we know it today, therefore, we have to contemplate the ebb and flow of penal politics in ages past, and become familiar with the seemingly circular, but usually asymmetrical, movements of ever-changing and inter-related modes of state and penal governance both nationally and globally. Presentation of contemporary penality's constitutive practices and ideologies – such as prison medicine, prison administration, competing conceptions of welfare and risk, penology and discourses of womanhood and femininity – is, furthermore, not made any easier by the constant evolution and transformation of the penal discourses within which those practices and ideologies are known. Instead of trying to depict a linear history of penal events and policies, the presentational techniques employed in this book will deliberately endeavour to picture the discontinuities, contradictions, fragmentation and transformations in women's imprisonment as they have been inscribed within state penality and popular consciousness. Let us therefore begin as we intend to go on, and start with the history of a major contradiction, one that has run through much penal discourse about women who break the law – the contradictory notion that women criminals are both women and not women (see Worrall 1990).

The first anomaly we describe in relation to women's imprisonment stems from the observation that although women in prison have always been treated primarily as prisoners, and then often as if they are *male* prisoners, their prison regimes have, at the same time, also been shaped by some of the most repressive, discriminatory and usually outdated ideologies of womanhood and femininity that have been prevalent in society at large. As a consequence of the prevalence, dominance and persistence of the social stereotypes which represent criminal women as being unnatural perversions of normal femininity, at least three separate, ideological strands concerning the nature of womanhood in general and 'criminal womanhood' in particular can be identified in the discourses of prison administrators and reformers who together have shaped women's imprisonment over the centuries:

1. The notion that as lawbreaking is most naturally a male activity, women who commit crime are doubly deviant, offending against both the law and their womanhood: they are bad citizens and unnatural women.

2. A recurrent pathologising and medicalisation of female inmates who, for one reason or another, have been seen to be less physically and mentally robust than male prisoners.

3. A continuing social welfare anxiety about the role of women in the family and society, and the extent to which prisons can, through their regimes and programmes, limit the damage done to women prisoners, their families and the society to which, sooner or later, most will return.

In short, the regimes of women prisoners, though subject to the general plethora of prison rules and security regulations, have been routinely fashioned by a mixture of ideologies of womanhood which portray women criminals as masculine, mad, menopausal and maladjusted to their roles in the family and labour market. Consequently, women in prison have not only been physically secured by all the hardware and disciplinary control paraphernalia of the men's establishments, they have, in addition, been psychologically interpellated (if not always constrained) by the triple disciplines of feminisation, domesticisation and medicalisation (see Smith 1962; Carlen 1983; Dobash et al., 1986).

The first objective of this chapter is to show why women's imprisonment in England takes the form it does, by demonstrating how the three historically-recurring strands of penal governance – feminisation, domesticisation and medicalisation – have contributed to the many and mixed meanings of women's imprisonment today. Other ideologies, discourses and modes of governance – such as changing conceptions of risk, welfare and punishment – have also made their mark, and these, too, will be considered towards the end of the chapter. However, before examining the making of women's imprisonment as we know it at the beginning of the twenty-first century, let us now look at the birth of the modern prison for women; and, also, at the modernising technologies of bureaucratised discipline which were, eventually, almost completely to supersede the corporal punishments of the pre-modern period.

The modernisers

Prior to the seventeenth century, women and men tended to be punished primarily by public shaming and bodily pain such as branding, whipping, mutilation, and a variety of horrible and long drawn-out deaths by burning, strangulation, hanging, beheading and even slower and more gruesome techniques of mutilation unto death. Women from wealthier families could be effectively confined in nunneries if their relatives refused to maintain them, while women from other classes were vulnerable to punishments meted out by both church and secular authorities. Two notorious punishments especially designed for women deemed to be 'common scolds' were the ducking stool and the painful 'scold's bridle' (see Dobash et al., 1986: 19). Gradually, however, these bodily punishments gave way to those of the modernisers.

Unlike their forebears, the penal administrators of nascent capitalism were less interested in attempting general deterrence through spectacular and fear-inducing public punishments, and more interested in using punishments productively – to instill habits of industry and self-control in the workforce. Nonetheless, and as Dobash et al., (1986: 23) point out, 'the newer mechanisms of systematic confinement did not supplant older forms of punishment and authority, but added them to the power of individual patriarchs and to the older public forms of punishment of the body'.

Modern approaches to punishment are usually portrayed as being more rooted in economically rational approaches to crime reduction than in the gut responses of pre-modern, retributivist and deterrent punishments. However, it is likely that (in addition to actual crime victimisation) fear of the stranger, the unknown and the deviant has always provoked reactions to crime which, in individuals at least, comprise a vengeful mixture of anger, hatred and helplessness. Modern governments have perennially been reminded by media and mob of the electoral saliency of such a potent mix. Certainly the more symbolic forms of punishment, such as the stocks and the pillory, were used in England right up to the end of the eighteenth century (Dobash et al., 1986: 18); and, with the advantage of hindsight we now know that the emotional, fearful, vengeful and spectacularly shaming responses which modernism taught us to think of as primitive and irrational were to have a widespread social renaissance during the economic uncertainties at the end of the twentieth century (see Pratt 2000, 2002). Since then, and in late-modern societies which Ulrich Beck (1992) has characterised as having a high consciousness of risk, anxieties about crime have been relentlessly played upon by, among others, the insurance and security industries, media and politicians. Such scare-mongering has, not surprisingly, resulted in an intensification of demand that governments more forcefully and effectively redress the criminal wrongs wrought upon a citizenry whose fears have nowadays been exacerbated by the spread of global terrorism.

But is it feasible for governments to attempt delivery of crime reduction through increased use of imprisonment? Unfortunately for advocates of such a 'common sense' approach to crime and punishment, incarceration of the criminal and long-term protection of the public through the general deterrent and/or individual rehabilitative effects of penal confinement do not necessarily go hand in hand. Harsh punishments may well fulfil a retributionist intent without making a blind bit of difference to crime rates. Sending a wrongdoer to prison may aggravate, rather than ameliorate, the psychological, economic and social factors which can predispose a woman to criminal activity in the first place (see Heidensohn 1986; Carlen 1988). (For the statistical evidence on the relationships between imprisonment and crime see Chapter 5.)

Another complication confronts governments wishing to appease a vengeful electorate. The development of liberal democracies in the nineteenth century gave birth to a new politico-legal concern: the requirement to legitimate the deprivation of a citizen's liberty by reference either to the greater good of the whole society or to the welfare of the prisoner – preferably both. But even utilitarian justifications for imprisonment are insufficient for those who question the fairness of the criminal justice system itself. Radical prison critics have always been quick to point out that imprisonment has never been used un-ambiguously and equitably for the punishment of *all* serious lawbreakers but also (and disproportionately) to warehouse the poor, the unemployed and the mentally ill. On this argument, which depends for its strength on what is known about the social composition of the prison population, (see Chapters 2 and 3) the ways in which imprisonment has been used over the years are presented as being fundamentally *illegitimate*.

A consequence of reform and rehabilitationist philosophies thus having their roots in the opposed legitimating and delegitimating rhetorics touched on above, is that, over the years, the justifications for imprisonment have become more and more complex, contradictory and, in some cases, only eccentrically related to the punishment of crime. In pure form they are usually listed under the headings of: retribution, reform, rehabilitation, social protection, deterrence (individual and general) and expiation. Chapter 4 provides fuller definitions and discussion of these justifications for imprisonment, though, for the reasons just discussed, they are nowadays seldom operationalised in pure form. The *modernisers'* emphasis on discipline had the ideological advantage of sidestepping questions of punishment and legitimacy by giving primacy to a prison and prisoner *disciplinary* mode of regulation seen to be equally desirable for all citizens, all social institutions and, indeed, for society as a whole. The *postmodernist* emphasis on the reconfigurability of all disciplines to meet multiple but differentiated 'need' provided more of the same but with a difference. All of the dominant ideological reconfigurations of official penal discourse over the last 400 years, have, in different ways, managed to avoid the question 'What are prisons *for*?'

Foucault's disciplinary thesis

The main concept to be used in this section on the modernisers is that of *'discipline'*, taken from a work which has achieved a prominence beyond all others in the modern sociology of punishment: *Discipline and Punish*, by the French philosopher Michel Foucault, first published in 1975 in French and translated into English in 1977. But why, you may well ask, is the concept of *'discipline'* of such importance in a section entitled 'the modernisers'? It is because just as Foucault was interested in the specific configuration of ideas (that is, sets of knowledges) and their accompanying social rules and related practices for getting things done (or, in other words, technologies) which were dominant at particular times, and which presented people with new ways of seeing old phenomena, so too have all the modernising prison reformers (whether state administrators or philanthropists of various persuasions) developed their own sets of knowledges about the rules according to which both prisons and prisoners should be governed? Thus, in *Discipline and Punish*, 'discipline' has a double meaning: connotationally, it embraces both a distinctive type of organisational knowledge – bureaucracy – (just as we sometimes talk of the 'discipline' of history or geography), and also its other meaning of 'bringing under a rule'.

In the eighteenth century, the spectacular and savage punishments originally intended as deterrent warnings to potential lawbreakers were increasingly being seen by the hungry masses as illegitimate weapons of repression. Brutal military suppression of civil unrest, coupled with judicial severity in the punishment of relatively minor crimes against the property of the wealthy, repeatedly aggravated already-inflamed situations and even provoked the bloody riots which most starkly called into question and threatened the legitimacy and continued existence of governments. And all at a time when rapid industrialisation was stoking demand for a self-disciplined and more reliable workforce! What was obviously required was a gentler, more effective and more subtle form of social regulation. Foucault's disciplinary thesis tells one story of how it was achieved.

In *Discipline and Punish*, Foucault argues that constant surveillance and ideological containment in a range of bureaucratically organised civil institutions such as schools and hospitals proved to be more effective techniques for the universal governance of the citizenry than sporadic incursions by the military and spectacular displays of savagery by the torturer and executioner. Modern modes of regulation, far from attempting to maim and kill, aimed for the creation of a self-disciplining labour force and citizenry which had so internalised the rules of disciplined social behaviour that the physical punishments inscribed upon the body, and which had aimed to terrorise (but had actually inflamed) the populace, should fall into disuse. The continuous technology of mass discipline, rather than depending upon physical terror, was to aim for psychological mastery. Its power was deemed to be inherent in the correct categorisation, placing, spacing , examination and timetabling of people according to rules which would ensure not only that everyone was kept in their proper place but also that everyone would internalise the rules specific to those proper places. According to Foucault, the birth of the modern prison as a *disciplinary* institution, as opposed to the mainly detentive lockup, Debtors Gaol and Bridewell which it superseded, had been made possible by forms of training that had already been perfected in army educational establishments.

Foucault's thesis is similar to Max Weber's previous depiction of bureaucracy (Weber, English translation 1947); while Erving Goffman's *Asylums* (1961), wherein the author developed the concept of *total institution* to demonstrate the near totality of control which can be exercised by institutions organised to suppress individuality and bring the lives of inmates under one rule, was another sociological classic which was prescient of much of Foucault's work on disciplinary control. Since the publication of *Discipline and Punish*, a range of authors has amended, built upon or criticised Foucault's disciplinary thesis, but it has seldom been ignored altogether by prison theorists and researchers. (See Howe (1994) for a feminist critique; see Dobash et al., (1986) and Bosworth (1999) for two books whose authors explicitly claim to have been influenced by the work of Michel Foucault.)

Around the same time that Foucault was writing *Discipline and Punish*, Dario Melossi and Massimo Pavarini were also writing about modern penal discipline in *The Prison and the Factory* (1977, English translation 1981). The story they tell, however, is slightly different. This is because *The Prison and the Factory* is a Marxist text which accords greater centrality to the material logic of capitalist production than to the proclaimed rationality of bureaucratic organisation in the development of modern penality. Thus, in addition to recognising the modern prison's disciplinary function, Melossi and Pavarini suggest that in sentencing a lawbreaker to a set period of imprisonment, politico/juridical rhetoric mimics the contractual logic of wage labour by translating time into a currency with which the imprisoned pays her dues to society (see Chapter 4 for a fuller discussion of Marxist theories of imprisonment).

Discipline through feminisation and domesticisation

The early penal reformer, John Howard (1727–1790), was primarily concerned that women should be housed apart from the contaminating presence of lewd and rowdy males. Separation of female from male prisoners was also the first and over-riding concern of the nineteenth-century female prison reformer, Elizabeth Fry (1780–1845). That this should be so is not surprising, given the idealised images of woman-hood that have been around from the seventeenth century onwards, and given also, the relatively small proportions of women in the total prison population since the end of the nineteenth century.

It has sometimes been assumed that after Elizabeth Fry had established separate and distinct regimes for imprisoned females in the mid-nineteenth century the women's prisons became entirely benign institutions, organised primarily for the 'gentling' of recalcitrant 'hussies' or the 'training' of 'unfortunate women' and that, as a consequence, they were devoid of those harsher or more counter-productive features which have always been known to characterise the men's gaols. Yet although, in the short term, Fry's campaigning did result in better living conditions for incarcerated women, and though, too, in her earliest writings she was committed to prisoners being democratically involved in the organisation of their own reform (compare this with the responsibilisation thesis discussed in Chapter 4), her later blueprints for women's penal regimes prescribed several of the disciplinary techniques which became hallmarks of the mid to late-twentieth-century institutions. For, as her work with women prisoners developed, Fry's concerns widened. From an initial desire to improve living conditions and provide useful work and education, she became more concerned with developing a technology of reform which would involve constant surveillance, the erasure of individuality and strict programmes of discipline. As we shall see later (in Chapters 4 and 6) this movement – from an emphasis on prison reform to an emphasis on prisoner reform – has been repeated more recently.

Dobash et al., have provided a succinct description of the state of the women's penal institutions in the mid-nineteenth century:

By mid-century, the British had created unique and austere institutions that usually provided secure, sanitary conditions for prisoners. Following the dictates of most reformers, they had separated women from men and appointed women warders, matrons and, later, lady superintendents to oversee the women's side. The corrupt and insanitary conditions that predominated in the late eighteenth and early nineteenth centuries had generally been replaced by new forbidding fortresses of discipline and punishment ... The new and improved prisons of this period combined degradation and humiliation with the positive elements of reform and discipline. In some ways the regimes were similar for men and women. Yet it is clear that patriarchal conceptions played a crucial role in the responses to women right from the beginning of the modern prison. The work provided for women was always predicated on assumptions about their natural skills and limitations, and the surveillance and regulation was always closer and more omnipresent than that usually directed at men. The personal and direct approach initially played an important role in some institutions. However, the impersonal and more abstract approaches increasingly gained acceptance along with an emphasis on humiliation, human accounting, hard useful labour and religious exhortation.

(Dobash et al., 1986: 61)

Thus, by 1850, two opposed trends in women's imprisonment could be detected; and they have persisted (sometimes in modified, sometimes in transformed, mode) right up to the present day. On the one hand it can be argued that the fundamental problem with women's prisons is that they are inappropriately modelled on institutions designed for men. On the other, it can be argued that the actual operation of the women's establishments has always been infused with both a paternalism and an actual recognition that women *are* different to men. In particular, the following features of nineteenth-century women's imprisonment have survived (or resurfaced) in one form or another until today:

- evidence of paternalistic and patriarchal attitudes on the part of the prison staff;

- closer surveillance and regulation of prisoners than in the men's prisons;

- the isolation of women from each other for much of the time, and their employment in low-paid 'women's work' or domesticity when they are in association;

- special accommodation for prisoners' children being incorporated into the living arrangements;

- self-mutilation and suicides by prisoners;

- a greater number of punishments for offences against prison discipline awarded to female prisoners than to males;

- a narrower range of facilities for women than for male prisoners;

- recurring concerns about sexual abuse of female prisoners by male officers; and most recently,

- the resurgence of 'programmes' claiming to repair women prisoners' posited psychological or reasoning deficits (see Kendall 2002).

Yet, although by 1850 male and female prisoners were being housed in separate accommodation, the regimes for women were only very slightly different to those designed specifically for men. Admittedly, women no longer suffered the corporal punishments still inflicted on male prisoners, and in some institutions were even allowed longer periods of association; but the dominant conception of lawbreaking women as being doubly deviant – as criminals and non-conforming women – was already established in penal discourse and was to persist and have effects throughout the twentieth century.

The second half of the nineteenth century saw a gradual decrease in the number of females imprisoned, and from 1895, when 50,000 women were received into prison (Heidensohn 1985: 60), until the 1970s, the prison population decreased remarkably:

> Over 33,000 women were imprisoned in 1913; by 1921 this figure had been reduced to 11,000; while in 1960 less than 2000 women were sentenced to imprisonment without the option of a fine.
>
> (Smith 1962: 187)

With the decrease in the numbers of women prisoners, several of the women's wings in men's prisons were closed down. Then, when in 1902 the last of the male prisoners were transferred to Brixton, Holloway became the main prison for women. Moreover, despite the complaint of the Chairman of the Prison Commission in 1942 that not enough attention had been paid to the specific problems of women in prison, a special agenda for the discipline and treatment of women in custody was gradually and silently being established (Smith 1962: 146).

Throughout the first part of the twentieth century, training in domesticity continued to be a central and most visible feature of life in the women's prisons. With the establishment of psychiatry in the prisons (Carlen 1986), however, the emergent, and (by the 1950s) dominant, discourse concerning women prisoners was that the majority of them were in need of some kind of psychiatric intervention or therapeutic treatment. It was this belief in the fundamental pathology of female prisoners that resulted in the 'new' Holloway being conceived not so much as a prison but more as a secure hospital for women in custody who, by definition, were presumed to be in need of therapy.

Discipline through medicalisation

> In 1968, the then Home Secretary announced that it was intended to reshape the whole system of the custodial treatment of female offenders and that, as part of this comprehensive change, Holloway Prison was to be completely redeveloped. A central feature of this development was to be provision of comprehensive medical, psychiatric and general hospital facilities for the whole of the women's prison service.
>
> (Home Office 1985: 5)

In the event, the building of the 'new' Holloway (Britain's largest prison for women) was not completed until 1985 (see Rock 1996 for an analysis of the rebuilding of Holloway).

As we have already suggested, it might have been expected that once the desirability of separate institutions for women prisoners had been accepted, it would also have been taken for granted that such institutions would be different to men's prisons. Yet, although in operation the women's prisons in England have always been different to the men's, the differences tend, by and large, to have been by default rather than by design and to have stemmed from the three main and distinguishing features of women's imprisonment:

1   The disproportionately small size of the female prison population compared with the men's.

2   The very different composition of the female prison population, especially distinguished by fewer recidivist criminals and far more women from abroad and from ethnic minority groups at home.

3   The informal way in which the women's regimes have been shaped by specific and ideological conceptions of femininity and womanhood.

The eighteenth- and early nineteenth-century reformers who had been anxious to segregate female prisoners from males had been more concerned about protecting public decency than about protecting the women themselves. As Ann Smith (1962) put it, female prisoners had first of all been seen by reformers as potential housemaids, and then, later, as potential housewives. It was not until the 1960s, when official prison policy started to redefine all women prisoners as potential mental patients, that an even newer generation of women's prison campaigners began to insist not only that women prisoners should be seen as having equal citizenship rights with male prisoners, but that recognition of these equal rights and responsibilities should also be tempered by a greater professional recognition of the special medical, emotional, psychological and social needs of female prisoners. These needs, however, which were, by and large, very different from those of male prisoners, were not seen by reformers to be *pathological* needs stemming from any inherently female form of inherent deviance or criminality, but rather were seen to be part and parcel of women's different biological make-up and different social conditioning and responsibilities. The reform emphasis was on *difference*, not *pathology*.

Throughout the period of Holloway's restructuring, groups like Radical Alternatives to Prison protested against the assumption that the petty persistent offenders constituting the bulk of the female prison population at that time really needed to be contained in a secure hospital, often pointing to Professor Gibbens' (1971) observation that 'although many women in prison look as mad as mad can be, they are really reacting to prison life'. Gradually, therefore, the notion of the 'therapeutic prison' for women was dropped by prison administrators. Nonetheless, although prison department officials came to admit that the majority of women in prison could not be presumed to be mentally ill, staff in the women's institutions continued to invoke the stereotype of the 'mad rather than bad' female prisoner in order to justify the rigid and infantile regimes for female inmates, regimes which would not have been tolerated in the men's prisons.

As the gap between the rhetoric of therapy and the reality of inadequate living conditions and debilitating regimes in the women's establishments became more visible, newer, and more vociferous, critics began to be heard (see Chapter 6), and by the end of the 1980s a substantial body of knowledge had been built up concerning the very specific ways in which women's imprisonment in England, Wales and Scotland is different to men's; and not merely because women are biologically different to men (though that is one important difference); nor because they have a different role to play in society (though that is another). But also because the social control of women in general is qualitatively different to the social control of men, the main qualitative difference being that women are socially regulated in many more informal ways outside the criminal justice system than men are. In particular, they are closely controlled by familial and gender ideologies, structures and processes (see Carlen 1995). Feeley and Little (1991) have even proposed that the relatively small proportions of women in prison in most western countries have come about as the informal controls on women have strengthened and tightened. The strategic relationships between the informal and formal social control of women and the ways in which they help explain the relatively small size of the female prison population are discussed in greater detail in Chapters 4 and 5. Suffice it to say here that, as a consequence of the matrix of popular theories about the nature of womanhood, femininity, women's crimes and women's imprisonment, the demographic composition of the women's prisons has been even more skewed than the men's: traditionally women's prisons have contained even more disproportionate numbers of women who have been in the care of local authorities, who are from ethnic minority groups, and who are mentally ill than have the men's establishments (see Chapter 2). Nonetheless, although the history of prison reform is at least as long as that of the modern prison, during most of the twentieth century women in prison tended to be the invisible prisoners, the women whom nobody wanted and almost everyone had forgotten.

The limits to modernism

In the mid-1980s, with the founding of the campaigning group Women in Prison, women's imprisonment in England became more visible and, as a result of a coalition of campaigners and concerned officials, was firmly on the prison reform agenda by the end of the 1980s. At that time, too, a philosophy of prison reductionism in general was enjoying a very brief renaissance. In 1988 Home Office officials had successfully challenged the government's policy of penal retributivism with the Green Paper *Custody in the Community* (Home Office 1988a; see also Rutherford 1996), and the Probation Service had been charged with preparing tough and effective community alternatives to imprisonment for all offenders convicted of less serious crimes. Many senior members of the Probation Service saw the new policies as being of especial importance to women, and were looking forward to shaping non-custodial programmes which might lead to a decrease in the size of the female prison population (see NAPO 1989: 18). Nacro (1991) set out a very positive and imaginative agenda entitled *A Fresh Start for Women Prisoners*.

There was also a slight loosening-up of regimes in the women's prisons, as more outside groups offering services to women prisoners were allowed into the establishments, and a greater emphasis was placed on 'throughcare' and the special medical needs of inmates. Although there was still much to be done to reduce the female prison population and remedy the inequities and poor facilities suffered by women in prison, there was also a pervasive optimism among those involved in innovative non-custodial and prison projects that things could only get better. That optimism was misplaced.

Even while probation services were drawing up plans for new non-custodial programmes of supervision, tougher economic and welfare climates were already threatening young people's ability to survive increasing unemployment and homelessness, and undermining, too, the best attempts of the probation and social services to keep vulnerable young people out of trouble. Young mothers living alone with their babies were beginning to be portrayed as representing a new threat both to family life and to the welfare economy, while the young people themselves painted a different picture – of unemployment, destitution and a despair about ever being able to secure a decent wage. The government's determination to minimalise the role of the welfare state was resulting in savage cuts in benefits and these punitive measures were falling most heavily upon women and young (especially black) people who, for one reason or another, were already suffering extremes of poverty (see Bull and Wilding 1983). Moreover, though the Conservative governments had backed detailed schemes purportedly designed to save money by reducing the prison population, they had, at the same time, counterproductively indulged in a scaremongering rhetoric about a 'breakdown in law and order' so as to divert attention from the failure of their economic, health and education policies. Such shortsighted and contradictory tactics (together with the sentencing and penal confusion they caused), played a major part in creating a new punitiveness, primarily directed towards young people in general, but also towards young, single mothers in particular. Thus, though 1992 did indeed see an overall decline in the prison population, 'by the early spring of 1993 it was clear that a number of countervailing forces were gaining ground rapidly ... (Rutherford 1996: 127). Almost before the prison reductionist Criminal Justice Act 1991 was on the statute book, magistrates, judges, police and media were clamouring against what was rather prematurely portrayed as a 'new leniency'. Vigilante groups were formed and applauded for patrolling the parts that the official police no longer seemed able to reach, and the government set about fashioning new and more punitive legislation.

New Home Secretary, Michael Howard, soon made clear his own position on penal policy. In a speech to the annual conference of the Conservative Party in 1993, he declaimed: 'Prison works. It ensures that we are protected from murderers, muggers and rapists – and it will make many who are tempted to commit crimes think twice' (Rutherford 1996: 128). The Director of Prisons was quick to support the Home Secretary in his attempts to make prisons more unpleasant than they already were (Lewis 1997). In a climate of economic uncertainty where the public were increasingly being enjoined to arm themselves against all kinds of risk – economic, criminal and unknown – the government at last appeared to have responded in kind to the populist punitiveness (Bottoms 1995) of its electorate.

This populist punitiveness had several inter-related dimensions, but the two that most affected women in the criminal justice and penal systems were: 'The New Folk Devils' (i.e. 'single mothers' and 'unattached male youth'); and 'The Fetishism of Prison Security'.

The new folk devils

It was in the period 1988–1994, during the time that three consecutive Conservative Home Secretaries were attempting to remodel penal administration in three fundamentally different ways (prison reductionism – Douglas Hurd; prison privatisation – Kenneth Clarke;

and security fetishism – Michael Howard) that two new sets of folk devils appeared: 'unattached youth' – quickly to become the butt of all kinds of penal fantasies – from hard labour for ten-year-olds, to bringing back both corporal and capital punishments; and, relatedly, 'single mothers' – to be 'deterred' from the single state by punitive changes in welfare and housing legislation.

The 1990s attack on single mothers in Britain was provoked by the stew of anti-poor prejudices that comprised right-wing versions of underclass theory. Basically, the rhetoric went like this: that, found in neighbourhoods containing high numbers of fatherless families headed by never-married mothers, 'underclass' poor are those who, having been reared by permissive mothers and a supportive welfare state, now refuse to work and, instead, engage in predatory, violent and society-threatening crime (Murray, 1994). Implicit in the theory was the old notion that all crime is explicable in terms of family structure and parenting, together with the even older calumny that women are the roots of all evil. (As Helena Kennedy's excellent 1992 book title puts it, *Eve Was Framed!*) It was undoubtedly some such atavistic conception of women's place that was responsible for the Conservative government's threat in the mid-1990s to bring in punitive legislation to deter single women unsupported by males from bearing children. As a host of studies had already suggested that sentencers were prejudiced against single women rearing children without men (Worrall 1981; Carlen 1983) it was likely that this generalised punitiveness towards single mothers (Dennis and Erdos 1992) would have further malign influence on their passage through the criminal justice and penal systems (Edwards 1984; Eaton 1986; Worrall 1990), and that, as a result, more young women would be sent to prison. As we shall see in the next chapter, between 1993 and 2001, the female prison population increased by over 145 per cent.

The fetishism of prison security

Whatever influence the New Punitiveness towards single mothers may or may not have had on the sentencing of female offenders, the dimension of the 'New Punitiveness' which had the greatest impact on the women's prisons in the 1990s was the fetishism of prison security (in terms of both the prevention of escapes and the crackdown on illicit drugs) which followed in the wake of escapes from two male prisons in the mid-1990s. Stories of the new degradations and pains to which women prisoners were being subjected came thick and fast. There were lurid stories about Holloway's new Dedicated Search Teams (dressed in tracksuits and baseball caps) making women submit to the most intimate and intimidating strip searches; about mothers being shackled in both labour and childbirth; and about Mandatory Drug Testing in some of the women's gaols not only requiring women to urinate in front of two female officers, but in requiring them to do so with their hands held up well above their heads.

> Women in Holloway prison are being subjected to an intensified and intimate form of strip-search by officers apparently looking for drugs, writes Lucy Johnston. In the past month, at least four women in the north London jail claim they have been made to bend over, spreadeagled and naked, while officers carry out vaginal inspections. The officers are believed to be part of a search team dubbed the 'squat team' 'or heavy mob' by inmates, introduced after the Whitemoor escape in 1994. Inmates describe the team as an intimidating group dressed in black PVC leggings, Doc Marten boots and baseball caps.
>
> (The *Observer*, 24 November 1996)

Meanwhile, however, official unease about, and media interest in, the women's prisons had been fanned by an extremely outspoken Chief Inspector of Prisons who, in December 1995, had made public his decision to walk out of an inspection of Holloway Prison in disgust at the prison's filthy state. When he followed this up with a very critical report, *Women in Prison: A Thematic Review* (HM Chief Inspector of Prisons 1997), a worried Prison Service responded to the mounting pressure by creating a special unit within the Service to be responsible for policy in the women's institutions.

The Women's Policy Group was established in January 1998 (and disbanded in 2004). From then on a new criminology of women's imprisonment was developed, one which mixed together pre-modern notions of populist retribution and criminogenic personalities with rationalist notions of need, rehabilitation and legitimate governance. The resulting translations of old concepts into new and inherently contradictory concepts with irresistible political and populist appeal was a triumph of postmodern creativity.

The postmodernists

It has already been suggested that by the mid-1990s, the British penal system was suffering a minor legitimacy crisis in relation to women's imprisonment, a crisis made worse by a growing popular awareness that women prisoners were more likely to be suffering from multiple problems of material deprivation than male prisoners and less likely than males to be 'career' or 'dangerous' criminals. Additionally, that as they were more likely than men to have dependent children for whom they were the main carers, their children at home could be expected to suffer all kinds of mental, emotional and psychological damage as a result of their mothers' imprisonment. At the same time, a contrary ideological trend encouraged a growth in punitiveness towards single mothers and an increasing number of sentencers who argued that if women wanted equality with men they should equally expect to receive equality of punishment with men when they broke the law. So, to satisfy both the punitive retributivists and the prison reformers, a new criminology of women's crime and women's imprisonment was stitched together by taking the vocabulary of the reformers, and placing it within an entirely new context while at the same time erasing from it all reference to inequities occasioned by economic inequality, sexism and racism. The resulting rhetoric (together with the sentencing innovations discussed in chapter 2) allowed more and more women to be imprisoned both *for their own good* (through access to a prison *programme* based on their *needs* they would, it was claimed, see their lawbreaking behaviour differently) and *for the general good* (they would, as a result of the *programme*, it was claimed, cease to recidivate).

In service of this new crimnology, words such as 'responsibility', 'victim', 'need', 'citizenship', 'risk', 'accountability' 'rehabilitation' and 'choice' were displaced from their original theoretical and campaigning contexts and took on very different meanings and referents; and the new meanings given to old campaigning words were destined to have entirely different effects from those envisaged by their radical authors. Carlen (2002g) has argued that during this time the main transformations in female prison reform discourse were as follows:

From 'Prison works' (Conservative Home Secretary, Michael Howard) to 'Prison doesn't work, but we'll make it work' (Labour Home Secretary, Jack Straw)

The thrust of much anti-prison campaigning in the early 1990s had been directed at refuting a Conservative Home Secretary's justification for increases in the prison population – the claim that 'prison works' in terms of reducing crime. In an address to the Howard League soon after the New Labour government came to power, the incoming Home Secretary amended that claim to: 'Prison doesn't work, but we will make it work'. The repairing gel, it was promised, was to be found in the magic of 'programming'. This move towards 'programming' could also claim to meet another objection to women's imprisonment: that the women most vulnerable to imprisonment were also those with multiple social problems and deprivations. 'Agreed,' said Prison Speak. 'Therefore we must develop programmes to address those needs, and this can be done better in prison than in the community where the resources are just not available.' But the needs addressed turned out to be only those which could be represented as related to 'criminogenic' behaviour, that is, 'needs' rooted in the women, rather than in their social circumstances (see Hudson 2002).

From the demand for prison accountability to the insistence on prisoner accountability

During the 1980s one recurring demand of reformers had been that prisons should be 'accountable', that structures should be put in place to safeguard prisoners' rights (Maguire et al., 1985), and that a charter of minimum prison standards should be published and made enforceable by the courts. By the 1990s the concept of 'accountability' was well embedded in prison ideology, but the emphasis now was on the 'accountability' of the prisoner – not only for her own behaviour, but, via prisoner compacts and the Incentives and Earned Privileges Scheme, for the standard of her prison conditions and access to prison 'privileges' too.

The *coup* for official discourse was inherent in the 'contractual' nature of the Incentives and Earned Privileges Scheme; it appealed to a liberal common-sense (about individual freedom and self-governance) and a feminist common-sense insistence that women take responsibility for their own lives and not be seen as victims. As David Garland (2001) has pointed out, contractual modes of governance appeal strongly to the middle classes because, in mimicking traditional middle-class forms of self-governance, they appear to be both 'obvious', and 'natural'. To give women in prison the opportunity to choose to govern their own lives may be a contradiction in terms, but if we add in the imagery of the discursive desire of anti-prison campaigners that women prisoners should have equal opportunities with all other women, in other words, *as if they were not in prison*, it becomes unassailable 'common-sense'. Ironically, it also means that, in prison, women whose common-sense tells them that they can have very little real choice about how to govern their lives as prisoners can continue to be punished in the name of therapy and by professional women, for the very same characteristic that sent many of them there in the first place – not being middle class, and, moreover, refusing to 'see things' as if they were.

From accountability to audit

The shift in emphasis from prison accountability to prisoner account-ability did not lessen the degree of control experienced by prison managements. Indeed, in the wake of the escapes from Parkhurst and Whitemoor Prisons, in the 1980s, centralised control was increased, its tone became more managerialist and, concomitantly, the degree of discretion allowed to prison governors in the general governance of the prison was set at a minimum (Carlen 2002b).

The concept of prison 'accountability' as employed by prisoners' rights lobbyists in the 1980s posited an obligation for prison authorities to give accounts which would justify penal policies in terms of known rules and contestable principles of penal justice and prison governance. This is a complex business, as Maguire et al., (1985) pointed out many years ago.

Garrett (1980) notes that many state departments are called upon to

> deliver services in which efficiency and economy cannot be measured directly in cost/output terms. They may provide services to which people are (to a more or less specified degree) entitled, or which must be distributed equitably within a fixed budget, or where provision to one group incurs disbenefits to others. In such cases accountability acquires social, political, legal and moral characteristics, raising difficult questions about the appropriate forms of audit and the yardsticks of assessment which should be employed.
>
> (Maguire et al., 1985: 2)

Auditability, however, unlike accountability, is not concerned with interpretation and debate. Instead, it demands that the workings of the system be made apparently transparent by being framed/measured within pregiven 'indicators' and 'standards'. Thus, while the concept of 'accountability' allows for openness and critique, audit via measure-ment closes off the possibility of critique by 'providing assurance that the system works well even when a substantive performance is poor' (Power 1997: 60). In the move from prisons accountability to prisons audit, the Key Performance Indicators and Standards which constitute the audit stifle critique by specifying in advance that only the working of the system is under investigation, not the system product.

From female prisoner resistance to class, gender and penal victimisation and oppression – to responsibilisation

One of the transformations in discourse about women's imprisonment which has been well-documented (see Hannah-Moffat 2001) is that which had its roots in feminist discourses which baulked at representations of female lawbreakers in the criminal justice system as being solely victims of class or racist discrimination, and instead insisted that they should also be represented as survivors with an agency capable of resisting the various forms of oppression to which, it was usually admitted, they had indeed been subject. At its extreme, this argument was also put forward as an organising principle to explain the experiences of women in prison (see Bosworth 1999). But although none of the writers who insisted that women in prison could choose to resist some of the prison's oppressive features denied that a majority of women prisoners had been subjected to various forms of oppression outside prison, many of them, especially if they held to a totally untheorized view of what prison actually entails – that is, punishment in the form of involuntary but secure custody – tended to underplay those aspects of custodial power which are necessarily activated and enhanced by prisoner resistance – in other words, the disciplinary and security mechanisms.

Within the women's prisons, a number of programmes were developed which, far from addressing the roots of women's oppression outside prison (and, incidentally, outside of their own, or any one individual's sphere of direct influence), focused instead on the prisoners' attitudes to their criminal behaviour – on the grounds that changing how prisoners thought (within the prison) about their behaviour (outside the prison), would reduce their lawbreaking behaviour upon release. Thus, a progressive feminist exhortation – that oppressed women should take charge of their own lives and act to resist oppression – was transformed into a 'responsibilisation' of prisoners which (through silencing all reference to structural constraints) implied that not only were they solely responsible for their own behavioural choices, but also for the conditions in which those choices were made (see Hannah-Moffat 2001). Unlike the prison governor quoted below, many who helped to frame these programmes just did not take note of the prison's controlling imperative. Prison staff, on the other hand, take it for granted that the demands of prison security and the demands of therapeutic practice are inevitably antagonistic:

We have the institutional dilemma of saying to women, 'Be assertive, be confident'. And as soon as they begin to exercise that assertiveness, staff say, 'Whoa. This is a prison. Get back there'.

(Male Prison Governor in Carlen 1998: 89;
see also Hannah-Moffat 2001: 18)

The translation of 'risk as dangerousness' into 'risk as need'

In the 1980s and early 1990s a number of campaigners against the imprisonment of minor female offenders had argued that women should only be imprisoned if they posed such a serious risk to public safety that a custodial sentence had to be imposed on the grounds of protection of the public. In the 1990s, however, 'risk' came to be translated into 'risk of committing another crime' and, especially in the case of women, 'risk to oneself'. Women with the greatest social needs were also seen as being those most 'at risk' of being in criminal trouble again in the future (see Hudson 2002). As this new interpretation of risk took hold, prison could be justified on two related grounds: if a woman's needs were such that she was at increased risk of committing crime in the future she should go to prison because, being needy, she posed a risk; and by going to prison she could have her needs addressed and the risk diminished. Needless to say, the needs to be addressed in prison were psychological needs relating to the adjustment of how the woman viewed her criminal behaviour and social situation; rather than the material needs that, according to the anti-prison campaigners had, in part, created the conditions conducive to many women's lawbreaking behaviour in the first place.

Holism and partnership operationalised as centralism

One of the key features of late-modern neo-liberal states according to Garland (1996) is the displacing of responsibility for crime control from the state to the citizen. The argument goes like this: given that the criminal justice system can no longer make good its claim to deliver order and security via policing, the courts and the prisons, citizens have been subjected to a responsibilisation strategy whereby responsible citizens are expected to help themselves in these matters, for instance, via increased private security, insurance and a reliance upon other private organisations with whom the state may or not claim to be 'in partnership'. In England, at the turn of the century, the Prison Service invited voluntary and other statutory organisations to join 'in partnership' in the design and running of many prison programmes and, because this was often done under the ideological signs of 'interagency' or 'co-ordination', anti-prison campaigners at first applauded the approach as being 'holistic'. Once again, their approval was premature.

A recurring criticism directed at services for female offenders during the 1990s related to the fragmented nature of service delivery. It was argued that too often provision by one agency undermined that of another; that although women in prison often required a great deal of specialist help, the expertise was not available within the prison and, furthermore, that although the relevant provision could be made by specialist agencies, the Prison Service did not make as much use of specialist agencies as it could. A third argument related to the need for 'one stop' provision – of information and all other types of service – so that ex-prisoners with children and/or a paucity of resources could easily identify and access their own specific mix of appropriate rehabilitative services. Proponents of these arguments confidently believed that a holistic approach would lead to more and more 'community' organisations going into prisons with a greater variety of approaches to prisoners' 'needs' being practised. The reverse happened. Harnessing the perennial campaigning rhetoric about the desirability of higher standards in prison provision to a justification for a new accreditation process, one designed to authorise and recognise (for funding purposes) only those programmes deemed by the accreditors to address offending behaviour, the Prison Service fashioned a new machinery for the three-fold centralisation of penological knowledge: causes of criminal behaviour were located in individual offenders; the best way to remedy these criminogenic tendencies was by cognitive behavioural technique (see Kendall 2002); and the best way to gain knowledge of anything penological whatsoever – success of therapeutic programmes, quality of prison and prison-officer performance – was to measure it.

From symbolic interactionism to construction of a new official criminology of women in prison

In the discourse of official knowledge there is a happy conjunction between necessity and desire. To be coherent, all discourse necessarily has to exclude certain statements and include others; to maintain its legitimacy, all official discourse desires to exclude oppositional knowledge of certain material conditions and replace it with an alternative world-view (see Burton and Carlen 1979). Most of the academic books and campaigning and semi-official reports of the last decades of the twentieth century implicitly challenged the legitimacy of continuing to imprison so many women with such appalling histories of histories of poverty and abuse as characterised the histories of a majority of women in prison. Having in part met the challenge by claiming that the justification for imprisoning such women was that their needs would be met by the new prison regimes and programmes, official assurance had to be made doubly sure: first, by discrediting the knowledge claims of those who argued that in-prison programmes run by psychologists would hardly address the poverty-stricken circumstances to which so many prisoners would return upon release; and second, by making sure that all of those running the new programmes held to an ontology and epistemology of women's crime which would further bolster the legitimacy of imprisoning them.

The basic ontology of the New Official Criminology of Women in Prison was expressed in a remarkably clever document entitled *The Government's Strategy for Female Offenders* (Home Office 2000a). In it, the arguments which had been put forward by some qualitative researchers that women committed crime because it appeared to them that they had few legitimate options (see Carlen 1988) were turned on their head. Implicitly allowing the symbolic-interactionist claim (and, incidentally, justification for qualitative, as opposed to quantitative, research) that their ways of seeing the world shape people's actions, the solution of the New Official Criminology for Women in Prison was simple. Change women prisoners' *beliefs* about the world; the problem is in their heads, not their social circumstances:

> The characteristics of women prisoners suggest that experiences such as poverty, abuse and drug addiction lead some women to *believe* that their options are limited. Many offending behaviour programmes are designed to help offenders see there are always positive choices open to them that do not involve crime. At the same time, across Government, we are tackling the aspects of social exclusion that make some women *believe* their options are limited.
>
> (Home Office 2000a: 7 emphases added)

This approach also justified the commissioning of new research into women's criminogenic needs, research which would produce 'research evidence on effective ways to tackle women's re-offending' (Home Office 2000a: 23). As the only programmes authorised for tackling women's offending behaviour were those which had been officially 'accredited', it seemed that, at the beginning of the twenty-first century, official discourse on women's imprisonment had indeed momentarily triumphed – at least until the unofficial, 'other' explanations of women's crime and imprisonment (see Chapter 7) had, in their turn, been incorporated or reincorporated into some even newer discourses and histories of women's imprisonment.

Summary

In his book *The Archaeology of Knowledge,* Michel Foucault (1972) uses the concept of the *archive* as a metaphor to illustrate his argument that modes of knowing are never totally superseded but remain in language as always transforming and transformative elements in the ever-reconfiguring conditions of old, new and emergent knowledge. In this chapter, instead of presenting the histories of women's imprisonment in England as a chronological pageant of penal tableaux, we have tried to sketch out *some* (we do not claim to know *all*) of the archival elements which, in ever-reconfigured discourses, have contributed to the making of women's imprisonment today.

Concepts to know

Students should ensure that they know the meanings of the concepts defined below as they have been used in this chapter. For fuller definitions of criminological concepts, students are advised to consult McLaughlin and Muncie (2001) *Sage Dictionary of Criminology.* For greater elucidation of the most important concepts, relevant books are also recommended below.

criminogenic: usually used to describe personality traits which predispose a person to criminal behaviour. Such traits can be inborn or acquired.

ideology: taken-for-granted, and, for the time being, unquestioned sets of knowledges; in other words, that which is already known, and which can, when questioned by theoretical critique, form the basis of new knowledge. Unquestioned, the new knowledge may, in its turn, constitute a new ideology. Most conceptualisations of ideology imply that ideological knowledge is *partial* knowledge: either because it is rooted in the experiences or interests of an individual, group or class (see Mannheim, (1960) *Ideology and Utopia*, and Lukacs, (1971) *History and Class Consciousness*) or because it has remained so locked into its own protocols for knowing that it has not been able to recognise the still newer ways of knowing made possible by its own (once new) conditions of existence (see Carlen 1998: 70–2).

discourse: a set of statements which has its own textual conditions of existence and the coherence of which depends as much upon what is not, as what is, said (see Foucault (1972) *The Archaeology of Knowledge*).

modernism: mode of social organisation ostensibly based on rational-scientific (as opposed to magical/religious) ways of knowing.

pathology: the study of disease. When it is asserted that a lawbreaker has been 'pathologised', it usually means first, that the criminal behaviour is seen as being humanly abnormal (rather than illegal); and second, and relatedly, that the criminal behaviour can therefore be best explained by some abnormality inherent in the genes, hormones, psyche or upbringing.

penality: analysis, modes of thinking about, and systems for imposing, formal and informal punishments, including analysis of the conditions of possibility of the various penologies (see Garland and Young (1983) *The Power to Punish*).

penology: the development, administration and justification of specific systems of punishment.

postmodernisms: modes of knowing which reject the modernist claim that science has been, or can be, governed and guaranteed by tried and tested rules and laws, and which instead insists upon the continuous and essential reconfigurability of all forms of knowledge and modes of knowing (see Lyotard (1984) *The Postmodern Condition: A Report on Knowledge*).

prison privatisation: the introduction of market mechanisms into previously publicly-controlled social provision. The main effect on English prisons was that some service delivery (i.e. the management and running of some prisons, and the partial provision of some services in others) was separated from policy making.

prison reductionism: penal policies which have deliberately aimed to reduce the numbers in prison.

rehabilitation: a non-custodial or custodial process which would (ideally) provide an offender with the material wherewithal to resist temptation to commit crime in the future. The concept of rehabilitation, unlike that of reform, focuses on the need to change the circumstances which might have predisposed the offender to lawbreaking, rather than on any 'reformable' characteristics of the offender herself (see Cullen and Gilbert (1982) *Reaffirming Rehabilitation*).

responsibilisation: an insistence by the state that people take responsibility for their own actions. As used in relation to women's imprisonment, see Hannah-Moffat (2001) *Punishment in Disguise*.

symbolic interactionism: a theoretical perspective that emphasised the relationships between the ways in which people see the world and the ways they act. For a fuller exposition of symbolic-interactionist perspectives in criminology see: Becker (1963) *Outsiders: Studies in the Sociology of Deviance*. For an excellent symbolic-interactionist study of female drug-users, see Rosenbaum (1983) *Women on Heroin*.

Further reading

Full references for books referred to in each chapter can be found in the bibliography at the back of the book. To deepen your understanding of the main themes of this chapter, the following books are especially recommended:

Carlen, P. (1983) *Women's Imprisonment*. London: Routledge
Carlen, P. (ed.) (2002d) *Women and Punishment: The Struggle for Justice*. Cullompton: Willan
Dobash, R.E., Dobash, R.P. and Gutteridge, S. (1986) *The Imprisonment of Women*. Oxford: Blackwell
Foucault, M. (1977) *Discipline and Punish*. London: Penguin
Hannah-Moffat, K. (2001) *Punishment in Disguise*. Toronto: University of Toronto Press
Rafter, N. (1992) *Partial Justice: Women, Prison and Social Control*. New Brunswick, NJ: Transaction Publishers
Smith, A. (1962) *Women in Prison*. London: Stevens
Zedner, L. (1991) *Women, Crime and Custody in Victorian England*. Oxford: Clarendon Press

Topics for discussion

1 Do you agree with the proposition that imprisonment is a more painful punishment for women than it is for men? Why?

2 Do people still think that it is more reprehensible for a woman to commit crime than it is for a man? Why?

Essay questions

1 Describe and explain the contradictions which have, historically, been inherent in prison regimes for women.
2 'Women's prison regimes have, historically, been organised to feminise, domesticise, medicalise and infantilise.' Explain and discuss.
3 To what extent, historically, were social stereotypes of femininity and the means for socially controlling women outside prison incorporated into the regimes for controlling women inside prison?

Chapter 2

Women in prison: the facts

Introduction

Women in prison are sent there by courts. This may seem an obvious statement but it is easy to forget that there is no inevitable or direct link between the crime a woman commits and her imprisonment. There are a number of stages and factors that intervene between crime and sentence and a number of choices to be made by a number of different people. In this chapter we will consider some of these factors in an attempt to understand why some women who commit crimes go to prison and others do not (we will return to sentences that do not involve imprisonment in Chapter 5). We will also explore the various ways of counting the number of women in prison. *The Prison Statistics for England and Wales* is published every year by the Home Office. The statistics are dominated by men in prison and it is not an easy task to extract data relating to women. In this chapter we will guide the reader through these statistics and highlight their most important features. Finally, we will provide some comparisons with policy and practice in other countries.

Sentencing women: chivalry or double jeopardy?

Hedderman and Gelsthorpe argue that:

> equal treatment for men and women is a matter of approach not outcome. The underlying assumption is that fairness consists of

people in similar circumstances being treated in similar ways, but it must be recognised that men and women do not necessarily appear in similar circumstances.

(1997: 1)

Despite periodic claims that women's offending is disproportionately under-reported (Pollak 1950; Mirrlees-Black 1999) there has never been any serious evidence to support this contention (see, for example, Gadd et al.'s (2002) attempt to follow up claims of domestic violence victimisation by men in the Scottish Crime Survey). In 2000, women accounted for 16 per cent of those arrested (Home Office 2002a). Within this small proportion, they tended to be over-represented in arrests for fraud and forgery (mainly falsely claiming social security) and theft and handling (mainly shoplifting). They were markedly under-represented in sexual offences and burglary.

Police decisions to proceed are influenced by a number of factors, including perceptions of the extent to which a woman fulfils gender role expectations and is therefore likely to respond to informal social controls, making formal controls unnecessary (Horn 1995). Over and above this consideration, women are more likely than men to admit their offences, making it easier for them to be cautioned (Phillips and Brown 1998). The reasons for women's apparent readiness to admit guilt are discussed in some detail by Worrall (1990) but may have less to do with an acceptance of legal guilt and more to do with, on the one hand, practical concerns about time and publicity and, on the other, an all-pervasive sense of guilt about being a failing wife and mother. Their additional reluctance to request a lawyer may be attributable to similar concerns, as well as (possibly misguided) concerns about the expense. What is clear from studies such as those by Phillips and Brown (1998) is that women feel – and, indeed, are – 'out-of-place' in the criminal justice system (Worrall 1981), unable to command the language and behaviour that will enable them to negotiate for themselves what passes for 'justice' in a male-dominated system.

On reaching court, women are more likely than men to receive conditional discharges and supervision, and less likely to receive fines and custody (Home Office 2002a). The overwhelming reasons for this apparent leniency are that women commit less serious offences and have fewer previous convictions than men. While one in three men is likely to have a conviction by the age of 40 years, this is true of only one in twelve women (Home Office 2002a). Women's criminal careers are also much shorter than men's, the vast majority lasting less than a year. Additionally, there has been a limited recognition in recent years of the 'criminalisation of female poverty' (Pantazis 1999) and women's relative inability to pay fines. There has been a consequent reluctance on the part of sentencers to burden women with fines (Hedderman and Gelsthorpe 1997) though the result has been that some women may experience the greater intrusiveness of supervision rather than the lesser sentence of a conditional discharge.

There may, however, be other 'non-legal' factors which influence the sentencing of women and these concern sentencers' perceptions of the women before them. These perceptions are, in turn, dependent on the kinds of information they have about the women and their own value judgements about what the woman 'needs' and/or 'deserves'. Only certain kinds of information are admissible in court. Most routinely, these kinds of information (or knowledge claims) are: lay 'common-sense' knowledge; legal knowledge; social psychological knowledge and (occasionally) medical knowledge (Worrall 1990). Any other information or knowledge claim (such as the defendant's own explanation or socio-political analyses of the defendant's circum-stances) are inadmissible unless re-presented in ways that are compatible with 'authorised' versions of events. This is what is meant when writers assert that 'women are socially constructed within discourses of femininity' (see Chapter 1). An alternative conception which is particularly apt for understanding women's experiences of court can be found in Ardener's work. Women, she claims, are frequently 'muted':

> The theory of mutedness ... does not require that the muted be actually silent. They may speak a great deal. The important issue is whether they are able to say all that they would wish to say, where and when they wish to say it. Must they, for instance, re-encode their thoughts to make them understood in the public domain? Are they able to think in ways which they would have thought had they been responsible for generating the linguistic tools with which to shape their thoughts? If they devise their own code will they be understood?
>
> (Ardener 1978: 21)

Sentencers tend to construct men and women differently, though it is arguable that those differences are diminishing and that it is this, rather than any changes in women's offending behaviour, that accounts for the increase in the numbers of women being sent to prison. This change has been termed the 'backlash' against feminist perspectives on women and crime, or the 'search for equivalence' (Worrall 2002a). Traditionally, sentencers have allowed considerations of women's domestic competence, sexual respectability and mental (in)stability (Eaton 1986; Allen 1987a; Worrall 1990; Hedderman and Gelsthorpe 1997) to inform their decisions to a greater extent than would be the case for men (where employment and general citizenship are considered to be more relevant) (Deane 2000; Horn and Evans 2000).

Notwithstanding all of the above, Hedderman and Gelsthorpe (1997) identified two groups of women for whom these considerations appeared to play little or no part in sentencing – women who commit drugs or violent offences. Although women are less likely than men to be sent to prison for their first drugs offence, repeat offenders are equally likely to receive a custodial sentence, regardless of other factors. The pattern is reversed in the case of violent offences. First-time violent female offenders are as likely as men to be sent to prison, though this is not true for repeat offenders. One can speculate that this is because women who commit violent offences are most likely to commit one very serious offence such as either homicide (of a male partner following years of his abuse, for example) or cruelty to a child. Those who engage in repeat but lower level violence may invite concerns about their mental stability and thus be diverted away from custody towards treatment (though see Chapter 3 for a fuller discussion of women's mental health issues and imprisonment).

Thomas (2002) is convinced that a major explanation for the increase in women's immediate imprisonment can be found in the decline in the use of the suspended prison sentence. If he is correct (and his argument appears to make numerical sense) then one aim of the Criminal Justice Act 1991[1] – to reduce the prison population – has been undermined by the restrictions placed on the use of the suspended sentence by that same Act. Prior to the Act, it had become received wisdom that suspended sentences simply postponed imprisonment and had a net-widening effect. In the case of women, however, because of their low re-offending rates, its use might well have prevented imprisonment. The case on which Thomas comments appears to have been an excellent example of this – a first offender with responsibility for children, committing a serious offence of dishonesty.

Discrimination and Section 95 publications

The Criminal Justice Act 1991 was a landmark in sentencing legislation and, despite being implemented by a Conservative government, was the most liberal piece of criminal legislation in the last quarter of the twentieth century (for a more detailed analysis of the Act and its implications, see Worrall 1997). Significant parts of the Act were subsequently revoked or amended in 1993 and the principles of the Act – that prison should be a sentence of last resort for only the most serious offenders – has been largely discredited by subsequent governments. However, one strange clause, which appeared as an ambiguous afterthought, has become established as part of the culture of Home Office statistical publications. Section 95 of the Act required the Secretary of State to 'publish such information as he considers expedient for the purpose of enabling persons engaged in the administration of justice to ... avoid discriminating against any persons on the ground of race or sex or any other improper ground'. Two publications now appear annually, on women and 'race' (Home Office 2002a, 2002b) which summarise, in an entirely descriptive but deliberately readable manner, selective statistical data on the experiences of women (and ethnic minorities) as offenders, victims and workers in the criminal justice system. The publications provide no new data, but are a useful supplement to the rather less accessible official statistics publications.

Counting women in prison

Average population

There are several ways of counting prisoners and this section will explain the main differences between the methods. The *average population* of prisoners derives from snapshots of all the people in prison on a given day. In England and Wales, the main day that is used for the production of annual prison statistics is 30 June. There are also monthly Prison Population Briefings which count prisoners on the last day of each month and the Prison Service now produces a weekly *average population* every Friday on its website (www.hmprisonservice.gov.uk). This method of counting will tell you how many people are in prison but it will not tell you how long they are in prison for. Counting the *average population* is a method which is biased in favour of people serving long sentences. For example, if a person is in prison for ten years, they will be counted ten times in the annual count at the end of June – and 120 times in the monthly briefings. On the other hand, if 52 people are sent to prison for seven days each (for example, for fine default) and they are sent one after another, only one of them will be counted at the end of June and only 12 will be counted for the monthly briefings. Only weekly counts would ensure that they were all counted.

So, long-term prisoners are over-represented in the *average population* count and short-term prisoners are under-represented.

Receptions

An alternative way of counting prisoners is by *receptions*. This method counts everyone who is sent to prison during a year, for whatever reason and for however long or short a term. This gives a much better picture of the number of people being sent to prison by the courts. However, this method is biased towards short-term prisoners, who are over-represented. To use the previous example, a person spending ten years in prison will only be counted as one reception in the first year and not counted at all in subsequent years. The 52 people serving seven days each will be counted 52 times. A good example of this difference can be found when considering *fine defaulters* and *life sentence prisoners*. Fine defaulters are people who fail to pay court fines and are subsequently sent to prison, often only for a few days until they pay the fine. On average, male fine defaulters spend six days in prison and female fine defaulters spend two days in prison (Home Office 2003a). In 2001, there were 1,460 *receptions* of fine defaulters, but an *average population* of only 43 (Home Office 2003a). At the opposite end of the spectrum from fine defaulters are *life sentence* prisoners, who serve indeterminate sentences for murder or other very serious offences of violence. In 2001, there were 512 *receptions* of life sentence prisoners but an *average population* of 4,810 (almost ten times *more* than the receptions). The difference between the figure for *receptions* and the figure for *average population* gives an indication of the length of prison sentences. The greater the difference in favour of *receptions*, the shorter will be the length of sentences; the greater the difference in favour of *average population,* the longer will be the length of the sentences.

An additional influence on this distinction is the differential parts played by the Magistrates' and Crown Courts. Magistrates deal with 75 per cent of all *imprisonable* cases coming to court. These are known generally as *indictable* offences, where the law allows for a sentence of imprisonment – many more cases dealt with by magistrates cannot result in a prison sentence by law. Although magistrates deal with the less serious cases, 16 per cent of them are given prison sentences. However, Magistrates' courts are limited by law in the length of prison sentence they can impose. So, magistrates send a large number of people to prison for short periods (on average less than six months) – thus having a strong influence on *receptions* to prison. The Crown Courts, on the other hand, deal with far fewer people but for more serious offences and send 64 per cent of them to prison for an average of two and a half years. So they have a strong influence on the *average population*. It is important to remember these distinctions when looking at official prison statistics.

Rates of imprisonment

A third method of counting prisoners has become increasingly popular in recent years, primarily because it allows for international comparisons. This method is known as *rates of imprisonment* and has become the internationally accepted method for comparing penal policy and practice. Absolute numbers of prisoners give no indication of the size of a country's overall population or the percentage of that population which is imprisoned. Normally based on the *average population* and the relevant overall population in a country, *rates of imprisonment* tell you how many people out of every 100,000 in a total population are sent to prison. This method allows for more accurate comparisons over time (trends – see below) as well as comparisons across populations. The simplest example is that of the ratio of overall prison populations to 100,000 of overall populations in 2001 (Home Office 2003a: Table 1:19):

England and Wales	127
Scotland	115
Northern Ireland	51
Australia	116
Canada	123
South Africa	392
USA	698
Russia	729

More detailed breakdowns give comparisons for different populations (for example, women, minority ethnic groups, and so on). Although *rates of imprisonment* are a useful tool for the reasons already given, it should be remembered that there is no internationally accepted method of recording imprisonment rates (Walmsley 2002), so some differences may be accounted for by different recording practices.

Trends

Finally, it is important to consider changes over time and these changes are known as *trends*. When looking at official statistics, many of the tables provide information over a number of years but some do not. It is sometimes necessary, therefore, to look back at previous issues of *Prison*

Statistics in order to get an accurate picture of the *pattern* of policy in relation to a particular aspect of imprisonment. In the 2001 edition of *Prison Statistics,* there is a very useful set of tables (to which we return below) showing *trends* in imprisonment for the whole of the twentieth century, for men and women.

How many women are there in prison?

The statistics in this section are all taken from *Prison Statistics for England and Wales 2001* (Home Office 2003a) and the tables and figures in brackets refer to the tables and figures in that document. These tables can be downloaded from the Home Office website (www.homeoffice.gov.uk/rds/). Click on 'subjects', then 'prisons'.

In 2001, the *average population* in prison was 66,301. Of these prisoners, 3,740 – or 5.6 per cent – were women (Home Office 2003a: Table 1.2a). During the previous ten years, the female prison population doubled, while the male population increased by about 50 per cent. But if we take a much longer-term view, it is clear from this same table and the accompanying figures (Figure 1:2a-d) that the *trend* or pattern of imprisonment for men and women was very different during the twentieth century. For men, the population increased from around 16,000 in 1901 to 62,500 in 2001. For women, the population declined from around 3,000 in 1901 to under 700 in the mid-1930s, then increased steadily thereafter. So, in 1901, there were as many women in prison as there are now and they represented over 16 per cent of the prison population, the majority being imprisoned for offences of drunkenness and prostitution (Home Office 2003a: 4).

The increase in the *average population* masks a different pattern of imprisonment, namely, changes in sentence length and time on remand. For this to be revealed, we need to consider *receptions* (Home Office 2003a: Table 1.1). In 2001, a total of 141,395 people were sent to prison and of these 11,946 were women – or around 8 per cent. Overall, there has been a large increase in *receptions* over the past ten years, but a small decline between 1999 and 2001. Nevertheless, the higher proportion of female receptions indicates (see previous section) that women are more likely than men to receive short sentences – or to be on remand.

Characteristics of women in prison

Prisoners fall into a number of different categories within the prison system, according to their age, type of offence, whether or not they are on remand or sentenced, the length of their sentence, and so on. Male prisoners are also categorised into one of four security categories (A – D) according to their assessed likelihood of escaping and the danger they would pose if they did escape. Women are only categorised as being suitable for closed (high security) or open (low security) conditions. It is not considered practical to categorise women in any greater detail because the numbers are so small that it would not be possible to provide sufficiently varied regimes to cater for more than two security categories. Thus, in theory, women might be either over- or under-categorised in terms of their security risk. In practice, the tendency is towards over-categorisation. However, only seven women have escaped from prison since 1995 (Home Office 2001d: Table 7.14[2]) compared with almost 200 men. The escape figures for men (though not for women) were considerably higher in previous years, but this did not prevent the Prison Service from instituting a security clamp-down in both male and female establishments following high profile escapes in 1994. Despite the overall increase in the number of women in prison, the number of 'open' places for women has declined from almost 500 prior to 2000 to fewer than 250. This has been due to the redesignation of Drake Hall prison in Staffordshire (formerly the largest open prison for women) as a 'semi-open' prison. The Prison Service claims that Drake Hall still caters for women suitable for open conditions, but the building of two security fences in 2001 makes this claim a dubious one (Worrall 2000a) (though it has to be conceded that 'minimum security' conditions in other countries often involve secure perimeters). A second women's prison, Morton Hall, has since been designated as 'semi-open'. Women are now held in 19 prisons, of which only 17 are designated as 'female establishments'. Two more women's prisons are due to be opened in 2004. The remainder are male establishments with separate female wings. In all, there are 139 prisons in England and Wales. Fewer than 10 per cent of women in prison are now in open conditions.

Age and motherhood

The age distribution of sentenced women in prison is similar to that of sentenced men (Home Office 2003a: Table 1.9). Over 80 per cent of the *average population* of both men and women in prison are under the age of 40 years. About 66 per cent of men and 70 per cent of women are aged between 21 and 40; about 4 per cent of men and 2.3 per cent of women are juveniles (under the age of 18). This distribution has not changed greatly over the past ten years. The significance of these figures is that at least 70 per cent of women in prison are of child-bearing age and, if we add those aged 18–20 and those aged 40–49, it is likely that 95 per cent of them could have dependent children. In fact, surveys show consistently (Caddle and Crisp 1997; HM Chief Inspector of Prisons 1997) that some two-thirds of women in prison have dependent children. While 90 per cent of fathers in prison expect their children to be cared for by the children's mother, only about 25 per cent of mothers in prison expect their children to be cared for by the children's father (Home Office 2002a), the remainder being cared for by grandmothers, female relatives and friends, or the local authority. There are currently around 70 places in four women's prisons (at Holloway, Styal, Askham Grange and New Hall prisons) for mothers to care for babies (HM Prison Service 1999) but the upper age limit for babies is 18 months. Provision for mothers to care for their babies in prison is a controversial issue, to which we return in Chapter 3.

Another feature of the age distribution of female prisoners is the very small number of young offenders – women aged between 15 and 20 years. In 2001 there were about 2,700 *receptions* in this age category (Home Office 2003a: Table 3.10) compared with about 39,000 young men. For both men and women, the *receptions* were divided half and half between remands and sentenced prisoners. All young offenders who are imprisoned are located in special Young Offender Institutions, designed to keep them away from the 'contamination' of older prisoners. However, there are no separate Young Offender Institutions in England and Wales for juvenile (under 18 years) women – or indeed for any female young offender (under 21 years). The plight of girls in prison was highlighted in 1997 by three events: a thematic review of women in prison by HM Chief Inspector of Prisons (1997), a report by the Howard League (1997) on the imprisonment of teenage girls and a High Court ruling that a teenage girl should not be held in an adult female prison (cited in Howard League 1997). It has become clear that holding girls under the age of 18 alongside adult prisoners contravenes the UN Convention on the Rights of the Child and fails to protect them from harm under the Children Act 1989. The Howard League has called for legislation prohibiting the use of prison custody for all girls aged under 18 years and the placing of 'those girls who genuinely require secure conditions in local authority secure accommodation units' (1997:11). After several U-turns, the government announced its intention to do just that in relation to 15- and 16-year-olds though probably not for several years. In March 2001, the Youth Justice Board announced its intention to build two new secure units for girls. In the meantime, Detention and Training Orders (introduced by the Crime and Disorder Act 1998) have resulted in the trebling of the numbers of juvenile girls in prison since 1993 (Home Office 2003a: Tables 3.11 and 3.12) and they are now held in separate wings of seven designated women's prisons. These are: Brockhill, Bullwood Hall, Eastwood Park, Holloway, Low Newton, New Hall and Styal. All are closed prisons, the argument being that there should be no need for juveniles to be held in open conditions, since juveniles suitable for open conditions should be dealt with by means of community penalties. There is no detailed research to indicate whether or not girls are being held in unnecessarily secure conditions. Everything we know about the backgrounds of adult women prisoners indicates that these girls will become the 'hard core' of recidivist women offenders destined for the revolving door of prison.

Finally, with regard to age, there is a very small group of juveniles who are imprisoned under Sections 90 and 91 of the Powers of Criminal Courts (Sentencing) Act 2000 (formerly Section 53 of the Children and Young Person Act 1933) for murder and other grave offences. This sentence is the equivalent of a life sentence for adults. In 2001, 438 boys and 15 girls were given such a sentence (Home Office 2003a: Table 3.12). Over the previous decade these numbers have fluctuated but, for both boys and girls, there has been a slight decline overall since 1997.

Ethnic group and nationality

In 2001, minority ethnic groups made up 21 per cent of the male and 26 per cent of the female *average population* in prison. In the general population of England and Wales, approximately 94 per cent is white, 2–3 per cent black, 2–3 per cent South Asian and 1 per cent Chinese and other ethnic groups (Home Office 2003a: Figure 6.2). However, the picture is complicated by the issue of *nationality*. In 2001, 10 per cent of the prison population was made up of foreign nationals, a few of whom would be classified as 'white', but most of whom would be from other ethnic groups. In total in 2001, there were 2,986 British national women in prison and 696 foreign national women. Of the former group, about 419 were black, South Asian, Chinese or other. Of the latter group, about 545 were in those categories. So, just under 1,000 'non-white' women are divided between British and foreign nationals in a ratio of roughly 45:55 (Home Office 2003a: Table 6.3). In terms of their offences, there are clear differences between British and foreign nationals and between white and 'non-white' prisoners (Home Office 2003a: Table 6.4). Eighty-one per cent of the foreign national women – and almost all (92 per cent) of the black foreign national women – are in prison for drugs offences. Only 30 per cent of the British national women – but over half (56 per cent) of the black British national women – are in prison for drugs offences. When countering allegations of racism, the government argues that black British and foreign national drug-offending women are inflating the otherwise insignificant numbers of women in prison and undermining an otherwise benign approach to the sentencing of women (Home Office 2001a). An alternative view is that, in the US-led war on drugs, black women and women of colour globally are increasingly becoming 'the raw material that fuels [the] expansion and profitability' of the 'global prison industrial complex' (Sudbury 2002:57).

Offences and previous convictions

Men and women are sent to prison for different offences (Home Office 2003a: Table 1.7). If we remove the 1,100 women in prison for drugs offences in 2001, the next largest group is the 439 in prison for violence, followed by the 434 in prison for theft and handling. This suggests that theft, handling and drugs offences account for over half the female prison population. For men, the picture is very different. The largest group of men in prison are there for violence (11,198), followed by burglary (8,361), with drugs accounting for the third largest group (7,936). Between them, these offences make up about 27,000 men, or half the sentenced population. Theft and handling come a long way down the list. The reason that women are sent to prison for different offences from men is because they *commit* different offences from men. Seventy per cent of all offences committed by women are for theft and handling, compared with less than half of those committed by men (Home Office 2002a). So it could be argued that the prison population is bound to reflect that difference. Nevertheless, it is important to recognise these differences when confronted with claims that 'women are getting more violent'. Even with the acknowledged concern about the increase in drugs offences committed by women, they still account for little more than 10 per cent of all drugs offenders in prison. Many statistical tables which purport to compare male and female offending are confusing because they deal in percentages rather than absolute numbers. It is wise to use the word 'proportionately' whenever you make com-parisons. For example, women commit *proportionately* more theft and handling offences than men, but they still commit far fewer such offences in absolute numbers.

Not only are women sent to prison for different offences from men, but they are also sent with fewer previous convictions. About one-third of women in prison are first offenders, compared with 13 per cent of men in prison (Home Office 2003a: Table 4.2). However, as many writers have pointed out (for example, Hedderman and Hough 1994) this does not mean that female first offenders are more likely than male first offenders to be sent to prison. The fact is that, because *most* women who appear in court are first offenders (Morgan 1997), first offenders will appear to be over-represented in *all* sentences on women.

Sentence lengths

On average, the sentences which women receive are shorter than those received by men (Home Office 2003a: Table 4.10), although both have increased steadily since 1995. In 2001 average sentences imposed on men by the Crown Court were 30 months and on women they were 26 months; sentences imposed by Magistrates' Courts were 4.4 months and 3.6 months respectively. However, this difference increases when one takes account of the fact that almost all short-term prisoners and many longer-term prisoners serve only half of their sentence in custody before being released on a supervised licence. Sometimes release is automatic; sometimes it depends on risk assessment (see Chapter 3 for further discussion of this term) (as with Home Detention Curfew and Parole). When these things are taken into account, women serve, on average, 50 per cent of their sentence length, while men serve 55 per cent (Home Office 2003a: Table 4.11). We have already seen that women serve, on average, two days for fine default, while men serve six days. In 2001, 73 women went to prison for fine default, compared with 1,380 men (Home Office 2003a: Table 1.14). At the other end of the spectrum, the average life sentence, for both men and women, is just over 13 years (Home Office 2003a: Table 5.8). Life sentences are indeterminate, which means that release is entirely dependent on progress in prison and risk assessment, once an individualised minimum time – or tariff – has been served (for the purposes of retribution). In 2001, the *average population* of female lifers was 162, out of a total of 4,810. In terms of *receptions*, 18 new women received life sentences that year, compared with 494 new men (Home Office 2003a: Table 5.1).

Suicide, disciplinary offences and reconvictions

Women prisoners don't riot – or so said Liebling (1994) after the Woolf Inquiry into the disturbances at Manchester prison in 1990. This, Liebling argued, is why they are so often overlooked. Women are more likely to self-harm and attempt suicide if they are distressed. Women are over-represented in self-inflicted deaths in prison, accounting for 9 per cent of such deaths (Home Office 2003a: Table 11.20) and, when one considers that, in the outside community, men commit suicide more than twice as frequently as women, this over-representation is even greater. Additionally, Liebling (1994, 1999) argues that women's apparent suicides in prison may attract verdicts such as 'misadventure', 'accidental' or 'open', due to assumptions of low intent (1999: 308).

However, it is certainly not true that women are not disruptive in response the experience of imprisonment. They may not respond collectively in the way that men do, but they commit more disciplinary offences per head than men do (Home Office 2003a: Table 8.1). In 2001, they averaged 2.3 offences, compared with 1.6 for men. But what sort of behaviour are we talking about here? Disciplinary offences consist of five broad categories – violence, escape, disobedience and disrespect, damage and unauthorised transactions (stealing or possessing un-authorised items including drugs) (Home Office 2003a: Table 8.3). Because of increased security, there are virtually no escapes from either male or female prisons these days. In all other categories, women commit more offences than men and young women commit the most offences. In contrast to male prisoners, white female prisoners are more likely than black female prisoners to commit disciplinary offences. But the most frequent category of offence for women is 'disobedience and disrespect'. From this, we can conclude one of two things – or a combination of both. First, women, and particularly young women, are not used to taking orders and do not like being told what to do, especially when prison rules appear to be unreasonable. Most frequently, women are charged with being in the wrong place at the wrong time, being late for work, being in a friend's cell or room at the wrong time, and so on. Alternatively, it has been argued (Denton 1992) that prison officers, and particularly female prison officers, tend to be stricter (or more 'petty') about imposing prison rules on women. Either way, it is clear that women do not cope well with the overt 'discipline' (see Chapter 1) of imprisonment and attempt to resist it, albeit in ultimately self-destructive ways. The most common punishment for both men and women was having extra days added to their sentence (Home Office 2003a: Table 8.4), although a European ruling in August 2002 has challenged the legality of prison governors using this punishment. On average, men in prison had 1 day added to their sentence and women had 1.2 days added. Other common punishments are forfeiture of privileges and loss of earnings – in both of which women outnumber men.

It has already been stated that women have fewer convictions and shorter criminal careers than men (Home Office 2002a). Women's reconviction rates within two years of discharge from prison are also lower, though perhaps not as markedly lower as one might expect, given their lower levels of previous offending. Of the men released from prison in 1999, 58 per cent had been reconvicted by 2001 (though that includes 73 per cent of young male offenders). Of the women released in 1999, 53 per cent had been reconvicted by 2001 (including 58 per cent of young female offenders) (Home Office 2003a: Table 9.1). When considered alongside the high level of disciplinary offences among women, there would seem to be at least some evidence to support the view that prison exacerbates whatever prior offending problems women might have had and, to adapt a phrase from the Government (Home Office 1990) 'makes bad/sad/mad women worse'.

Drugs, sexual abuse and mental health

Leaving aside, for the moment, the numbers of women who are in prison specifically for drugs offences, the Prison Service now estimates that almost all prisoners have problems with alcohol, drugs and/or mental illness. Women in prison are more likely than men to report having had a drugs dependency before coming to prison and they are also more likely to report having had treatment for some form of mental ill-health prior to imprisonment. The latter is not a surprising observation since women not in prison are more likely than men in the community to seek help for mental ill-health (predominantly depression and anxiety) (Chesler 1974; Allen 1987a; Department of Health 2002). Having said this, one in five women in prison has spent some time as an in-patient in a psychiatric hospital (Prison Reform Trust 2000a), which is a higher proportion than in the population at large. Many writers (Carlen 1988; Howard League 1997; Prison Reform Trust 2000a) have pointed to the fact that many women in prison report having been sexually abused at some time in their childhood or adult lives. A high proportion have been subject to local authority care, thus moving from one institution to another on reaching adulthood (Carlen 1988). (For an analysis of the gender, ethnicity and vulnerability of young women in local authority care, see Lees 2002.)

It is clear from all the above that most women in prison have grown up in multiply disadvantaged environments and, given their relatively low levels of offending, have spent much of their lives struggling to live within the law. Although they still represent a very small proportion of the prison population, there is no rational reason why that proportion should not be even smaller. Instead, it is slowly but surely increasing and, as we shall see now, this is not a problem confined to England and Wales.

International comparisons

'Nowhere in the world do women make up more than one in ten of the whole prison population' (Stern 1998:138). In many countries the proportion is nearer one in twenty and in some it is even fewer. This consistency in the face of widely differing overall prison populations around the world suggests some universality of attitudes towards women who commit crimes, though, as we shall see, there also exists a false consensus of concerns which denies the specificity of women's imprisonment in differing social and political contexts in an attempt to (mis)recognise a globalised penal discourse (Worrall 1998, 2000b). The examples that will be used in this section are taken from Australia, Canada and the USA. For a broader overview of women's imprisonment around the world, see Chapter 7 of Stern (1998).

In Australia, women represent about 6 per cent of the prison population. Their *rate of imprisonment* has increased from 9.2 (per 100,000 of the female population) in 1991 to 15.3 in 1999. However, the latter rate masks a vast differential in the imprisonment rates of Aboriginal and Torres Strait Islander (ATSI) women – a rate of 206.5 per 100,000 of female ATSI population – and non-ATSI women – a rate of 11.8 (Cameron 2001; Pickering and Alder 2000). In Canada, women represented 5.4 per cent of the federal prison population in 2000-2001 but that proportion has increased from 4 per cent in 1996–1997 (Solicitor General Canada 2001). About 15 per cent of those women are Aboriginal (compared with 2 per cent of the general population) – a proportion similar to that of ATSI women imprisoned in Australia (though in Western Australia the proportion is 50 per cent). In the USA, more than 10 per cent of the jail population and more than 6 per cent of the prison population now consists of women (Zatz 2002). The *rate of imprisonment* for women has increased from 11 per 100,000 in 1980 to 51 in 1996 – a change of 364 per cent (Blumstein and Beck 1999). Latinas and African-American women make up 60 per cent of the female prison population (Sudbury 2002).

Crude as these statistics are, they present a universal dilemma. On the one hand, they confirm a perception of women – even those who commit crimes – as posing far less of a threat to a nation's law and order than men. On the other hand, that threat is perceived to be increasing disproportionately. Investigating these figures exposes a seemingly universal chivalry which belies a mixture of benign (and malign) neglect, paternalistic (and maternalistic) medicalisation, fear and genuine bewilderment about what constitutes the 'right treatment' of imprisoned women. In the next chapter, we examine these 'universal concerns' and ask to what extent they are indeed 'universal' and to what extent they constitute a 'false consensus' that disregards the specificity of the local social, economic and political context of women's imprisonment.

Conclusion

The aim of this chapter has been to provide the reader with sufficient 'facts' about women in prison to make sense of the debates that follow in this book and to enable them to understand how some of the more extreme statements that are made about women offenders in the media come to be made. As I write this, I am reading a front page headline in the *West Australian* (19 October 2002) which declares: 'Prison Luxury'. It proceeds thus:

> The 103 inmates at Bandyup women's prison will be back on instant coffee after Justice Minister Jim McGinty took away their $3,200 professional cappuccino machine. The Justice Department said the machine was bought for prisoner training, a plan praised by caterers. But Mr McGinty said it was not a suitable use of taxpayers' money. 'To have a cappuccino machine available to prisoners would be perceived in the broader community as being inappropriate and providing prisoners with luxuries,' he said.

It could be argued that Mr McGinty is right on 'less eligibility' grounds. The poorest honest person in the community probably does not have a cappuccino machine, so why should prisoners – for whatever reason? On the other hand, it might be in the community's long-term interests for women to learn how to make a good cup of coffee and thus be better qualified for a job in the hospitality industry on release (as the article goes on to explain). But what is undoubtedly true is that Mr McGinty's action – and its calculated reporting – will reinforce community prejudices that prisoners, and particularly women prisoners, will always be pampered by liberal-minded prison authorities, unless those authorities are constantly and rigorously held to account. As the article reports unsurprisingly:

> WA Prison Officers' Union president Phil Giblett welcomed the machine's removal. 'It's another example of the wastage of money

in the department when it is making uniformed staff accountable for every cent and cutting us back in major areas of security concerns,' he said.

At the same time, the Inspector of Custodial Services in Western Australia (the equivalent of Her Majesty's Inspector of Prisons in England and Wales) was inspecting the prison. In a report which makes a major contribution to the debate on women's imprisonment, the Inspector concludes:

> The Inspector is supportive of new arrangements at the community hall and recreation centre, such as the coffee shop and a canteen [prison shop] where prisoners 'shop' in a manner that is more commercial (and 'normal') than institutional. However, it is the unfortunate rationale for these quite commendable endeavours that has disappointed the Inspection Team. Allowing prisoners to buy coffees, and other prisoners to make and serve them, *are reasonable activities in themselves.* They should not have to be justified in terms of stereotyped models of women as shoppers and potential waitresses.
>
> (Inspector of Custodial Services, WA 2003: 75)

Notes

1   At the time of writing, this Act is still the governing sentencing legislation. However, a new Criminal Justice Bill is proceeding through Parliament which will modify the aims of sentencing. It is unlikely that this new Act will contribute to any reduction in the prison population.
2   A comparable table does not appear in the statistics for 2001. This is a good example of the lack of consistency in the presentation of official statistics, making the task of establishing trends a complex and difficult one.

Concepts to know

average prison population: derived from snapshots of the prison population at any particular time; influenced more by length of sentence than by numbers of prisoners passing through.

receptions: counting every prisoner who is received into prison during a time period; influenced more by numbers passing through than by length of sentence.

rates of imprisonment: counting how many people are imprisoned per 100,000 of any relevant population; allows for comparisons across populations even where the actual numbers of prisoners involved may differ widely.

trends: comparing changes in any of the above methods of counting over time.

less eligibility: a penal philosophical term, derived from the principles of the Victorian workhouse, which argues that provision within institutions for paupers or criminals should be no better than that which exists in the community for the poorest respectable citizen. If this differential is not maintained, it is argued that there is no incentive in society for the poor to be honest.

net-widening: the unintended consequence of a policy designed to reduce imprisonment. When new sentencing options are introduced as alternatives to prison, there is a risk that sentencers will use these for offenders who would otherwise have received a more lenient sentence. For example, the suspended prison sentence was frequently used for offenders who might otherwise have received a fine, thus making it more, not less, likely that they would go to prison when/if they re-offend.

Further reading

Gelsthorpe, L. and Morris, A. (2002) 'Women's imprisonment in England and Wales: A penal paradox', *Criminal Justice*, 2(3): 277–301

Hedderman, C. and Gelsthorpe, L. (1997) *Understanding the Sentencing of Women*, Home Office Research Study 170. London: Home Office

Home Office (2003) *Prison Statistics for England and Wales 2001*, Cm 5743. London: The Stationery Office

Stern, V. (1998) *A Sin Against the Future: Imprisonment in the World*. London: Penguin, Chapter 7

Topics for discussion

1 What are the advantages and disadvantages of different methods of 'counting prisoners'?
2 What different explanations are there for the increase in the female prison population in westernised countries?
3 What are the main social characteristics of the female prison population in England and Wales?

Essay questions

1 What challenges and opportunities are presented to criminal justice systems by the recent increases in the populations of women prisoners in many countries?
2 What changes, if any, should be made to sentencing practice to ensure the absence of discrimination against female offenders?

Chapter 3

Women in prison: contemporary issues

From the moment of reception, barring court appearances, visits, segregation or jail transfers, your days blur into a cycle: rising at 6.30 am, muster [roll call] at 7.00 am, breakfast, 8.30 am pill parade and, if you're fortunate, off to work or class, sandwich lunch and muster, work till 3 pm, back to the wing, 3.30 pm pill parade, cook or collect meals from the kitchen, eat, muster, lock-in wing at 4 pm and in cell at 6 pm and the same again tomorrow.

(Hampton 1993: 45)

Introduction

Women are imprisoned as a punishment. In the previous chapter we made the point that there is no direct or positivistic (causal) relationship between women's lawbreaking behaviour and their imprisonment. The process of criminal justice constructs the imprisonable woman, and the seriousness of her crime is but one factor in this construction. Judicial attitudes towards women and changes in sentencing policies and patterns (some of which have not been gender-specific) also play their part (Gelsthorpe and Morris 2002), as do political priorities about the kind of offenders who should be incarcerated at any given time (Worrall 2002a). The decision to imprison women is also influenced by changes in judicial beliefs about what prison can achieve *for* women. As we have seen, there have always been paternalistic and maternalistic tendencies to believe that women can be sent to prison 'for their own good' (Carlen 1983; 1990; 1998) to be made into better women, better wives, better mothers, better daughters. It is easy therefore to forget that women's prisons are not hospitals, clinics, finishing schools, colleges or health farms. In this chapter we discuss a range of issues that characterise women's prisons in England and, where relevant, draw on examples from other jurisdictions to illustrate the extent to which these issues transcend national boundaries. Hannah-Moffat and Shaw (2000b) call them 'systemic concerns'. In order to avoid simply listing these issues as though they are unrelated, we use a concept favoured by the former HM Chief Inspector of Prisons for England and Wales, Sir David Ramsbotham – that of the 'healthy prison', and we ask the question: Can women's prisons be healthy prisons?

The concept of a 'healthy prison'

The concept of 'healthy prisons' did not originate in England and Wales, nor is it unique to that jurisdiction. The World Health Organisation has been promoting the concept for a number of years (Smith 2000). Within England and Wales, however, it became established in penal policy thinking following its elaboration in the HM Inspectorate of Prisons' Thematic Review, *Suicide is Everyone's Concern* (1999a). Building on previous research (e.g. Liebling 1992) that suicide in prison is influenced by the prison environment and not just by the vulnerability of the individual prisoner, the Chief Inspector identified four key constituents of a 'healthy prison':

1 A safe environment.
2 Treating people with respect.
3 A full, constructive and purposeful regime.
4 Resettlement training to prevent re-offending.

He concluded that the concept of a 'healthy prison' was relevant not just to an understanding of prison suicide but that it should be the 'cornerstone of future prison inspections' and a model 'upon which whole prisons may be accredited' (1999a: para. 7.38). As such, it reflects a recent tradition in England and Wales of both justifying imprisonment and seeking to minimise its harm, which has been adopted by officially-appointed critics since the seminal report by Lord Woolf (1991) following the Strangeways riot. The Woolf Report argued for a need to balance security, control and justice within prisons in order to prevent escapes, disruption and re-offending (for a fuller discussion of the report, see Cavadino and Dignan 2000). Such critiques have attempted to acknowledge that the prison environment is more than the sum of its constituent parts and that a holistic approach to prison and prisoner management is required, which consistently links attention to detail with overall purpose. Symbolic of that paradigmatic shift in penal thinking was the post-Woolf introduction of the Prison Service's Statement of Purpose that appears outside (and inside) every prison:

> Her Majesty's Prison Service serves the public by keeping in custody those committed by the courts. Our duty is to look after them with humanity and help them lead law-abiding and useful lives in custody and after release.

Healthy prisons: an oxymoron?

David Ramsbotham (the former Chief Inspector responsible for the central position that the term has achieved in contemporary debates about prison conditions) acknowledges that his use of the term 'healthy prison' must be qualified and that it 'in no way implies that prisons, even those that are very well run, are "healthy" in the full sense of the word' (1999a: para. 7.12). Nevertheless, he considers it to be a useful gauge of the comparative state of the well-being of prisoners. Subsequently, policy makers have tended to confine the use of the term to specific discussions about health care provision in prisons. However, two writers – Carlen (2001a) and Smith (2000) – have taken up the broader definition of the term 'health' in the prison context. Although Carlen does not use the term 'healthy prison', she recognises that suicide and self-harm are not discrete problems but are indicators of the general 'health' of a prison and argues for a 'holistic' approach to the care of women in prison, which is aimed not just at those women considered 'at risk' of suicide but at the whole prison culture and organisational style. This approach, she argues, should be regarded as *a good in itself* (2001a: 462) and not simply as a means to an end, however worthy that end might be. There is therefore a distinction to be made between the question of the morality of imprisonment (or its moral justifications) and the question of probity in prison management (or what can be done to prisoners *with probity*). The argument that certain things should happen in prison because they are 'good in themselves' and not because they can be justified in terms of 'outcomes' (preventing suicide, reducing re-offending, and so on) reflects the classical debate about the justification of punishment itself. Retributivism asserts that punishing the wrong-doer is a moral duty which is not dependent on what the punishment achieves in terms of future conduct. In contrast, utilitarianism asserts that punishment can only be justified if it achieves a 'greater good' – the reduction of crime (through deterrence, incapacitation or rehabilitation – see Chapter 4 for an explanation and discussion of the classical justifications for imprisonment). By the same token, it can be argued that there is a moral duty to treat prisoners as 'ends in themselves' and not as 'means to an end'. This touches on the second key constituent of a 'healthy prison' – the requirement for respect – which will be considered in more detail later.

Smith (2000) provides an interesting critique of the concept of 'healthy prisons', with some significant references to its implications for women in prison. She highlights the dangers of initially laudable health-promoting initiatives turning into 'surveillance medicine' or 'health policing' (2000:343) with women being held responsible (but without power) for their own health in an environment which is intrinsically 'disadvantageous ... for good health' (2000: 349). An example is the increasing trend to ban smoking in the visits areas of prisons. Of itself, this is a laudable policy, since smoke-filled visiting halls are undoubtedly very unpleasant and unhealthy environments. Never-theless, they are also extremely stressful places for prisoners and visitors alike and smoking prohibitions add to that stress for many. There can be no right answer because the situation is inherently 'unhealthy' in the first place. A further example is the promotion of 'healthy eating' among women in prison. Women are exhorted to eat healthily yet the quality of prison food and the limited availability of salads and fresh fruit make this very difficult. Women in prison have little control over the food that is available to them and in closed prisons often have to eat it in their cells, on their beds and next to their toilets:

> The food is far too stodgy, and if, on top of that, they're not getting any physical activity many of them are concerned about their weight. It's all self-image. If you're feeling particularly low, often one of the things you try to do is to maintain your own physical appearance as a way of combating the low self-esteem that you feel ... Women would be more than happy with salads and sandwiches, rather than having three cooked meals in a day [but] three cooked meals is what they get. And obviously quite high in calories.
>
> (Governor cited in Carlen 1998: 92)

In its mildest form, health promotion in prison may constitute an invasion of privacy; less benignly, some procedures (such as the mandatory drug testing of women) may infringe human rights and may also be counter-productive. In the oppressive environment of prison, the constant focus on 'unhealthy' behaviours (such as smoking, drugs and over-eating) may actually serve to increase their attractiveness when other options are so limited (Smith 2000:350).

What can be meant by the term 'healthy prison'?

We now consider each of the Chief Inspector's key constituents of a 'healthy prison'. As we do so, it is important to bear in mind that there are at least two perspectives on every issue: the prison's perspective and the prisoner's perspective. Much contemporary official rhetoric assumes that the interests of the prison (and, by implication, the community as a whole) and the interests of the 'responsible' prisoner are the same. The 'responsible' prisoner accepts that their punishment is just and seeks to co-operate with the prison in taking every opportunity to 'pay their debt' and rehabilitate themselves. Within this discourse, there is no conflict of interest and the only debate is about the pragmatics of implementation. For many prisoners, the experience *and meaning* of imprisonment is more complex and contradictory.

A safe environment

Security

The term 'security' may mean at least two things within the context of imprisonment. For the prison, it usually means ensuring that prisoners do not escape. This may be achieved in a number of ways – physical measures (high walls, razor wire, locks, keys, dogs, patrols, head counts, restrictions of movement, and so on); dynamic measures (staff–prisoner relationships, constructive regimes, in-cell television, visits, incentives, and so on) and security categorisation (assessing the likelihood of a prisoner attempting to escape and placing them in appropriate accommodation). As we have seen in the previous chapter, women tend not to escape and, if they do, they are very unlikely to be any danger to the community. They will almost always escape (or, more often, abscond from an otherwise legitimate outside visit) in order to go home to see children or to sort out family problems. It is not uncommon for women to abscond for a few days and then return voluntarily to prison to face their inevitable punishment.

While male prisoners are categorised from A to D, reflecting a relatively wide spectrum of security risk (maximum to open), women are categorised only as being suitable for 'closed' or 'open' conditions, and there are now very few 'open' places remaining in the system (see Chapter 2). But, as the recent inspection report on women's imprisonment in Western Australia concludes, a 'maximum security' prison *for women* is not the same as a maximum security prison for men, even when the same terminology is used (Inspector of Custodial Services, WA 2003). The system tacitly acknowledges that women do not present the same security risk as men, yet this is not translated into any explicit policy – and when women themselves are labelled 'maximum security' the public assumes, understandably, that they pose the same danger as a man with the same categorisation. An example of the difference is the blanket policy for all life sentence prisoners to begin their sentence as though they require 'maximum security', even though most homicides committed by women take place within a domestic context (see discussion later in this chapter on female lifers). Women prisoners in England and Wales also suffered disproportionately from the security clamp-down in the mid-1990s following the escapes of men from Whitemoor and Parkhurst prisons (Carlen 1998) and they continue to be held in conditions of higher security than is warranted because of the Prison Service's unwillingness to take the issue of women's different security categorisation seriously.

Assessing the risk posed by women prisoners is presented as a scientific exercise (Clark and Howden-Windell 1999) but is, in reality, an artificial one for a number of reasons. First, regardless of assessed risk, the location of women is heavily dependent on the number and type of places available across the female prison estate. Second, there is a constant conflation of the terms 'risk' and 'need' in the assessment of women (Hannah-Moffat 1999). Women in greatest 'need' are frequently assessed as being, almost by definition, those of highest 'risk'. Mental health, drugs, abuse and parenting 'needs' are translated into issues of 'risk', requiring high levels of security. The vocabulary of 'risk' and 'need' involves two parallel meanings. From the prisoner's perspective, she may view herself as being 'at risk', that is, vulnerable to a range of personal and socio-economic factors that threaten her health and well-being, and thus 'in need' of help. Those same terms, however, may be used by the prison to identify the prisoner as being 'at risk' of escape, disruption or re-offending, and thus being 'in need' of discipline and control.

But 'security' has another meaning for the prisoner, which is more closely associated with 'personal safety'. The Chief Inspector recognised that 'by their nature prisons are unsafe places in which to live' (HM Inspectorate of Prisons 1999a: para. 7.13) Sykes (1971) recognised this when he identified a 'lack of security' as one of the 'pains of imprisonment'. By 'security' he was not referring to the physical security of the prison which prevents escapes. He was concerned about what we might call a 'sense of security'. He pointed out that prison requires people to live in close proximity with other people who may well threaten their personal safety or just be routinely uncongenial in their behaviour and conversation. This enforced association often results in bullying, sexual assault and general intimidation, the implications of which for women will be discussed below.

Control

'Control' is another word with several meanings. For the prison, 'control' means the prevention of disruption, at both a collective and an individual level. This is achieved largely through prison discipline which itself may mean several things (see Chapter 1). A 'disciplined' prison is, arguably, a well-run and purposeful prison where everyone – staff and prisoners – knows what is expected of them, what they should be doing, when and where. In a well-run prison, the formal discipline system, which punishes specified prison 'offences' serves to buttress a disciplined environment but is not regarded as the sole guarantor of such an environment. Routinely high levels of disciplinary offences indicate an undisciplined prison, rather than its opposite. As we have seen, women routinely commit almost twice as many disciplinary offences as men. The prison may interpret this as meaning that women prisoners are more disturbed and difficult to manage; women prisoners may interpret this as meaning that discipline in women's prisons is more petty or that the pains of imprisonment are more unbearable – or both.

Accommodating women prisoners

What, then, constitutes an appropriate physical environment for women prisoners? Because of the small numbers, it is difficult to decide whether women should be accommodated together centrally where it *may*, but rarely *is* possible to provide a greater variety of facilities, or in small groups attached to men's prisons, which might be nearer to their homes but provide much poorer facilities. An example of the latter 'solution' can be found in Western Australia where Aboriginal women from remote areas are located in appalling conditions in remote men's prisons in order to be relatively near their families, rather than being transferred to central Perth where facilities are considerably better (Inspector of Custodial Services, WA 2003). In Hawaii, women were moved into men's prisons precisely in order to access better facilities but the reality was that women had less freedom of movement and ended up with less provision (Chesney-Lind and Rodriguez 2004). In England, increasing numbers of men's prisons are being required to accommodate a small number of women prisoners who invariably become 'second-class citizens' within the prison complexes, having less access to the best jobs, education and recreational facilities than the men – and there is no guarantee that they will end up being any nearer to their families (Carlen 1998).

Architecturally, prisons are not designed with women in mind (though some may argue that they are simply not designed with *people* in mind). Until recently, almost all women's prisons in England (with the notable and disastrous exception of Holloway – see Chapter 1) were either previously used as men's prisons or were used for completely different purposes historically. All three of the women's open prisons fall into the latter category. Askham Grange and East Sutton Park are stately homes and Drake Hall (now a closed prison) was originally a hostel for munitions workers in World War II. In fairness to Drake Hall, a major rebuild in the mid-1990s did attempt to provide village-type house blocks with green spaces and pathways. Unfortunately, most of the old accommodation remained in use, which rather detracted from the limited but welcomed vision. The approach to accommodating women prisoners has taken one of two forms: women are either considered to be no different from men and have been housed in identical structures, or they have been subjected to a paternalistic belief that if they are in 'nice' surroundings, they will feel less imprisoned. Nothing could be further from the truth. Women from inner London are often desolate and disorientated when located in the unfamiliar rural setting of Drake Hall (in North Staffordshire) and many request to be transferred back to Holloway, despite its worse conditions (Worrall 2000a).

The Woolf Report did not consider women's prisons explicitly because no serious collective disturbances have ever taken place in a women's prison in England and Wales. Nevertheless, the implications of his principles for women's prisons, and his advocacy of 'community prisons', were discussed creatively (Nacro 1991; Player 1994; Hayman 1996). In particular, one interpretation of the concept of 'community prisons' was the proposal for a large number of locally-based houses set aside for the purpose, where women would reside (possibly with their children) making use of community facilities and resources to provide their daily regime (Nacro 1991). Examples of such 'transitional' arrangements exist in other countries, such as the Netherlands (see Hayman 1996) and parts of Australia (Carlen 2002h) but in this country opposition by campaigning groups (on the grounds that such provision might increase the numbers of women sent to prison) and the general under-funding and neglect of hostel provision for women offenders (Howard League 2000) means that there has been no innovative residential provision for women offenders.

Sexuality and cross-gender posting

Since 1988 the Prison Service has officially adopted an equal opportunities approach to staff posting, which enables women officers to work in men's prisons and men officers in women's prisons (Carlen 1998). Despite this, only 17 per cent of prison officers are female and the proportion of female officers ranges from 3 per cent in one men's prison to 90 per cent in one open women's prison (Liebling and Price 2001). The introduction of female officers to men's prisons has generally been welcomed and viewed as having a 'normalising' effect on the prison environment, though their presence has challenged the male-dominated culture of prisons in much the same way as female police officers challenge 'cop culture' (Liebling and Price 2001; Walklate 2001).

Far less has been written about the impact of male prison officers in women's prisons. In US prisons, there is ample evidence of routine sexual assault of female prisoners by male guards, to the extent that the issue has attracted the attention of Human Rights Watch (Chesney-Lind and Pasko 2004). In her research of women's imprisonment at the millennium in England, Pat Carlen (1998) found that, although women prisoners did not object to male officers *per se,* they were often uncomfortable about their presence in the residential parts of the prison. As we have already seen, many women prisoners have past experiences of violent and abusive relationships with men that make them wary of contact with men in their living quarters. For such women, knowing that male officers are authorised to be involved in their daily routines causes anxiety. The counter-argument is that it might be beneficial for such women to experience men 'who are good role models, because a lot of these women have never met a decent man or a man who can keep his trousers zipped up' (Prison governor cited in Carlen 1998: 142). Beyond that specific anxiety, however, it could be argued that, since all women are socialised into being modest and private about their bodies, the prospect of unknown men being able both to discuss and to view them in various states of (un)dress, health and hygiene, is not unreasonably a matter of concern for them:

I've no objection to the employment of men in the prison. In some ways it's quite good. Nice to have some male conversation now and then. But I do object when two men do the patrols on the houses at night. Especially at four o'clock in the morning, they either tip the curtain back and shine a torch in, or they actually walk into the room. I don't like that. It could be very awkward.

(Amanda, cited in Carlen 1998: 139)

While the presence of male officers in women's prisons throws the issue of sexuality and sexual relations into sharp relief, there is 'a silence' about the numbers of lesbian officers working in women's prisons (Carlen 1998:143). There is no evidence to suggest that prison officers in England – male or female, heterosexual or lesbian – are any more sexually predatory than anyone else, but that is not the point. The point is that women who already feel vulnerable by reason of their imprisonment have to contend additionally with a routinised and structured loss of privacy which, quite literally, requires them to be naked before a 'legitimated punitive stare' (Carlen 1998: 142).

Drugs, bullying and violence

The history of women's imprisonment has been a history of the medicalisation of women's problems (Carlen 1983, 1998; Sim 1990) or, as Hannah-Moffat puts it, the power of *pastoralism* – the secular version of concern for the soul of the individual (2000: 8). The rebuilding of Holloway Prison in the 1970s was based on the assumption that women in prison needed medical and psychiatric facilities rather than punishment. Women's prisons were at the top of the prison 'league table' for the prescription of drugs that affected the central nervous system and the psychiatric control of difficult women through medication became one of the main concerns of the campaigning group *Women in Prison* in the 1980s. But, even at the height of this concern, it was acknowledged that prisons were doing no more than reflecting women's widespread dependency on prescribed drugs and that prison doctors were in a 'no win' situation:

If the prison doctor then stops prescribing drugs which the women have been legitimately prescribed outside s/he is likely to be accused of being punitive. If, on the other hand, s/he continues to prescribe large doses of drugs then s/he is likely to be accused of drugging women solely for penal control purposes.

(O'Dwyer and Carlen 1985: 165)

Increasingly, the view was formed among both those working in prisons and in campaigning groups that women turned to drugs – both prescribed and illegitimately obtained – in order to survive the pains of imprisonment. What was not conceded at that time was that women were themselves *drug offenders.*

The recognition, or over-recognition, of women as drug offenders came with the emergence into professional discourse of anti-discriminatory practice and anti-racism training in the late 1980s and early 1990s (see Chapter 2). By the mid-1990s, concern about drugs in women's prisons reached the point where the Chief Inspector of Prisons expressed the view, after visiting one women's prison, that it was possible for a woman 'to enter a shoplifter and leave an addict' (cited in Malloch 2000: 7). This level of illicit drug use in women's prisons was leading to bullying, trading and violent sexual assault among women (conducting internal searches on other women) (Malloch 2000). Officers began to view drug-users as the most aggressive and disruptive women in the prison: 'the biggest problem in here isn't the murderers, it's the addicts – they're far more devious' (Malloch 2000: 113).

Levels of substance misuse among prisoners are roughly comparable for men and women (Howard League 2000: 5), though women are proportionately more likely than men to be users of opiates and crack cocaine – the drugs most strongly associated with offending (Ramsey 2003; Home Office 2003b). For this reason, the Prison Service Women's Policy Group regards the misuse of drugs as a 'major issue for women in prison' (Stewart 2000: 42) and increasing resources are being made available for drugs treatment in women's prisons. But there is now a danger that courts will send more women to prison precisely because this is the one place in the criminal justice system where such treatment may be available (see Chapter 5 for a discussion of drugs treatment in the community). However, the limited availability of such treatment in prison means that many are simply condemned to an environment of violence and intimidation where their drugs problems worsen rather than improve.

Mandatory drugs testing (MDT) was introduced into prisons in England and Wales in 1995, with little consideration given to its differential impact on men and women (Carlen 1998). Ensuring the provision of an uncontaminated urine sample is a more intrusive process for women than for men – watching women urinate is less socially acceptable than watching men do so! It requires a level of disrespect for privacy that, arguably, comes close to infringing human rights (Smith 2000). MDT may be carried out on prisoners suspected of drugs involvement but it can also be carried out randomly and the legality of compulsory urinalysis has been successfully challenged in Canada (Smith 2000). Although the argument in favour of MDT is often couched in terms of health promotion and the protection of prisoners, it raises the question of the extent to which compulsorily detained people can be subjected to 'further involuntary interventions in their lives' (Smith 2000: 348). This issue of compulsory treatment (whether medical or psychological) is one to which we return later in this chapter when we discuss 'empowerment' and 'responsibilisation' in the context of cognitive behavioural programmes for women prisoners. We turn now to the Chief Inspector's second key constituent of a 'healthy prison'.

Treating people with respect

'The ways in which a prison can demonstrate respect for prisoners are many and various', according to the Chief Inspector (HM Inspectorate of Prisons 1999a: para.7.19). Decent accommodation and food, privacy, cleanliness, courtesy, a constructive regime and appropriate facilities for physical and mental well-being are all ways in which prisoners recognise that they are being treated with respect – and many books and articles have been devoted to discussing these aspects of imprisonment. What concerns us here are the ways in which *women* in prison may experience gender-specific respect or disrespect and our key argument is that women experience disrespect overwhelmingly when they are treated as *either* being no different from men in prison *or* as being *so* different from men in prison that paternalistic and maternalistic stereotypes of 'what women need' dictate what happens to them. Despite (or perhaps because of) a steady flow of research studies, official reports and reforming campaigns there has been little change in official responses to female offending. Instead, penal repression has been overlaid with 'the trappings of bureaucratic legitimacy' that require prisoners to be 'further humiliated by being forced to collude in their own repression' (Carlen 1998: 144). The potential for disrespect (and even infringement of human rights) now exists in a number of seemingly constructive initiatives within both male and female prisons and we discuss some of these below. But first we argue that the very recognition of 'women in prison' is in danger of becoming a stultified and disrespectful 'add-on' within global penal discourse (Worrall 2000b).

Universal concerns or false consensus?

At one time, writers on imprisonment made little reference to women prisoners who, as Stern says, 'nowhere in the world ... make up more than one in ten of the whole prison population' (1998: 138) and, in many countries, make up less than five per cent of that population. But that is no longer the case. Discussion of 'women in prison' is now an indispensable part of penology's global trading language and many common concerns appear to transcend national boundaries – inappropriate accommodation, distances from families, disproportionate numbers of indigenous, foreign and ethnic minority prisoners, provision for mothers and babies, health care, drugs problems and prison employment (Worrall 1998). Most women in prison around the world are there for crimes of poverty or drugs-related crimes and most crimes of violence are more likely to be intimate and retaliatory following years of abuse.

Alongside these apparently universal concerns, however, every country imprisons women for reasons that are embedded in local legal, social and political contexts (for example, the disproportionate imprisonment of female members of Shining Path – a terrorist group – in Peru, or of Aboriginal women for public order offences in Western Australia). The use of common terminology may mask very different understandings and approaches. Phrases like 'working with women in small groups', 'suitable clothing', 'allowing contact with families', 'suitable work', 'access to education' and so on, may mean very different things in different jurisdictions (Worrall 1998). Alternatively, similar practices may be justified on very different grounds. Teaching women to cook, sew and wash their clothes better may be described by one regime as making them better wives and mothers and by another as giving them survival skills for everyday living. Allowing women to keep their babies in prison may be justified as ensuring mother–child bonding or as being a woman's 'right'. Not keeping babies in prison may be seen as being in the child's best interests or as a means of putting pressure on courts not to send women with small babies to prison – which may, in turn, be seen as encouraging discrimination against women without small children. Maintaining close contact with families may be viewed as essential for the well being of both the woman and her family – or it may be a viewed as a way of preventing or minimising lesbianism (Worrall 1998)! Calling women prisoners by their first (rather than last) names may be interpreted as a sign of respect (HM Inspectorate of Prisons 1999) or an infantilising lack of respect (especially when coupled with reference to women as 'girls').

Traditional resistance from public sector prison officers to the use of 'Mr', 'Mrs' or 'Miss', let alone 'Ms', is one of the first 'pains of imprisonment' that all prisoners encounter.

Health care

The Prison Health Care Service is not yet part of the National Health Service although it employs many NHS-trained staff and aspires to provide a comparable standard of care. In April 2003 responsibility for funding for prison health services was transferred from the Home Office to the Department of Health and it is planned that within five years NHS Primary Health Care Trusts will be responsible for health care provision in prisons in their area. Given the notorious reputation of health care in prisons, this has to be good news, though whether such provision commands any priority within the NHS remains to be seen.

It is generally accepted that women's health-care needs in prison – both physical and mental – are more various and complex than men's (Alemagno and Dickie 2002) but the overwhelming experience of women in prison is that their health needs are not consistently dealt with in a respectful and appropriate way. The handcuffing of women in labour is but an extreme example (HM Chief Inspector of Prisons 1997) of a general attitude that regards women's unpredictable bodies as, at best, a nuisance and, at worst, a threat to security. In addition to the respect required in relation to routine menstruation needs, women require special attention in relation to pregnancy, cervical cytology and breast cancer screening, and miscellaneous hormonally-triggered 'women's ailments', which may include chronic mundane conditions such as constipation and other digestive problems. Attention to diet and nutrition generally is of particular importance for women and, given the stressful relationship which so many women have with food and body image outside prison, it is not surprising that eating disorders abound in women's prisons (Carlen 1998: 92).

It is also part of received wisdom that women prisoners suffer a higher level of mental illness than do men prisoners, though it is necessary to examine this claim in more detail. For example, Maden et al., (1994) found an equal prevalence of psychosis in male and female prisoners but women had a higher prevalence of learning difficulties, personality disorder, neurotic disorder (anxiety and depression) and substance abuse. The extent to which the prison environment creates such conditions and the extent to which it exacerbates pre-existing conditions is a matter of debate, though women in prison are twice as likely as men in prison to report having received help for a mental/

emotional problem in the 12 months before entering prison (Department of Health 2002). Maden et al., among many other writers, argue that many women in prison should either be in hospital or be treated in the community (Department of Health 2002).

Racism

In Chapter 2 we discussed the disproportionate number of black, indigenous and other ethnic minority women in prison around the world and made the distinction (predominantly a drugs-related one) between British and foreign national women in prisons in England and Wales. Here we consider the very limited literature that exists on the experiences of ethnic minority women in prison. The Prison Service has an extensive race relations policy which is designed to prevent direct and indirect (institutional) racism. For example, the ethnic mix in accommodation and work locations is monitored to ensure that no ghettos or exclusions develop and that all prisoners have equal access to the best accommodation and employment opportunities. Prison chaplains are responsible for ensuring that all prisoners are able to worship according to, and have access to an official from, their religion. Caterers are expected to make reasonable provision for culturally diverse diets and many prisons try to recognise a range of cultural and religious festivals. At the same time, however, prison canteens (shops) in women's prisons continue to resist stocking a full range of hair and skin products suitable for black women (Agozino 1997; Worrall 2000a). Women prisoners are allowed to wear their own clothes but foreign national women may have no one to buy clothes for them (Agozino 1997). Black women may be perceived to be aggressive and difficult and therefore less likely to be accepted for education lists, especially if they are not fluent in English (Chiqwada-Bailey 1997). Health-care staff may be lacking in knowledge about illnesses to which black and ethnic minority women are prone. In Western Australia, Aboriginal women are routinely disadvantaged in relation to the better accommodation and work because they are considered not to meet requirements of tidiness, hygiene, attitude or work ethic (Inspector of Custodial Services, WA 2003). By the same token, they are less likely to be moved to minimum security conditions, despite the fact that their offences are consistently more minor and their sentences consistently shorter in length than non-Aboriginal women. In addition to these experiences of indirect or institutional racism, direct racism – racial abuse and disrespect – continues to be a routine part of the experiences of black women in prison (Agozino 1997; Chiqwada-Bailey 1997; Nacro 2001; Inspector of Custodial Services, WA 2003; Henriques and Manatu-Rupert 2004).

Human rights

The Human Rights Act 1998 came into force in England and Wales in 2000. This did not introduce any new rights, laws or procedures but, for the first time, made it possible for the European Convention on Human Rights (to which the UK has always been a signatory) to be enforced in UK national courts. There are numerous books which provide the detail of the Convention but we are concerned here with its impact on the imprisonment of women. The rights are set out in a series of Articles and those which have proved of most relevance to prisoners in the UK have so far been:

- Article 3: the prohibition of torture, inhuman and degrading treatment
- Article 6: the right to a fair trial
- Article 7: the prohibition of punishment without law
- Article 8: the right to private and family life.

Not all the rights are 'absolute' and the 'rule of law' in a civilised society limits and qualifies some of them. Consequently, the Prison Service has been complacent about the impact of the Human Rights Act. Nevertheless, cases are now being brought which challenge prison treatment generally (under Article 3), the prison disciplinary system (under Articles 6 and 7) and restrictions on contact with families (under Article 8). The latter may prove to be of particular significance for women prisoners.

Imprisoning mothers

It is estimated that in England and Wales at least 100,000 children a year experience their father's imprisonment and more than 6,000 children a year are affected by maternal imprisonment (Lloyd 1995). In 1991 the first National Prison Survey interviewed 4,000 prisoners and found that 43 per cent said a family member had criminal convictions, compared with 16 per cent of the general population, and 35 per cent had another family member in prison. Among young prisoners the figures were even higher – 53 per cent had relatives with criminal convictions and 44 per cent had a family member who had been in prison. At the very broadest level therefore having a parent in prison is likely to increase the chances of a child ending up in prison themselves. Pelligrini (1997) interviewed children whose fathers had been imprisoned and she concluded that they went through five stages of adjustment:

establishing the meaning of the father's action; acknowledging the separation from the father and adapting daily activities to the new situation; managing feelings elicited by the situation; accepting the father's temporary separation; and re-adjusting to the father's return. The role of the child's mother in ensuring that adjustment was crucial and, although Pelligrini did not interview the children of imprisoned mothers, one cannot imagine that the impact of maternal imprisonment would be any less. The loss of their role as mother is considered by most prison administrations to be a significant 'pain of imprisonment' for women (Woodrow 1992). But this is not just an individual problem for mother and child. The impact of maternal separation on the future well-being of the state and its citizens is also a consideration.

According to a Caddle and Crisp (1997) 61 per cent of women in prison in England in 1994 were mothers. Between them, these 1,000 women had over 2,000 children and nearly one-third of these were under five years old. While men in prison normally expect their children to be cared for by their female partners, women in prison are heavily dependent on temporary carers such as grandparents or other female relations. The same study noted that children of imprisoned mothers were reported as having a variety of behavioural problems resulting from the separation, including becoming withdrawn, sleeping and eating problems, bed-wetting and problems in making and keeping friends.

So administrators of women's prisons feel obliged to find ways of allowing imprisoned women as much contact as possible with their families. This is done in four ways. First, women are afforded a variety of 'temporary releases' to spend time at home. Second, special facilities are made available to enable families to visit women in prison. Bandyup's Family Support Centre is a good example – a well-equipped and well-maintained building just outside the prison. Here, visitors can relax and obtain refreshment after a long journey to the prison. They can also obtain advice and help with any concerns they have. Children can be cared for while parents visit the prison, or collected from a visit half way through. The Centre is run by a non-governmental organisation, which also runs rehabilitation courses for the women, such as offending behaviour courses (Inspector of Custodial Services, WA 2003). Several women's prisons in England run whole day visits for children. Third and most rarely, women are allowed to postpone their prison sentences until suitable child care arrangements can be made. Fourth, and most controversially, women are allowed to keep their children with them in prison up to a certain age.

In England, there are currently four prisons which accommodate mothers with babies – Holloway, Styal, New Hall and Askham Grange – providing 69 places, although there are plans for two further units to be opened in 2004, offering 22 more places. Babies are allowed to stay up to 9 months in the three closed prisons and 18 months at Askham Grange, which is an open prison. The units are staffed by trained prison officers and employ professional nursery nurses. The prison accepts a duty of care towards the baby in relation to health issues. Abroad, there are many variations of provision (Caddle 1998) and the Ter Peel experiment in the Netherlands is often cited as a model of provision. Here, children remain with their mothers up to the age of four years but attend nurseries outside the prison on a daily basis. Similar provision exists in parts of Australia (Farrell 1998; Carlen 2002h), although the nursery at Bandyup Prison is considered to be problematic. Here there are no suitably trained staff and the health care centre refuses to provide medical care beyond primary health care. If a child is sick, a relative has to be contacted to collect the child from the prison, which is clearly an unsatisfactory and potentially dangerous situation. Lack of supervision has also resulted in babies being vulnerable to abuse (Inspector of Custodial Services, WA 2003).

The debate about mother and baby units is an unresolved one. It can be argued that a baby has the right not to start its life in prison and there has been much criticism of the standards of care and stimulation in units (Department of Health 1994), although there have been many improvements in recent years (HM Prison Service 1999). Their very existence is also said to encourage courts to send mothers with babies to prison instead of seeking out the alternatives. A study by Catan (1992) compares the development of two groups of babies – one in a unit and one cared for by temporary carers. Although the motor development of the group in the unit was slower, they quickly caught up once the mother was released, and this was off-set by a much greater stability of social environment and continuity of care. Many of the separated babies experienced changes of carers and were less likely to be reunited with their mothers. Even those mothers who did resume care of their babies had difficulties in sustaining the parental relationship.

Against this background, what rights do prisoners' children have? The answer is, not many. The UN Convention on the Rights of the Child is important in that it emphasises that all the rights it identifies apply to all children and that there should be no discrimination on the grounds of the activities or status of the child's parents. The key right is in Article 9 of the Convention which is the right to maintain regular contact with both parents unless it is contrary to the child's interests. The Children Act 1989 similarly emphasises the right of regular contact. A useful set of principles is proposed by Save the Children (Pelligrini 1997):

1   The interests of the child are paramount. Children should be helped to understand what is going on and be consulted about and involved in all decisions that affect them.

2   The child should suffer minimal disruption when a parent is imprisoned.

3   The child of an imprisoned parent should have good quality regular access to his or her imprisoned parent.

4   The parental responsibilities of the prisoner should be taken into account at the time of arrest and in any subsequent proceedings.

5   The support needs of the parent or carer looking after the child of an imprisoned parent should be recognised by social services departments, the probation service and other support agencies, and the response co-ordinated.

6   The maintenance of life within the child's established home and community should be given priority in any arrangements made concerning her or him. This requires co-ordination of services and sensitivity, awareness and training for all agencies concerned.

It could be argued that 'treating people with respect' is an overarching theme, rather than individual component, of a 'healthy prison'. Nevertheless, we turn now to the third key feature – that of providing a 'full, constructive and purposeful' regime.

A full, constructive and purposeful regime

There are a number of arguments in favour of keeping prisoners fully occupied. From the prison's perspective it makes control of the prison easier and less confrontational than simply locking prisoners up – it is part of 'dynamic' or interactional security. It is likely to give a prisoner some limited sense of purpose and thus help to reduce self-harming and suicidal behaviour. Prison work provides a modest but important source of income. Finally, education, work skills and other activities (such as programmes) might contribute, either directly or indirectly, towards the reduction of re-offending once a prisoner is released. In other words, keeping a prisoner constructively occupied is regarded as a 'good in itself' and its efficacy should not have to be proven. The underlying argument in this section is that, all too often, keeping women constructively occupied in prison is not viewed with the same (admittedly limited) priority as keeping men occupied. The moral (or capitalist) imperative to produce disciplined members of the work force is less strong for women than for men and the assumption that women will 'make do' with poorer prison provision is tenacious.

Employment and education

Much has been written about the paucity of the regimes in many women's prisons and the driving assumption that women in prison need to be made into better wives and mothers by improving their domestic skills of sewing, cooking, cleaning and, less frequently, gardening (Carlen 1990; Carlen and Tchaikovsky 1996). Kitchens, laundries and sewing workshops are the main sources of employment, though it might be argued that this is true also of men's prisons. It is the greater shortage of alternatives that is the distinctive feature of women's prisons and the overall shortage of employment provision. Including an element of training and recognisable qualification is a feature of some women's prisons, though its level and purpose varies greatly. Clerical qualifications and NVQs in hairdressing, catering and computers are among the most common, though there is a high level of unmet need (Hamlyn and Lewis 2000). Standards of education in women's prisons also vary, though the contracting out of education services in England and Wales to colleges of further education has brought an improvement in the range of provision. Despite this, there is little integration of work and education opportunities and many women are disadvantaged because of the short length of their sentences (Hamlyn and Lewis 2000). The opportunity to work outside the prison is a privilege reserved for minimum-security women. Community work in local shops, factories and, in some cases, schools and care homes, is facilitated in some prisons, though security concerns have meant that the practice is less widespread than in the past .

Programmes

Over the past decade, the central plank of rehabilitative work within prisons in England and Wales has been a range of cognitive behavioural programmes, devised and supervised by psychologists and delivered by specially trained prison and prison welfare (probation) officers.

These programmes may be offence-specific, such as the Sex Offender Treatment Programme, Anger Management Programme or Violent Offender Programme, or they may be generic, such as the Reasoning and Rehabilitation or Enhanced Thinking Skills programmes. Cognitive behavioural programmes are premised on social learning theory and a belief that offenders have cognitive deficits, that they view the world differently from non-offenders and that their cognitive distortions can be un-learned. The link between 'anti-social thinking' and 'anti-social behaviour' is said, by programme advocates, to be well established and the aim of programmes is the laudable one of helping prisoners to improve their problem-solving abilities through developing better information gathering, analytical and social skills. Beyond being regarded as something which may be 'good in itself', however, programmes claim to instil 'correct' or 'pro-social' thinking and to reduce re-offending as a direct consequence of their completion. The programmes have a long history in Canada, where most originate, and there is extensive published evidence of their efficacy (see the website for the Correctional Services of Canada, www.csc-scc.gc.ca). Until recently, the generic cognitive skills programmes have been considered to be particularly successful in England and Wales (Friendship et al. 2002). They are, however, very controversial, even when applied to white, male prisoners, (Cann et al. 2003) but criticism is dismissed as 'knowledge destruction' by some of their more extreme protagonists (Andrews and Bonta 1998). Questions about the 'voluntariness' of participation and the inconsistency of programme availability across prisons also raise human rights issues, especially when the completion of programmes is a key factor in Parole Board considerations about early release. Further reading relating to this important and fascinating debate is recommended at the end of this chapter. Our concern here is to examine the implications of such programmes for women in prison, where the evidence of efficacy is far scarcer, as indeed it is in relation to indigenous and other ethnic minority prisoners.

Although there is nothing inherently wrong in helping women prisoners to 'think better', nor is it suggested that women 'think differently' from men in any essentialist sense, there has been a great deal of criticism about the suitability of cognitive behavioural programmes as vehicles for the rehabilitation of women in prison. There are two broad criticisms. First, it is argued that the delivery of the programmes is inappropriate – that they do not take account of women's *responsivity*. By this is meant that the programmes need to be *adapted* for use with women, taking account of women's different life experiences, providing examples to which women are more likely to relate, perhaps even adopting a different tone and style of tutoring. This is the official Prison Service response to criticism (Clark and Howden-Windell 1999) and some psychologists are prepared to go even further in recognising the difficulties in running programmes for women:

> It is often found with individual women that it is impossible to dismiss the distress element and ignore the continually repeated background history of abuse or domestic violence. We find that women bring emotional distress into offending behaviour group programmes such as R & R. If this is not addressed outside the programme, they may be unable or unwilling to engage cognitively.
>
> (King and Brosnan 1998: 14)

One of us has visited a programme which will not accept pregnant women on the grounds that the other women will always want to talk about pregnancy, childbirth, child-rearing and related topics and that this will be a distraction from the business of discussing offending.

But underlying this response is a resistance to the suggestion that women's crime may have different causes from men's crime. To use the correct parlance, women have broadly the same 'criminogenic needs' as men (Clark and Howden-Windell 1999).

The second, and more radical, criticism is that cognitive behavioural programmes, at a fundamental level, fail to contextualise women's offending within their often long-term victimisation, and insist that they have more rational choices in their lives than they do. In a now much-quoted government statement, it is asserted that women only *believe* that their options are limited' by 'poverty, abuse and drug addiction' (Home Office 2000a: 7). A number of writers (Hannah-Moffat and Shaw 2000a; Kendall 2002; Carlen 2002c) have argued that such programmes are not part of the process of the 'empowerment' of women, but rather of their 'responsibilisation'. Instead of empowering women to make genuine choices, cognitive behavioural programmes hold women responsible for their own rehabilitation. It is accepted, even by advocates, that there is a lack of evidence to support the effectiveness of programmes for women but this is, perhaps unsurprisingly, regarded with some complacency (Worrall 2003).

Resettlement training to prevent re-offending

So, finally, we reach the fourth component of Sir David's 'healthy prison'.

Preparation for release

The Social Exclusion Unit (2002) published a report entitled 'Reducing re-offending by ex-prisoners' in which it identified nine key factors that influence the 'revolving door' of prison-release-re-offending-prison for both men and women . These were:

1   Education.
2   Employment.
3   Drug and alcohol misuse.
4   Mental and physical health.
5   Attitudes and self-control.
6   Institutionalisation and life-skills.
7   Housing.
8   Financial support and debt.
9   Family networks.

The report goes on, using these indicators, to demonstrate how much of a socially-excluded group ex-prisoners are and how little chance they stand of not re-offending unless these issues are addressed (see also HM Inspectorates of Prisons and Probation 2001). It includes an Annex which specifically discusses women prisoners, summarising the high level of disruption they experience even in relation to short sentences, often losing housing and children in an impact that is disproportionate to the sentence itself (see also Nacro 2001). Employer attitudes to women with prison records further disadvantages them in the job market on release and child-care costs prevent many from taking up employment, even when they were working before their sentence. Hamlyn and Lewis (2000) found that 44 per cent of the women in their survey had worked in the 12 months prior to their sentence, but, although 90 per cent of them worked in prison, only 37 per cent found work on release and that was through friends and family – and largely related to their pre-sentence work. They did not feel they had learned any useful new work skills in prison. Many of them claimed that they would not re-offend but this was because they had found prison such a negative experience, not through any positive gains from work or programmes.

Planning for release is a difficult task even when a woman knows the exact date of her release. One particular group of prisoners remains in prison for many years without knowing their release date. These are life sentence prisoners, whose length of stay in prison is indeterminate and we turn now to a case study of female life sentence prisoners.

Indeterminacy – the case of the female lifer

A life sentence is a sentence like no other. The ultimate weapon in the penal armoury of England and Wales, its uniqueness lies in its indeterminacy, a feature which sets it apart from even the longest determinate sentence. In populist punitive discourses it remains the Other of the capital punishment debate – the overly lenient and undeserved escape from death for those who have taken or endangered the lives of 'the innocent'. In 2001 there were 4,810 life sentence prisoners in England and Wales (see Chapter 2). The population of male lifers has increased from 2,800 in 1991 to 4,648 in 2001, while the population of female lifers has increased from 96 in 1991 to 162 in 2001. The number of prison receptions sentenced to life imprisonment has doubled from 1991 to 2001, with male receptions increasing from 246 in 1991 to 512 in 2001 but the trend in receptions is less clear for women. Because the numbers are so small, they fluctuate from year to year but the highest figure was 22 in 2000.

Drawing on interviews undertaken with 47 (about half) of the female lifers incarcerated in the mid-1990s, Walker and Worrall (2000) identified some of the gendered 'pains of imprisonment' that were specific to the experiences of female life sentence prisoners. Much has been written about the 'pains of imprisonment' experienced by both men and women, particularly those serving long sentences who, in addition to those losses experienced by all prisoners (for example, privacy, autonomy, heterosexual relations, family contact, personal security, and so on) also experience a great fear of physical and mental deterioration. What remains relatively unexplored are the losses specifically associated with indeterminate sentences – the losses that become more, rather than less, difficult to bear with time because there is no known release date, no end point to be worked towards. For women, many of these losses are bound up with motherhood. Even – perhaps especially – those women who do not have children suffer extensive gender-specific loss as the result of a life sentence. For example, the ticking of the 'biological clock' means that women serving life sentences may be deprived of the chance to have children directly as a result of their sentence. They may also 'lose' their children to long-term foster care or adoption because of their inability to plan for their return home. For those who retain contact with their children, there is the additional pain of seeing them brought up – sometimes for the whole of their childhood – by other people. Since many female lifers have killed the father of their children, their sense of guilt at seeing their children lose both parents for an unknown number of years is the single most painful aspect of their sentence.

Lifers can be certain of only one thing – that nothing is certain. Tariff dates offer only tantalising and slender hope of release. All life sentence prisoners come to learn, as they are socialised into lifer culture, that tariffs may be extended, provisional release dates withdrawn and release criteria altered. The life sentence prisoner is 'helpless in a world of nightmare uncertainties' (Sapsford 1983: 19) When (if) released, the life sentence prisoner remains on *life licence* for the rest of her life and is subject to recall to prison at any time, if she commits an offence or otherwise fails to comply with the conditions of her licence. According to Kershaw et al., (1997), 9 per cent of lifers released between 1972 and 1993 were recalled within two years and 17 per cent within five years. A more startling statistic is that, of the 52 female lifers released since 1981, no reconvictions for a standard list offence had been recorded against them by 1995 (HM Inspectorate of Prisons 1999b). By and large, then, life licensees, and particularly women, are a compliant and conforming group of ex-prisoners (Woodward 1999) who settle back into the community well and are 'indistinguishable from other members of the public' (Coker and Martin 1985: 235).

Coping with a life sentence has been likened to coming to terms with having a terminal illness – a living death – but without the sympathy and support afforded to the terminally ill (Jose-Kampfner 1990). Women lifers, who most often kill close relatives, are additionally vilified for being responsible for the lasting damage caused to their children. They are viewed as having forfeited their right to 'grieve for the loss of themselves and their outside world' (1990: 112). Building on the widely accepted stages of grieving, Jose-Kampfner argues that female lifers (should be allowed to) experience (not necessarily sequentially) *denial, anger, depression, mourning, acceptance* and *hope.*

The prison environment, however, is uniquely unsuited to such a process. Lowthian (2002: 177) summarises the concerns which make it disingenuous to describe women's prisons as 'healthy':

- Deterioration in standards of healthcare and hygiene

- Pressures relating to staff shortages resulting in non-mandatory tasks (e.g. housing and resettlement support) being dropped in order to ensure that statutory functions (e.g. security and discipline) are carried out

- Inappropriate allocation of prisoners due to the inexorable demand for places

- Staffing shortages resulting in the failure to maintain adequate standards of care and thus increasing the risk of bullying, self-harm and suicide

- Staffing shortages reducing cover to the extent that regime activities and education are curtailed since women cannot be unlocked

- Focus on offending behaviour and other accredited cognitive behavioural programmes resulting in a lack of holistic, needs-based programmes for women.

Conclusion

Prison authorities often argue that the women they have to deal with are already so damaged that it is extraordinarily difficult for them to achieve anything approaching genuine rehabilitation. One has to sympathise with this argument to some extent. But when Ruth Wyner (2003) was imprisoned under highly controversial circumstances, she found her intelligence, education and management skills wholly inadequate for personal survival. Her profound sense of shock and injustice suffuses her account, as does the evidence of the real and lasting damage caused to her by her imprisonment.

A professional charity worker, Wyner was imprisoned for failing to disclose to the police the names of drug dealers *who had been banned* from the shelter for which she was responsible. Leaving aside the issue of whether or not she should have been imprisoned at all, her story provides an almost clinical case study of the impact of prison on an otherwise 'normal' woman. Her story is one of an assault on identity that affected both her mental and physical health in ways from which she is still recovering. In addition to the routine physical privations detailed in this chapter, it was also clear that the prison was incapable of dealing with her in anything other than a wholly standardised way. As a trained journalist, Wyner offered to be a 'classroom assistant' on the English courses but was apparently told that this could not be allowed ('It seems that as well as being unable to help myself, I am not allowed to help anyone else' [p.66]). Almost 20 years on, Carlen's observation (above) about 'good prisoners' not thinking themselves better than other women still seems pertinent. Instead Wyner was obliged to attend an art class in which she had no interest and for which she had no aptitude, and to work in the gardens which, as it happened, turned into something of an oasis of sanity for her. That Wyner suffered with migraines and depression throughout her sentence appears to have been a matter of little concern to the medical authorities in the prison.

That she was offered an offending behaviour course for drug importers ('"I'm not in for that", I protest. "It's all we have to offer", the probation officer replies' [p.131]) illustrates the absurdity of inflexible approaches to offender rehabilitation. That, as a Jewish woman, she had to subject herself to a regime of evangelical Christianity in order to live in half-decent surroundings could be viewed as an abuse of Human Rights.

The prison authorities would probably say that Ruth Wyner was a 'difficult' woman because she challenged every perceived incident of disrespect (including being referred to as a 'girl' rather than a 'woman') and she occasionally seems to have stirred up her fellow prisoners. But, by and large, this is an account of a woman trying to be professionally, if not personally, conciliatory – as much for her own survival as for the benefit of others – and feeling herself thwarted on every hand. Presumably, it was her attempt to relate to prison staff in a 'professional' manner that most irritated them. When she was reduced to a crying or giggling 'girl', she was easier to handle.

This chapter has not aimed to provide a comprehensive list of every issue and concern relating to women's prisons. There is a wealth of literature from many countries to which the reader can turn for that level of detail – and we provide a full bibliography at the end of this book. Instead, we have sought to highlight some of the more controversial issues and to place those within a conceptual framework that will allow readers to go beyond bemoaning the inadequate provision in women's prisons to a more thoughtful exploration of the purpose of women's imprisonment and the extent to which women's prisons can be regarded as 'healthy' environments.

Concepts to know

black: the term 'black' is often used (as here) politically to denote an opposition to 'white' and as a common term for women of African, Caribbean and Asian origin. The term 'women of colour' is the preferred term in the USA since the term 'black' there refers only to women of African origin. 'Aboriginal' (with a capital 'A') and 'indigenous' are the respectful terms for the first inhabitants of Canada, the USA, Australia and New Zealand. The term 'First Nation' is also used in the North America and 'Maori' in New Zealand. It is important to recognise that the terminology is contested but the term 'coloured' is unacceptable.

cognitive behavioural approaches: treatment programmes based on social learning theory which argue that offenders have cognitive deficits and need help to change the distorted thinking that is claimed to be the major cause of anti-social behaviour.

criminogenic needs: factors regarded officially to be linked directly with offending (such as poor thinking skills, criminal associates, impulsivity, lack of self-control, poor educational attainment). Non-criminogenic needs are viewed as those that contribute only indirectly to offending (such as low self-esteem, a history of abuse, depression and anxiety and structural factors like race, gender and class).

empowerment: a term which has been (mis)appropriated from feminist discourse by prison managers to imply that it is possible to organise women's imprisonment in such a way as to enable women to make genuine choices about how they live their lives in prison and in preparation for release.

indirect or institutional racism: features or regulations in an organisation which, while not overtly advantaging particular groups, nevertheless make it likely that other particular groups will be unable to fulfil the requirements. In this context, an example would be giving the best prison accommodation to kitchen workers, knowing that black prisoners are under represented as kitchen workers.

responsibilisation: the consequences, whether intentional or not, of advocating 'empowerment' within an environment of total constraint. Prisoners (male and female) are required to accept responsibility for their own health, well-being and rehabilitation but without any genuine power to make the necessary choices.

risk assessment: an actuarial approach to predicting likelihood of recidivism (re-offending); static (fixed) factors such as age, gender and criminal history are quantified alongside dynamic (personal and social) factors to produce a predictive score which is used for a variety of purposes within the prison system (for more detail see Kemshall 1995).

social exclusion: in this context, a term that indicates the marginalisation of ex-prisoners and their likely re-offending as a result of a range of unaddressed social and personal needs.

tariff: the length of time (set by the trial judge) that a life sentence prisoner has to serve for purposes of retribution before their release can start to be considered.

Further reading

Caddle, D. and Crisp, D. (1997) *Imprisoned Women and Mothers.* Home Office Research Study 162. London: Home Office

Carlen, P. (ed.) (2002d) *Women and Punishment: The Struggle for Justice.* Cullompton: Willan.

Fox, K.J. (1999) 'Changing violent minds: Discursive correction and resistance in the cognitive treatment of violent offenders in prison'. *Social Problems*, 46(1): 88–103

HM Prison Service (1999) *Report of a Review of Principles, Policies and Procedures on Mothers and Babies/Children in Prison.* London: HM Prison Service (available to download from www.hmprisonservice.gov.uk)

Inspector of Custodial Services, Western Australia (2003) *Bandyup Prison and the Imprisonment of Women in Western Australia*, Perth (available to download from www.custodialinspector.wa.gov.au)

McGuire, J. (ed.) (1995) *What Works: Reducing Re-offending.* New York, NY: Wiley and Sons

Social Exclusion Unit (2002) *Reducing Re-offending by Ex-prisoners.* London: Cabinet Office (available to download from www.cabinet-office.gov.uk/seu/publications)

Topics for discussion

1 Which common concerns about women in prison appear to transcend national boundaries?
2 How useful is the concept of a 'healthy prison' in understanding women's experiences of imprisonment?
3 Explore the arguments put forward by writers who contend that the use of the term 'empowerment' in relation to women's imprisonment is disingenuous.

Essay questions

1 To what extent is it possible for women's prisons to be 'healthy prisons'?
2 'It is no more important for prisons to take account of a woman's role as a mother than a man's role as a father'. Discuss.
3 Describe and analyse the main features of cognitive behavioural programmes for prisoners. In what ways are these programmes suitable for women and in what ways might they be unsuitable?

Chapter 4

Theories of women's imprisonment

Introduction

Theories provide explanations. In sociology they attempt to answer questions about the origins, constitution, functions or possible meanings of social phenomena. However, because social phenomena are always and already presented to us laden with historical and cultural meanings, a sociologist has to take some pains to define what is to be explained, and then use very specifically delineated and clearly related concepts to answer questions about a phenomenon's provenance, construction, functionalities or possibilities. What, nominally, may appear to be the same social phenomenon may be differently specified in different theories, according to the domain assumptions made by the theorist. This difference in definition and the assumptions behind it then of course shapes the rest of the 'story' about what *in theory* has, within a newly-imposed theoretical framework, now shed its common-sense meaning and become an object of knowledge. Theoretical work therefore is not aimed at finding 'truth', but at helping to create new knowledge of why things take the form they do.

In looking at (or rather *for*) theories of women's imprisonment we are soon confronted by the realisation that most theories of imprisonment are not gender-specific. They are not always only about male imprisonment either; some are gender-neutral (see Cousins 1980). Nor, because of the lack of symmetry between lawbreaking and the severity of punishment, is it much help, when looking for theories of women's *imprisonment* to look at explanations of women's *crime*. A theory purporting to explain why certain women break the law will not explain why they receive, or do not receive, a custodial sentence. Explaining lawbreaking behaviour tells us nothing about why any particular woman goes to prison, nor about the meanings of penal incarceration. In this chapter therefore the strategy will be to harness both general and gender-specific theories of penal incarceration to a discussion of how they have been, or might be, used to inform analyses of the forms and functions of women's imprisonment. This will often necessitate outlining general theories of imprisonment before highlighting the ways in which they have been used (or criticised, transformed, rejected or ignored) in relation to theories about the imprisonment of women.

The questions that sociologists have asked, either implicitly or explicitly, about women's imprisonment have been many and varied. We are going to parcel up and summarise their answers under three main questions of our own:

1   Why do women's prisons take the forms they do?
2   What are women's prisons for?
3   Why do relatively few women go to prison?

In this chapter we will describe and discuss a range of texts to suggest the breadth, depth and relevance of the vast literature which might be drawn upon to answer questions 1and 2. Question 3 will be addressed in Chapter 5. There will, however, necessarily be much overlap between the different sections in this chapter and, indeed, between all the chapters in this book. The best authors and theories can seldom be neatly pigeon-holed, and so it is with the wide spectrum of writings which analyse the complex social phenomena constituting imprisonment in general and women's imprisonment in particular.

Why do women's prisons take the forms they do?

In the literature which might be used to answer this first question, four themes are dominant: prisonisation; discrimination; resistance; and carceral clawback. The first three themes are all concerned with the ways in which prisoners respond to being in prison. The fourth, carceral clawback, refers to the way in which the prison's fundamental function (to keep prisoners in secure custody) is ultimately the final arbiter in relationships between prison staff and prisoners. In addition to their contribution to these themes, most of the books and articles cited below are rich in information about life in women's prisons. So, even if they are only mentioned in connection with one or two themes here, all of them will repay further study.

Prisonisation

Either the process whereby a prisoner adopts the behavioural style and values of the 'inmate culture'; or where, as an adaptive response to imprisonment, the prisoner behaves in ways at variance with her usual behavioural style outside prison.

Early sociological studies of imprisonment in the 1950s and 1960s tended to focus on the ways in which prisoners *adapt* to incarceration. Many of them took the concept of 'prisonisation' from Donald Clemmer's 1930s study of a male prison (Clemmer 1940) and tried both to explain why a distinctive inmate culture emerges in prison and to assess to what extent this inmate culture is responsible for inmate behaviour, norms and values. Analysing the relationships between social structure and individual behaviour has been a traditional task for sociologists and it is not surprising that this theme has been of either major or minor concern in many empirical studies of imprisonment right up to the present day. However, and as will be suggested below, even when studies share a (greater or lesser) focus on 'prisonisation' they, nonetheless, may take very different forms and draw very different conclusions. For whereas earlier studies tended to focus on the potency of inmate culture as the source of anti-institutional behaviour in prison, later studies were more inclined to focus on the nature of the prison regimes themselves – or at least on the interaction between different types of regime and different prisoner personalities. Indeed, even in relation to disturbed behaviour, by the early 1970s, the psychiatrist T.C.N. Gibbens (1971) was remarking of women in Holloway Prison, London, that 'although their behaviour looks as mad as mad can be, [they] are really reacting to prison life.'

The two books discussed below are both 'interactionist' studies insofar as they examine the interaction between individuals and organisational behaviour. Where they differ is that whereas the first sees the inmate culture as the prime motivator of inmate behaviour, the second sees the disciplinary regimes of the institutions themselves as being the most potent determinant of how inmates behave.

D. Ward and G. Kassebaum, *Women's Prison: Sex and Social Structure.* London: Weidenfeld and Nicolson, 1966

Research for Ward and Kassebaum's *Women's Prison* was conducted in Frontera Prison in California, and it was one of the first sociological studies to recognise that the needs of women in prison are different to those of male prisoners and that incarcerated women are much more adversely affected by loss of family and friends than are males. They had actually set out to investigate whether women's modes of adaptation to prison life were similar to men's and they quickly discovered that they were not. However, there the similarity with later studies ended. For *Women's Prison* (like prison studies before and since) was a product of its time, and, just as previous and contemporary explanations of women's crime had focused on female sexuality (for example, Lombroso and Ferrero 1895; Thomas 1923; Pollak 1950), so did Ward and Kassebaum when it came to explaining the different modes of adaptation to institutional life of women prisoners. They saw a link between the homosexual relationships which they observed in women's prisons and women prisoners' reiteration of their deep sense of loss of family and friends. A similar argument was put forward by Rose Giallombardo (1966, 1974) who was studying the US Federal Penitentiary for women around the same time.

Ward and Kassebaum can be criticised for abandoning too soon their analysis of the social structure of the prison and rooting their explanation in stereotypical views of some essentialised female psychology which implies that all women want the same things from life and, moreover, that when they are deprived of these essentials, will all seek solace in identical ways. For, as later theorists were to point out, how women adapt to imprisonment will depend upon their past histories, their education and many other factors. Unfortunately, the fascination of Ward, Kassebaum and Giallombardo with the dynamics of homosexual relationships in the end told us less about the nature of women's imprisonment and more about relationships between women which may or may not have been peculiar to the imprisonment environment, but which certainly seemed to be in what Alvin Gouldner (1968: 121–2) once called the 'zoo-keeping' [voyeuristic] tradition of criminological research. At the same time, and in defence of Ward, Kassebaum and Giallombardo, it has to be noted that several studies of the sentencing of women have suggested that women without men are more at risk of custodial sentences than are their sisters living in male-related domesticity (Worrall 1981; Carlen 1983), a finding which might mean that prisons are more likely to house disproportionate numbers of homosexual women. Moreover, it is certainly the case that prison authorities in England have for years been concerned about homosexuality among female prison staff and the effect this has on prison organisation. Even so, taken together, these two observations only add up to saying that, for various reasons, disproportionate numbers of women are, at certain times in history and in specific cultures, likely to be of homosexual orientation before they enter prison, rather than to any convincing evidence that, among women prisoners homosexual relationships are more prevalent than among male prisoners; or that, for women, homosexual activities and relationships are the dominant (rather than just one among several) modes of coping with the pains of imprisonment.

Alexandra Mandaraka-Sheppard, *The Dynamics of Aggression in Women's Prisons in England.* **Aldershot: Gower, 1986**

As the title of her book suggests, Mandaraka-Sheppard's main objective in studying the 'dynamics of aggression' in six women's prisons in England was to ascertain to what extent, and how, organisational responses to prisoners' misbehaviour affected their future behaviour. Arguing that previous studies of 'prisonisation' had failed to identify which aspects of a custodial environment resulted in a response from prisoners which was specifically the result of their being in prison, in 1979 Mandaraka-Sheppard interviewed 50 per cent of women in six English prisons (three open and three closed). Altogether, 326 prisoners were interviewed. They were asked about the establishment's rules and punishments, about their responses to the prison discipline, and also about their relationships with the other prisoners. Detailed statistical analysis of the results supported the claim of previous 'prisonisation' studies that institutional factors exert a significant influence upon inmate behaviour, but only in interaction with their own previous socio-biographies and the varying discipline systems of the different prisons. For example: young, single and childless women were found to be more badly behaved in prison than older women and mothers; and there were significant differences between the prisons which had the most severe punishment systems and those where the disciplinary procedures were more lenient. Prisons with the harshest methods of punishment had the most instances of bad behaviour. Thus, although the overall findings of Mandaraka-Sheppard's study suggested that a certain 'prisonisation' of prisoners does occur, they did not confirm previous claims that the cause of in-prison rule-breaking behaviour is primarily attributable to inmate subculture. Misbehaviour among the prisoners in this study tended to be an individualist response to institutional factors emanating from the disciplinary system and staff attitudes. In her discussion of the findings, Mandaraka-Sheppard argues that 'prisonisation' of prisoners is neither uniform not inevitable. However, insofar as this argument ignores the fact that security in prisons is a logical necessity (rather than an optional extra which might be dispensed with) it is likely that while prisons exist, some degree of 'prisonisation' is likely to occur (see section on *carceral clawback* pp. 90–1).

Discrimination

One of the most persistent themes in both historical and contemporary stories of women's imprisonment has been that of *discrimination*, telling the story of how women in prison have always been treated differently to male prisoners, though not usually in ways which have been to their advantage, and, paradoxically, often at the same time as they were, arguably, also being treated as if they were men! Each of the following books broke new ground in analysing discrimination in the women's prisons.

Pat Carlen, *Women's Imprisonment: A Study in Social Control.* **London: Routledge and Kegan Paul, 1983**

Pat Carlen's *Women's Imprisonment* was not conceived as a 'feminist' project, but rather as an investigation and theorization of what imprisonment 'means' in the sense of its predeterminants (i.e. which women go to prison and why) and its effects on the women's lives after prison. For that reason, only one chapter of the book was actually about Scotland's women's prison, Cornton Vale, where interviews were conducted with 20 women prisoners over the age of 21. (The other chapters covered such topics as family life and conceptions of masculinity in Scottish culture, mental illness and medico-legal conceptions of personality disorder and social work in Scotland – all of which, it was argued, were effective in making the meanings of women's imprisonment in Scotland take the form they did.)

The chapter on imprisonment focused primarily on the ways in which women prisoners were treated unfavourably within the prison system, mainly because there were relatively few of them, but also because of the debilitating and contradictory assumptions which have been inherent in social constructions of femininity and female subjectivity.

The relatively small size of most women's prison systems when compared with men's have routinely had effects which were apparent in Scotland in 1982 when the research was reported and which are still apparent in many prison systems today:

- Women prisoners tend to be invisible to the general population and therefore their needs are often neglected

- It is often assumed (erroneously) by the public that because relatively few women go to prison, those who do must have committed very serious crimes

- Women prisoners tend to be imprisoned at greater distances from their homes

- The range of regimes and training activities within regimes tend to be more restricted because there are fewer economies of scale

- The women's prisons are often organised in exactly the same way as the men's, thereby not recognising women's different needs stemming from differential physical and medical need, differential family responsibilities and differential cultural assumptions

- There are fewer and geographically sparsely spread facilities for women when they come out of prison

- Released women prisoners are likely to suffer greater social stigma than male prisoners. This is primarily because a male convict is seen only as being a bad citizen whereas, because women criminals have traditionally been seen to be 'unnatural' women, a woman prisoner is likely to be seen as being both a bad citizen and an unnatural woman. Not only has she offended against the state; she has also offended against her femininity

It was in analysing what the women told her about the way in which they were treated within the prison that Carlen came to the conclusion that one of the reasons why the prisoners felt so tense (and why, too, the peculiar behaviour which some women in prison exhibit leads to them all being stereotyped as being either mad or sad) was because they were, as she put it, constantly being defined as being 'both within and without sociability; both within and without femininity; and … both within and without adulthood' (p. 90). In other words, although the women were frequently characterised by prison personnel as being 'unsocialised', 'unfeminine' and 'childish', Carlen was able to demonstrate that many aspects of the regime provoked the very types of 'other' behaviour which the prison's disciplinary pedagogy condemned. In sum, her analyses led her to conclude that whereas the motto of those charged with the penal regulation of deviant men and boys may well have been 'discipline and punish', the motto of those involved in overseeing the imprisonment of women and girls may, arguably, have been 'discipline, medicalise, domesticise, psychiatrise and infantilise'.

Nicole Rafter, *Partial Justice: Women in State Prisons 1800–1935.* **Boston: Northeastern University Press, 1985**

Nicole Rafter's *Partial Justice* is a relatively early and seminal work in the international literature on women's imprisonment. Although it is about women in state prisons in America, throughout the whole of the nineteenth century to 1935, the specifics of women's penal custody which Rafter details have many resonances with stories of women's imprisonment elsewhere, both then and now. Writing of women's custodial institutions in the early to mid-nineteenth century she described them thus:

> The custodial model was a masculine model: derived from men's prisons, it adopted their characteristics – retributive purpose, high-security architecture, a male-dominated authority structure, programmes that stressed earnings and harsh discipline ... women's custodial institutions treated women like men. But ... this did not mean that women's care and experience of incarceration were identical to those of males. Probably lonelier and certainly more vulnerable to sexual exploitation, easier to ignore because so few in number, and viewed with distaste by prison officials, women in custodial units were treated as the dregs of the state prisoner population.
>
> (Rafter 1985: 21)

Throughout her analyses Rafter emphasises that gender differentiation in relation to state punishment is always intertwined with class differentiations and the discriminations emanating from racism, for instance:

> After the Civil War, southern judges sent black women to prison for minor thefts while finding alternative dispositions for all but the most serious white female offenders. The reformatory movement drew in large numbers of working-class women, even though their misbehaviours were trivial. And officials seem to have reacted less harshly ... to married than to single women, who also tended to be black and poor.
>
> (Rafter 1985: 178; see also Worrall 1981 and Carlen 1983)

Specifically, the author highlights the historical differences which have persisted within the women's penal system in the USA as being related to: their small numbers; the bifurcation of the system according to race; and the bifurcation of the prisoner population into women who were 'saveable' and those who were not. This historical instance of bifurcation is very similar to that discussed by Kelly Hannah-Moffat (2001) in her book *Punishment in Disguise*, where she describes how women in Canadian prisons who have not responded well to the reformers' programmes of 'empowerment' have been labelled as being 'unempowerable'.

Rafter's major contribution is twofold: in *Partial Justice* she provides a valuable historical perspective on the differential and discriminatory treatment of women and girls in penal custody which is lacking in Carlen (1983 and subsequently); and she was one of the first to recognise that the differential treatment of imprisoned females requires analyses of its intertwined class, race and gender dimensions, and not merely according to gender differentiation. Carlen's (1983) analysis was along class and gender lines, but, because the population of the Scottish women's prison was at that time homogenously white Scottish, the likely effects of racism on penal justice were not confronted – an example of one limitation of the case-study method.

Margaret Malloch, *Women, Drugs and Custody: The Experience of Women Drug Users in Prison*. **Winchester: Waterside Press, 2000**

The literature referred to at the beginning of *Women, Drugs and Custody* suggests that Malloch's book about the experiences of women drugs-users in prison was also written in the tradition of studies which emphasised the difference between the prison experiences of women and men. However, after her very competent theoretical chapters on the ways in which women's difference results in them being structurally discriminated against in prison regimes designed for men, most of the analysis of the empirical data could apply equally well to the experiences of male and female prisoners. Indeed, even though she quotes Howe (1994) on the bodily intrusions which women in particular suffer in prison, she fails to address some of the gender-specific indignities which women in prison in England have suffered as a result of being defined at the intersection of medical and juridical discourses (Allen 1987a, 1987b). Indeed, students wishing to discover more about the specifics of the medical treatment and medicalisation of women prisoners, will need to peruse Sim (1990: 129–176) for more theoretically informed analyses of how general penal/medical policies, including those relating to imprisoned drug-users impact differently on women; and Carlen (1998: 116–123; 138–144) for how the mandatory drugs testing (MDT) introduced into all British prisons in the 1990s especially discriminated against women prisoners' culturally acquired conceptions of female modesty. For as Carlen found,

> The women themselves expressed concern … about the violation of the social convention that dictates that women should usually

take pains to hide their sexual parts from all but their chosen sexual partners or a medical practitioner ... But when a woman is forced to expose her body (in a strip search), to engage in supervised urinating (in the MDT test), or to live in constant fear that she will be involuntarily exposed to the surveillance of a prison officer (male or female) who may or may not look upon her with the gaze of a voyeur – but who will certainly look upon her with a legitimated punitive stare – it is arguable that she, sensing a perversion of both legitimate punishment and legitimate sex, will feel an intense humiliation.

(Carlen 1998: 142)

Yet, despite the author's failure to integrate the book's theoretical knowledge with the study's empirical findings, *Women, Drugs and Custody* is an important book because it is (at the time of writing) the only book which is directed solely at analysing the prison experiences of female drug-users in Britain. Even its failure to explain the women drug-users' in-prison experiences in gender terms makes the book interesting, because it implicitly raises the question of the extent to which it is always possible or desirable to privilege gender differences in relation to women's imprisonment. (For further discussion of this point see pp. 110–11 this chapter.)

Resistance (The capacity to oppose)

The fundamental capacity of human beings to survive by resisting oppression has been one of literature's persistent and most uplifting *motifs*. Ioan Davies' *Writers in Prison* (1990) is a valuable collection of extracts which well displays the tenacity of the human spirit to survive the pains of custody, while Jane Robinson's *Pandora's Daughters* (2002) presents a range of feisty women (some of whom landed up in gaol) from 5 BC to the early twentieth century to indicate that western women of all classes have always resisted their male oppressors and the discriminatory gender conventions of their day.

In sociology the term 'resistance' has been used specifically as a corrective to those sociological theories which, in emphasising the power of social structural factors (such as class and gender) and cultural factors (such as language and law) to shape individual biographies, have appeared to minimise, or ignore altogether, the power of individuals to *act*, to fight back and erode the power of the powerful social institutions which otherwise would dominate them. In sociology this debate has tended to be characterised as the 'agency versus social structure debate'. In its philosophical wraps it translates into questions about 'free will or determinism'. In interpretive sociology the dichotomy was almost (but not quite) collapsed in symbolic inter-actionist theories (Mead 1934) which emphasised that, in interaction with each other and the societies into which they are born, human beings constantly, through the power of language, constitute and reconstitute themselves and their societies at the same time as they themselves are reconstituted within the unintended social products of that interaction.

Symbolic interactionist theories, however, were unable to explain why some contested meanings won out and became embedded in powerful institutions (such as law) while others were suppressed. In other words, critics claimed that symbolic interactionism could not explain power.

Symbolic interactionism has wielded a powerful and creative influence on the sociology of crime and deviance from the end of the 1960s onwards, being responsible in particular for the following now taken-for-granted assumptions underlying much criminological research: that the ways in which people see the world and their own experiences should be taken seriously because their perceptions help shape (and therefore will, in part, explain) their actions, however incomprehensible those actions might otherwise appear to an observer; that to begin to understand both the eccentricities and systemicities in people's individual behaviours criminologists need also to study all the social factors to which that behaviour may, in part, be a response.

In symbolic interactionist approaches to sociological investigation, the emphasis has always been on looking at both sides of the 'self and society' dichotomy. Nonetheless, in actual theoretical practice, it seems inevitable that, when explaining a social phenomenon, theorists tend to put more emphasis on either individual agency or on social structure – primarily because if they did not, they would go round in circular fashion, merely refining their analytic descriptions. (Though many interpretive sociologists have been content to do just that – to engage in the complex, and often highly technical task of exploring symbols and meanings, leaving it to others to 'explain' them.)

In actual research practice, whether an emphasis is put on structure or agency tends to be decided by the 'object of knowledge' under investigation. Thus, in their classic text *Psychological Survival* (where the objective was to describe how long-term prisoners psychologically survive their imprisonment without becoming institutionalised zombies) Cohen and Taylor (1972) focused on the power of prisoners to fight back against the 'total institution' described so well by Goffman

(1961) in his *Asylums* (see Chapter 1 pp. 6–7). Conversely, because Goffman's own objective in *Asylums* had been to explain the power of total institutions to transform individuals into their own obedient creatures (a process known in sociological criminology as *institutionalisation*) he, of course, emphasised the power of social structure and institutional process to transform (apparently) lawless convicts into (apparently) docile and rule-governed prisoners.

The point of the foregoing two examples is to illustrate that sociology does not aim merely to describe, to take comprehensive and literal snapshots of social phenomena. Nor does sociology claim that there is ever a one-to-one relationship between the social phenomenon and the object of knowledge.

As the German sociologist Alfred Schutz (1962) pointed out long ago, sociological concepts, however carefully honed for theoretical purposes, are 'second degree' concepts, they tend to be words which come already laden with cultural meanings. A theorist has to transform the common-sense word into a concept by indicating how, because of its relationships with other concepts in the conceptual framework specified, it will inform the analysis and explanation of the very narrowly-defined and specific process under investigation. But unless the theorist works entirely with neologisms, the other cultural meanings will continue to intrude. Hence this long explanation of the pre-history and specific utility of the word 'resistance' in sociology and criminology!

In criminology 'resistance' has retained its dictionary meaning, as given above, but it has also acquired an especial utility and significance for feminist writers. Concerned that portrayals of women as victims (of domestic violence, or of poverty-stricken material conditions which make lawbreaking appear an attractive option, or of harsh prison regimes which neglect women's special needs) were playing into traditional and sexist misrepresentations of women as the weak sex (physically, emotionally and morally) several writers set out to redress the balance by showing that even under the most violent and repressive conditions women can resist their violent oppressors (Mama 1989) and both contest and evade the rules which would grind them down (Carlen et al., 1985; Worrall 1990; Bosworth 1999; Denton 2001).

Yet, whatever the reasons for highlighting women's known strength in adversity, in the general prison literature a staple theme has always concerned the various ways in which prisoners have fought against institutionalisation by refusing to let the system grind them down: sometimes through the maintenance of prisoner subcultures (Clemmer 1940; Ward and Kassesbaum 1966), sometimes by adherence to strict psychological disciplines (Cohen and Taylor 1973; Peckham 1985) and sometimes by violent protest (Boyle 1977; O'Dwyer and Carlen 1985).

Two turn-of-the century studies which have contested the notion that women in prison are 'victims' are: Mary Bosworth's (1999) *Engendering Resistance: Agency and Power in Women's Prisons*; and Denton's (2001) *Dealing: Women in the Drug Economy*. In the former Bosworth argued that far from being oppressed by idealised notions of femininity, as Carlen (1983) had argued, women use those same notions of femininity themselves in order to resist oppression (Bosworth 1999: 4). In the latter, Denton (2001: 158) concluded that when women drug dealers are in custody they manage to 'have an active and robust prison culture and social organisation that is at least as complex and viable as that of their male counterparts'. Yet, as was pointed out in relation to Cohen and Taylor (1973) and Goffman (1961) the varied conclusions theorists reach are often not directly comparable because they are trying to construct entirely different objects of knowledge (in these cases, different dimensions of the same phenomenon). Thus, whereas Carlen's (1983) study set out to provide a structural account of the 'moment of prison' for a group of short-term prisoners who were in and out of prison primarily *because* of their poor social circumstances rather than for the seriousness of their crimes, both Bosworth (1999) and Denton (2001) are telling us about women who were in prison for longer and who, by their own account, also had more going for them on the outside. By and large, it is usually inappropriate to compare studies which are empirically different or (when there are no empirical differences) are asking entirely different theoretical questions of only a few dimensions of an empirical phenomenon. Thus Carlen (1983), an anti-prison campaigner and primarily interested in class oppression (and therefore as a socialist feminist, primarily interested in working-class women) tends to use different concepts to Bosworth (1999) who, writing from a declared feminist and Foucauldian perspective (see below), has a commitment to demonstrating women's strength in adversity. Perhaps Denton best sums up why good research must stand on its own rather than attempting to depend for its significance on carving out a space where all previous research is seen to have failed to capture some imaginary truth of some imaginary reality – a point we return to in the section on feminist theories. Denton writes:

> I am not attempting to suggest all previous research was wrong, biased or distorted. Rather it seems to me that the illicit drug industry is likely to be highly diverse, and that what emerges will depend on who you select as examples, what contexts are to be studied, what sources of information are consulted and so on. In selecting successful women, naturally I will not have produced the

'real truth' about *all* women participants in illicit drug use and distribution settings. Nevertheless, what emerges in this account provides an important counterbalance to the notion that women in the drug industry cannot be competent and successful participants.

(Denton 2001: 172)

However, whatever the theoretical issues are in relation to prisoner resistance, there are also a number of political issues, especially when it comes to the strategies to be employed by anti-prison campaigners intent on improving conditions for prisoners (see Chapter 6).

In concluding this section on resistance, we should note that, in the literature on women's prisons, as in the literature on men's, there has been a constant fascination with the interaction between prisoner and prison. The three main processes identified have been those of:

1 *adaptation*: as in 'prisonisation', when by the formation of prison subcultures prisoners manage to adjust the rules to serve their own ends);

2 *institutionalization*: when prisoners become rule-governed in at least some aspects of their behaviour – though seldom all;

3 *resistance*: when prisoners directly evade or disobey rules; or engage in psychological strategies for the maintenance of identity and self-esteem.

Carceral clawback

The set of constantly changing ideological mechanisms necessary to the existence of the maintenance of prisons. Because prison logically involves the notion that prisoners must be kept in, a necessary condition of the prison's continued existence is that reforms which erode prison security be suppressed or modified. This suppression tends, in modern times, to be achieved discursively.

The concept of *carceral clawback* was first developed by Pat Carlen (2002a) when reviewing Kelly Hannah-Moffat's book *Punishment in Disguise* together with her other book, co-edited with Margaret Shaw and entitled *Ideal Prison* (Hannah-Moffat and Shaw 2001). It was subsequently expanded and refined (Carlen 2002c), and was based on the assumption that, as it is a logical necessity for prisons to keep people *in* prison (otherwise the prison would no longer be a prison but something else) it is a necessary (rather than a contingent) requirement that all threats to prison security be suppressed. The concept was inspired by Hannah-Moffat's *Punishment in Disguise* because, in describing the history and eventual demise of the attempts to operationalise the reforms put forward in the radical *Report of the Task Force on Federally Sentenced Women: Creating Choices* (Task Force on Federally Sentenced Women 1990) the author shows how, despite the lip service paid to reform, the prisons' security priorities never did effectively change. The authorities attributed the failure of reform to the basic inability of some of the prisoners to take responsibility for their own *empowerment*. Hannah-Moffat summed up her own analysis of the causes of the failure differently. After criticising the reformers for never challenging the actual *use* of imprisonment as a legitimate punishment, she went on to argue that:

> Another major barrier to the realisation of the women-centred ideal … is that it denies the material and legal realities of carceral relations. … Prisons are governed by material structures, cultural sensibilities and material realities that limit the extent to which the content of a regime can be changed.
>
> (Hannah-Moffat 2002: 197)

The concept of *carceral clawback* describes just one of the limitations on regime change. Others are discussed in Chapter 6. (The important work of Kelly Hannah-Moffat is also discussed in greater detail later in this chapter and in Chapter 6.)

What are women's prisons for?

As we have seen, much of the early work on women's prisons was concerned with describing the way in which prisoners interact with each other, and with prison staff, and then trying to explain those relationships. Studies of that type are still conducted (see, for instance, Girshick 1999; Malloch 2000) and policy makers and anti-prison campaigners consider them important sources of information about what goes on behind the prison walls – because, like other institutions, prisons are constantly adapting to their political environments.

In most of the empirical investigations of prisons the primary emphasis is on the prisoners, prison staff, individual custodial establishments and/or specific prison systems, rather than on the institution of imprisonment itself. Yet, and as we have seen, even when the main research focus is prison-based, a range of theories may be employed to inform analyses of the empirical data in such a way that important generalisations can be made.

In order to answer the very different question, 'What are women's prisons for?' it is necessary to move away from the empirical focus on prisoners, their gaolers and penal regimes, towards explanation of the meanings of imprisonment in terms of its social, economic and political functions. The various answers to the question posed are derived either from philosophies of punishment or from theoretical and statistical analyses of the purposes, origins, effects and inmate population demographics of specific prison systems. Additionally, though the theories most frequently put forward may well draw upon qualitative or quantitative empirical data in support of their arguments, all employ either philosophical justifications for punishment or macro sociological theories of the relationships between law, state and economy.

Political explanations

At the most fundamental level, the question 'What are prisons for?' has been interpreted as a political question about the state's justification for taking upon itself the right to deprive citizens of their liberty. Contemporary justifications of the state's right to punish stem from the contract theories of, for example, Hobbes (1968/1651) and Locke (1967/1690).

In contract theory, the state's right to punish is predicated upon a conceit that the state is founded upon the citizens' consensual agreement to surrender to state agencies their individual capacities to redress wrongs done to them. In return, citizens have a right to expect the state to protect their lives and property. In democratic societies the state agencies are themselves expected to be subject to due legal process. In welfare states an expectation has also been raised that citizens will receive 'minimal need satisfaction' (Doyal and Gough 1991: 92). Thus a moral reciprocity is set up: the state is to satisfy the minimum needs of citizens, protect their lives and property from attack, and avenge crimes committed against them; citizens, for their part, are to fulfil obligations to obey the law, to keep the peace by not taking the law into their own hands against transgressors, and to fulfil other obligations incurred by virtue of their citizenship. The state's power to imprison is just one of an array of punitive strategies which it has a right (indeed, a contractual obligation) to employ in fulfilment of its commitment to protect the public, reduce crime, reform, deter and/or rehabilitate criminals, denounce villainy and avenge crimes on behalf of the victims.

The obvious flaw in contract theory as far as the legitimacy of government is concerned, is that, if the contract were a reality rather than a myth, at any time citizens should be able to make effective claim that proven failure on the part of the state to fulfil the contract in terms of protection or provision of the necessities of life either licenses citizens to avenge wrongs committed against them (vigilantism), or to commit crime for the purpose of satisfying their unrequited basic needs. As we will see throughout this book, a continuing argument against the imprisonment of women has been that the majority of females locked up are those who are among the most materially deprived and disadvantaged in society. It is primarily for that reason that the demographic characteristics of female prison populations (already outlined and discussed in Chapter 2) so frequently feature as either starting points for, or evidence in support of, all the more radical explanations of women's imprisonment which are described and analysed below, after the less radical penal explanations have been outlined and discussed.

Penological explanations

Since the mid-eighteenth century, jurisprudentialists and penologists have treated the question 'What are prisons for?' as a functionalist one that calls for state punishments, including imprisonment, not only to be legitimated in terms of the right of the state to punish, but also to be continually *re*legitimated in terms of secondary penal and social objectives which, it is implied, will contribute towards the state's overall goal of honouring its obligation to protect citizens by fighting crime on their behalf. For, bald assertions of the state's sovereignty over criminal matters are no longer enough. In modern consumer societies 'law 'n' order' has become a central electioneering issue. With rising crime rates at home and a global climate of fear about an international terrorist threat abroad which might materialise anywhere, most governments cannot credibly claim that their crime reduction strategies deliver citizen security and peace of mind (see Garland 1996). Instead, rhetorics of crime control become more and more complex and, in addition to doubts about imprisonment's saliency as a deterrent punishment, there are the recurring civil liberties questions to be addressed.

Imprisonment so nearly violates so many human rights, and is so painful that, ever since the mid-eighteenth century, democratic governments have attempted justification of the systematic and almost exclusive use of prison against certain classes and categories of lawbreakers for quite minor crimes, by claiming that prisons can achieve social goods other than punishment. And, as we saw in Chapter

1, whenever oppositional claims are made questioning imprisonment's legitimacy (in terms of its political propriety) and validity (in terms of its contribution to crime reduction), those old philosophical justifications are strengthened through their discursive realignment within new penal discourses aimed at pacifying the critics and mobilising popular electoral support.

Yet, despite recurring questions about the political legitimacy and dubious achievements of penal incarceration, the functionalist justifications for state punishment (including imprisonment) also persist. They are generally listed in terms of one or more forensic objectives (these being seven in all) though some of them (for example, expiation) are seldom invoked nowadays, while others have, within their discursive histories, taken on meanings which, at first sight, seem far removed from the original. For as the penal ambitions of the state have increased, the listed objectives of imprisonment have perennially changed and multiplied and, where more than one objective has been put forward in specific sentencing policies, have frequently contradicted or subverted each other. At the same time, much of the administrative audit of imprisonment has been in terms of its success or not in reducing crime via deterrence, reform, rehabilitation or other modern variants of one or more of the classic strategies (for example, the 'programming' that has replaced 'reform' and was discussed in Chapter 1). As a consequence of this persistent political desire to justify imprisonment as an efficacious weapon in the 'fight against crime', the main forms of measurement have been indices of recidivism. These are usually obtained by comparing the reconviction rates of offenders with similar profiles receiving either custodial or non-custodial sentences for the same types of offence. In this book comparative recidivism rates are presented and analysed in Chapter 5. Here, the seven justificatory objectives of imprisonment are now defined and discussed below.

Expiation: *the making of amends in return for a wrong committed.*
This moral justification for punishment focuses on both offender and victim of a crime: the offender is given a chance to redress the wrong, while the victim receives satisfaction that the offender has recognised the wrongdoing and, through punishment, has paid a price for the transgression. Although the term 'expiation' used to be especially associated with religious discourses, its connotations (though not the terminology) can nowadays be seen in the various programmes of 'restorative justice' which have built upon John Braithwaite's original thesis put forward in his book *Crime, Shame and Reintegration*. Braithwaite (1989) argued that the recognition and righting of a wrong

is a necessary prerequisite to the future well-being of both crime perpetrator and crime victim.

Denunciation:
although it must be assumed that all punishments are denunciatory in the sense that imposition of a penalty signifies social disapproval, a punishment may be described as being purely denunciatory when a court wishes to signal disapprobation and yet cannot see any other purpose to be achieved. An example here might be the case of aged war criminals brought to court years after their crimes had been committed; and where it might be argued that the imposition of punishment served no useful purpose except to signify social abhorrence of the crimes and recognition of the sufferings of the victims. (As we will see below, for the French social theorist Emile Durkheim (1969/1895), denunciation was the primary purpose of punishment.)

Retribution: Retributive punishments are based on the moral position that an offender deserves punishment in proportion to the offence committed, and that a society has a moral duty to both offender and victim to ensure that the offender pay for (expiate) his or her crime. This moral justification is further buttressed when combined with political claims and counter claims (based on contract theory) about the obligations of the state to protect citizens by punishing criminals and keeping the peace.

Retributionism is probably the most widely-held and common-sensical justification for punishment, and underpins most populist campaigns for harsher penalties for lawbreaking. However, retributionism is undermined (or at least tempered) by a variety of other viewpoints on punishment. They include: Christian notions of forgiveness; a variety of theories which argue that not all offenders can be held totally responsible for their crimes (for example, when they are crimes of survival – see Carlen 1988; 1996); theories which contend that when the state fails to keep its side of the contract in terms of minimum needs satisfaction, citizens are justified in not keeping theirs (see Hudson 1996 for an excellent analysis of the main critiques of retributivism); policy makers whose experience suggests that certain punishments, and especially imprisonment, may well reduce the likelihood of an offender 'going straight' in the future, thereby subverting the crime reduction objective which is the funda-mental justification nowadays for most custodial sentences where the crime is not so heinous that protection of the public is the taken-for-granted justification; and finally by the difficulty of ensuring that the retributive punishment is in proportion to the crime.

Retributivists will usually point out that the principle of *proportionality* central to a retributivist punishment endows it with a rationality (and thereby a justice) which is absent from the emotionalism seen to be both the key instigator and characteristic of revenge punishments, as well as the chief cause of their being so frequently *disproportionate* in their ferocity. But 'proportionate' to what? Should the punishment be proportionate to the degree of criminal *intent* of the perpetrator of the offence or to the degree of *loss* or *pain* suffered by the victim?

The degrees of criminal intent involved in criminal actions and the degrees of loss or pain suffered by the victims of those same criminal actions are seldom commensurable. Nor is it easy to assess the relative losses or pains of victims of crime who are differently circumstanced. For example: a very poor (or already depressed) mother living alone with her children may suffer much more loss or pain from a burglary involving goods of low financial value than a wealthy woman protected by servants or living with other adults might suffer from a burglary involving greater financial loss.

On the other side of the coin, punishments may not cause the same amounts of pain to people differently circumstanced. Indeed, it has been a constant claim that women in prison suffer more acutely from being separated from their children and from the invasion of bodily privacy done in the name of prison security than do male prisoners (Carlen 1998). Turning now from gender difference to class difference, it should be noted that there have also been recurring debates about how to make financial penalties equitable across all income groups. Attempts to solve this conundrum have been fraught with difficulties and these will be discussed further when the issue of proportionality in relation to non-custodial sentences is discussed further in Chapter 5.

Deterrence: *deterrence theories of crime come in two guises: general and individual.* **General deterrence** *assumes that the main purposes of the criminal and penal systems is symbolic, their function being to warn the 'others' of what will happen to them if they break the law.* **Individual deterrence** *theories either make the assumption that offenders are rational people who will change their criminal ways as a result of reflecting on the punishment meted out to them last time they broke the law; or the implication is that the punishment will be so salutary that the offender's behaviour will be modified in the future.*

The problem with deterrence theory is that the assumptions it makes about rational actors and/or conditioned behaviour just do not mesh with what is known about the conditions in which lawbreaking occurs and is then recognised and denounced as a crime. Much crime (such as burglary and petty theft) is opportunist; some, like assault, is situational; other types, like drugs and receiving, might be called lifestyle crimes (see Carlen 1988). Moreover, as the majority of lawbreakers are not apprehended, it might be entirely rational for a destitute person to obtain goods by illicit means. Finally, when it comes to imprisonment, there is seldom a guaranteed symmetry between crime seriousness and whether or not a person goes to gaol, and, even when there is, the person's criminal career may indicate an uneven drift towards the custody end of the crime seriousness scale, rather than a steady escalation (see Matza 1969; Rosenbaum 1983).

Public protection/offender incapacitation: as a justification for imprisonment, this means exactly what it says: that because certain offenders are so dangerous or persistently criminal that they pose a serious threat to life, property or polity they have to be prevented from committing crimes by being locked up.

(However, in recent years the Probation Service in England and Wales has argued that non-custodial penalties can also have an incapacitative effect; see Chapter 5.)

One of the major problems with justifying imprisonment on the grounds that prisons put dangerous prisoners out of action for the period of their sentence inheres in the difficulties of defining dangerousness (Bottoms (1977). Hilary Allen (1987a) has demonstrated that in the cases of certain women the seriousness of the crime – even when it involves the death of the victim – is no guarantee of a prison sentence for the convicted offender, especially if she can be defined (stereotypically) as not being responsible for her actions by virtue of her gender and stressful life circumstances. Similarly, a range of feminist authors has indicated that, traditionally and routinely, men who beat or even kill their wives or partners receive far more lenient sentences than might have been expected if the assault, manslaughter or murder had not been viewed as 'domestic'. Presumably in all these cases, the concept of 'public protection' did not extend behind the front door into the marital home or joint household, thus maintaining the rigid distinction between 'public' and 'private' which, many argue, has been so damaging for women, and certainly a prime cause of the state's failure to protect them against male violence.

Most recently, the case of Garry David in Australia has again raised questions about dangerousness from a different standpoint: about the extent to which culturally incomprehensible behaviour may be punished as being a sign of potential dangerousness, even when the presenting behaviour is neither illegal nor dangerous (to others) as presently defined in law (Greig 2002). The way in which the state went to extreme and novel lengths to pander to popular fears by suspending due process and redefining both legislation and mental illness in attempts to ensure David's continued detention, demonstrates the vulnerability of all those other (and non-criminal) 'others' whose difference makes them vulnerable to popular fears that their 'otherness' is dangerous (Chevigny 2003). In societies manifesting high levels of anxiety about hidden and ill-defined dangers, such fears of otherness may be one factor in the relatively high imprisonment rates of immigrant workers, gypsies and ethnic minority women (Cippolini et al. 1989; Sim et al. 1995; Mauer 1999).

The problem with using prison to incapacitate *persistent* offenders, is that because some of the most persistent offenders are also some of those who commit the least serious crimes, in imprisoning them the courts are violating the principle of *proportionality*. In fact, the use of imprisonment for minor, persistent offenders is one reason for the increase in the imprisonment of female offenders since 1990 (see Hudson 2002 and section 5).

Reform: *the changing of the criminal's character so that he or she chooses to embrace a law-abiding life in the future.*

From the 1960s until the end of the 1990s there was, for most of the time in England, a greater emphasis on rehabilitation than reform. However, the inception and prevalence of cognitive behavioural programmes in recent years has meant, in effect, that the primary rehabilitative effort is focused on attempts to change prisoners' views of themselves, the worlds in which they live outside prison, and their attitudes towards their own lawbreaking behaviour.

Cognitive behaviourist programmes are based on positivistic assumptions about criminogenic patterns of behaviour and faulty modes of thinking, as well as on empiricist assumptions about how changes in thinking about behaviour can be measured (see Friendship et al., 2002 for a positive evaluation of these programmes). However, in a trenchant critique, Kendall has described their underlying logic as follows:

> Offenders fail to learn particular cognitive skills as a consequence of the interplay between problematic psychological and environmental factors. Treatment therefore should aim to provide them with these skills by teaching criminals how to think.
>
> (2002: 188; see also, Vanstone 2000)

A constant criticism of these programmes in relation to women is that women already know how to *think* about their problems, their failure is to *act* or to have the opportunity to *act*. Hence the feminists' emphasis on assertiveness training programmes for women, on anger management and on activities which enhance women's skills and experiences.

Rehabilitation: *Strictly speaking, rehabilitation refers to attempts to restore prisoners to their former status after their imprisonment, or to make them fit to live again in society after a period of incarceration. However, it is often used more loosely to refer to any attempt to equip prisoners with the wherewithal – skills, material goods, principles – to lead crime-free lives after prison.*

As so many people in prison, especially women, are almost destitute when they enter prison, and then lose their remaining relationships and possessions while they are serving their sentence (Carlen 1983; Devlin 1998; Cook and Davies 1999) it is, on the strict definition of 'rehabilitation', difficult to envisage what it is that women coming out of prison are to be rehabilitated *to*. Indeed, Eaton (1993: 57) has argued that upon release from prison, the woman ex-prisoner 'dislocated and disempowered … has to set about making a place for herself'. When interpreted within decarcerative penal policies, however, (as opposed to in-prison programming or prison aftercare policies), the 'rehabilitative ideal' – that no one is so steeped in crime that they cannot be turned towards a law-abiding path once the root causes of their offending have been identified and addressed – has resulted in all kinds of non-custodial alternatives to prison (see Allen 1981; Worrall 1997; Chapter 5 of this volume). Within prisons, the activation of the rehabilitative ideal has resulted in a variety of a work programmes for prisoners, though a constant criticism of the work provided in women's prisons is that it is too oriented towards the acquisition of women's traditional work skills (see Carlen 1983; Dobash et al., 1986; Comack 1996; Devlin 1998). However, it has also been noted that, even when prisons do offer less traditional job training, women prisoners themselves still 'usually choose stereotypically female jobs within the already narrow range of options provided' (Girshick 1999: 140–1).

Criticisms of the penological explanations of imprisonment

The traditional penological explanations of imprisonment explain the existence of penal incarceration by reference to its objectives. Such an explanation, which explains the origins of something in terms of its future or present function, is called a *teleological* or *functionalist* explana-tion. Insofar as penological explanations explain the existence of imprisonment by reference to the future achievement of some present objectives, they are also *idealist*. Internal criticisms of this type of functionalist explanation have therefore always been directed at assessment of the extent to which imprisonment has in practice, or can logically be expected to, meet those objectives. The overwhelming assessment has been that imprisonment does not and cannot meet its traditional objectives: first, because penal custody cannot effectively synthesise the contradictory objectives which the prison's legitimating rhetoric has traditionally required it to pursue; and, second, because all objectives which might more broadly be characterised as 'crime reducing attempts' via reform or rehabilitation of the prisoner, tend to be undermined. Initially reform programmes are eroded by security constraints within the prison (see Hannah-Moffat 2001). Subsequently, the adverse social conditions to which so many prisoners return after release are very often directly inimical to their best attempts to lead law-abiding lives.

Does prison work? Practical assessments

Retribution, expiation, denunciation, protection/incapacitation

There is no doubt that prison is painful, that its corrosive effects may be experienced long after the prisoner has been released, and that therefore, in the vast majority of cases, a sentence of imprisonment achieves its retributive aim (see Boyle 1985; Cook and Davies 1999). Insofar as victims are satisfied that the prisoner received his/her just deserts, it may also be reasonably claimed that through imprisonment the state denounces the crime and the offender expiates the offence. Certainly also, when criminals who have committed serious crimes are in custody the public is protected from them until they re-emerge. Of course, gaoled offenders may be committing crimes against fellow-prisoners while in prison and their experiences while in custody may make them more predatory when they are released. Moreover, and as we saw in Chapter 2, the majority of people receiving a prison sentence have not committed crimes of violence or serious property crimes. Nonetheless, when a criminally violent person is in custody, the public (at least) is protected from that individual's violence for the duration of the sentence. Whether that, in itself, also reduces the public sense of risk and anxiety is, however, unlikely. In reporting on the responses to a series of questions on sentencing contained in the 1996 British Crime Survey, Hough and Roberts (1999: 11) comment that the answers elicited revealed that, 'the public systematically underestimate the severity of sentencing patterns'.

Reform, rehabilitation, deterrence

Claims that prison can reform or rehabilitate are hardly justified by the evidence. As far as general deterrence is concerned, we can, of course never know to what extent the very existence of the whole criminal justice and penal apparatus deters people from committing crime. Hale (1998: 40), moreover, has argued that, because of the low numbers (4.9 per cent) of offences known to the police which are ever cleared up (and the even lower numbers (2 per cent) which result in a conviction, 'increasing either the numbers imprisoned or the average sentence length is unlikely to have a major impact upon the level of crime'.

As for individual deterrence, there is some evidence from the autobiographical accounts of male and female criminals that once youngsters have tasted custody they are less afraid of it in the future (Boyle 1977; O'Dwyer and Carlen 1985; Carlen 1988), and even more evidence that, by young people in certain areas, their imprisonment may be seen as a welcome rite of passage into the adult criminal world.

In England, at the end of the twentieth century, 58 per cent of men and nearly half of all women released from prison in 1997 were reconvicted within two years (Social Exclusion Unit 2002: 5, 136).

Does prison work? Penal theorists' assessments

Three very different recent critiques of the penological justifications for imprisonment have been made by the following: David Garland (1996, 2001); Thomas Mathiesen (2000); and a range of theorists analysing the failure of attempted reforms of women's imprisonment in Scotland and Canada (Hannah-Moffat and Shaw 2000; Hannah-Moffatt 2001; Carlen 2002d). All argue that prison obviously does not work on its own in terms of reducing crime, though all additionally argue that prison's classic justifications do work at the symbolic level, as rhetorical or therapeutic components of the prison's iconography.

Thomas Mathiesen (2000/1990) has made the most sustained critique of the classic claims that prison protects by rehabilitating, deterring and incapacitating offenders. In his book *Prison on Trial* he uses the metaphor of the trial to examine the claims of the prison to rehabilitate, deter and incapacitate. As far as *rehabilitation* is concerned, Mathiesen argues that throughout the history of the ideology of rehabilitation, 'the prison has never actually rehabilitated people in practice' (Mathiesen 2000: 46) and provides evidence for that assertion from three main sources: statistical evidence which indicates that rehabilitative programmes have had little effect on recidivism rates (for example, Martinson 1974), prison studies indicating that prisons have security and other features (such as over-crowding, bullying, violence) which subvert rehabilitation programmes and render them ineffective; (Mathiesen does not give any examples here but Carlen 1998: 83 describes the corrosive fear that most women experience in prison and which is not conducive to an increase in their confidence or self-esteem); and prison studies which indicate that in order to defend themselves against the pains of imprisonment prisoners form an inmate culture which militates against prisoner responsiveness to official programmes of rehabilitation (for example, Clemmer 1940; Sykes 1958).

Mathiesen does not refer to any similar studies of resistance to official intervention in women's prisons but, as we have already discussed, Carlen (1985) Bosworth (1999) and Denton (2001) have provided analyses of women's resistance to prison which, though different in focus to the early studies of male prisons, suggest that, in their attempts to evade and resist the prisons' attempts at total control and surveillance, many women prisoners are also not amenable to prisons' rehabilitation attempts. (For more detailed discussion of the work of Bosworth and Denton, see the section on *resistance* on pp. 86–90). When this happens, the failure of rehabilitation is likely to be blamed on the women, as has happened in the most recent past in Canada, where women who did not respond to official programmes of empowerment were defined as failing to take responsibility for their own lives and thereby demonstrating that they were non-empowerable (see Hannah-Moffatt 2002 and the discussion at the end of Chapter 1 of this volume).

Having rejected the claims of rehabilitationism as a justification for imprisonment, Mathiesen turns to the case for *general deterrence*. He minutely examines a range of statistical studies and arguments in relation to punishment's deterrent symbolic and moral functions, but again concludes that a case cannot be made for imprisonment:

all available research results, as well as international comparisons show that the development of crime is not related in any definite way to the level maintained in the number of incarcerations and their length.

(Mathiesen 2000: 84)

Finally it is the turn of *incapacitation* (or protection of the public through the use of imprisonment to reduce an offender's capacity to commit crimes in the future). Here Mathiesen argues that there are two issues: one of *accuracy* – the difficulty of predicting who is likely to commit crime in the future; the other of *principle* – what justification is there for actuarial punishment, that is, of determining punishment of a past offence on the basis of a dubious calculation about the likely criminality of future action? Following on from Feeley and Simon's (1992) seminal article on actuarial justice, other commentators have noted that this predictive, actuarial justice, whereby whole categories of 'risky' people are selected for increased surveillance and incapacitative incarceration, has become a hallmark of late-modern high anxiety societies. However, as Mathiesen (2000: 95) adds, when it is noted that: 'the individuals thus sentenced to a large extent are poor, socially handicapped and stigmatized … the moral issue becomes acute'. But, it might be objected, surely no one can deny that when a specific dangerous offender is locked up – (*selective incapacitation* as distinguished from the *general incapacitation* of the actuarial model) – the state would be failing in its duty of citizen protection were it not to take the common-sense step of attempting physically to prevent (through incarceration) the same offender committing the same (or a worse) offence in the future.

Mathiesen provides three main arguments to indicate that, as so often is the case in relation to other social phenomena, common-sense about *selective incapacitation* is wrong. First, he draws on the work of Andrew von Hirsch (1986: 105–7) to show that prediction studies of the future behaviour of offenders have been irremediably flawed at the methodological level, and, consequently, have been found to have low predictive accuracy. Second, he argues that once social factors are used to predict recidivism (that is, when what is known about present offenders is used to predict those most likely to become recidivists in the future) there is an inevitability about more and more of the poor being candidates for incarceration. Third, he argues that most dangerous acts are situational and therefore defy prediction.

Overall, then, it seems that the explanations for imprisonment which take the penological justifications for imprisonment as an answer to the question, 'What are prisons for?' are unsustainable in light of studies which set out to see if prisons could actually deliver the penological objectives promised. The appeal of those common-sense justifications, though, have saliency through their symbolic efficacy in sustaining the existence of prisons in spite of all critique.

The symbolic importance of the prison is emphasised by Mathiesen throughout *Prison on Trial*, and the iconography of the prison will be touched on again below, when we consider the perspective of Emile Durkheim. Let us now, however, turn to the work of David Garland who, along with other risk theorists, argues that the contemporary persistence and increase in the use of imprisonment can be fundamentally explained by the arguable (and certainly perceived) failure of the state to protect citizens through the criminal justice and penal systems.

Cultural explanations

These are analytic approaches which highlight the role of changing penal discourses in the context of changing economic and or political conditions.

David Garland (1996, 2001) views the classic justifications for imprisonment as being provocative of the populist demand that imprisonment be used to reduce the sense of risk and fear of others which, according to many theorists, characterises high modern societies. In times of widespread unemployment, constant threat of war, a pervasive fear of terrorism and ever quickening cycles of economic uncertainties, only the prison seems capable of providing punitive security and just deserts in an insecure and unjust world (Becket and Sasson 2000; Waquant 2003). When a prisoner is released, or when an offence is really too trivial to merit custody for its perpetrator, a transcarceralist approach (Lowman et al., 1987) to so-called community penalties attempts to bring the pains of imprisonment out beyond the prison walls so that, as in pre-modern times, the already socially-excluded can be named and shamed and banished still further from the usual citizenship privileges of civil society. See the discussion of Cohen (1985) in Chapter 5; for further examples, read Pratt (2002).

Writing of the prison at the beginning of the new millennium, Garland describes how:

> In the penal-welfare system [1920s–1980s] the prison functioned as the deep end of the correctional sector, dealing with those offenders who failed to respond to the reformatory measures of other institutions. In theory, if not in practice, it represented itself as the last-resort terminus on a continuum of treatment. Today it is conceived much more explicitly as a mechanism of exclusion and control. Treatment modalities still operate within its walls, and lip service is still paid to the ideal of the rehabilitative prison. But the

walls themselves are the institution's most important and valuable element ... the walls have been fortified, literally and figuratively ... The prison is used today as a kind of reservation, a quarantine zone in which purportedly dangerous individuals are segregated in the name of public safety. Those offenders who are released into the community are subject to much tighter control than previously ...

(Garland 2001: 177–178)

In relation to women's imprisonment, Barbara Hudson (2002a), Anne Worrall (2002) and Kelly Hannah-Moffat (2001) have illustrated how the new 'populist punitiveness' has invoked some of the old penological explanations for imprisonment to justify more and more women being sent to prison for relatively minor crimes.

Barbara Hudson (2002) painstakingly analysed policy directives to demonstrate that whereas the concept of 'need' was previously utilised in welfare discourses to justify the non-imprisonment of women committing minor offences, within the new discourses of risk in criminal justice systems pandering to a populist punitiveness, social need has nowadays been redefined as an indicator of likely recidivism which can be best prevented by incarceration of the needy woman.

Anne Worrall's (2002a) analysis in the same collection of articles also showed how discourses change over time, and demonstrated, too, how official penal discourses in the 1990s in England selectively incorporated elements of feminist discourses in order to argue that men and women in the criminal justice and penal systems should be treated equally – an invocation of the formal notion of *equivalence of punishment for like crimes*. But, as Worrall points out, the 1990s' renewed emphasis on equivalence in penal justice, blatantly ignored all the classic difficulties involved in the substantive calculation of equivalences of punishment (already discussed above). The resultant simplistic adherence to the equivalence doctrine, when applied as equivalence of punishment for men and women, has allowed more and more women to be sent to prison without their specific circumstances *as women in crime* being taken into account. A perverse reading of feminist discourses which argue that *women in general* should be empowered to take responsibility for their own actions was also sometimes invoked by those wishing to justify this more punitive sentencing approach to all female offenders.

Kelly Hannah-Moffatt (2001) has forcefully illustrated, and in great detail, that, when confronted by the carceral imperative of the prison, all reforming discourses, including feminist and anti-racist discourses, are likely to be neutralised: either by being cleverly incorporated into official penal discourse in such a way that, divorced from their originating discursive contexts, their original meanings are completely changed; or by a government's failure to provide material support for reform implementation being redefined as prisoner failure to take advantage of reform initiatives. (For further discussion of Hannah-Moffat's book *Punishment in Disguise* see below and Chapter 6.)

Classical approaches

Although (to our knowledge) there are no published studies of women's imprisonment claiming to be either 'Durkheimian' or 'Marxian', the influences of Durkheim and Marx on the study of penality are outlined here primarily because Durkheim's writing on crime and punishment and Marx's on the nature of capitalism have permeated much modern and postmodern thought both about why crime and punishment take the forms they do, and about what imprisonment is for.

The legacy of Emile Durkheim (1858–1917)

Emile Durkheim's main writings on crime and punishment are contained in *Rules of Sociological Method* (1969/1895: chapter 3) and his article *Two Laws of Penal Evolution* (1998/1900). In all his writings he showed more interest in the nature of punishment than in the causes of lawbreaking.

In *The Rules,* Durkheim argued that the function of punishment was twofold: the promotion of social solidarity via the exclusion of deviant persons from society; and the conferral of moral identity upon a society through the punitive designation of its moral boundaries. The relevance of this thesis should by now already be clear to readers of this book: throughout history, the demographics of women who have been imprisoned have demonstrated very clearly that societies have had different moral standards for men and women, and that those female lawbreakers who have been sent to prison have been those who have been seen to have posed the greatest threat to moral order by violating the norms of femininity as much as, or even more than, the criminal law.

In the *Two Laws of Penal Evolution* Durkheim demonstrated that, in the study of punishment, two questions have to be distinguished: those relating to the *quality* (type) of punishment; and those about the *quantity* of punishment imposed in societies in specific eras. Quality and quantity of punishment are, of course, related, as analysis of social control and the different quality and quantity of punishment of women illustrates. The main *qualitative* difference between the social control of women and the social control of men is that women are regulated in many more informal ways outside the criminal justice and penal systems than are men. In particular, they are closely controlled by familial and gender ideologies, structures and processes (see Carlen 1995). This difference in type of social control has, arguably, had a direct influence upon the *quantity* of penal incarceration which women have experienced. Indeed, Feeley and Little (1991) have proposed that the relatively small proportions of women in prison in most western countries have come about as the informal controls on women have strengthened and tightened. In the same vein, Scottish judges interviewed by Carlen (1983) were in agreement that they would be more likely to send a woman to prison if she appeared to be without family ties. It is certainly arguable that the steep increases in women's imprisonment in the 1990s were occasioned by: first, heightened publicity about increases in single motherhood and, (contradictorily) popular fears that young girls were growing up with fewer familial controls being exercised upon them than had been operative in previous eras (Carlen; 1998; Worrall 2002a); and second, an actuarialism in relation to imprisonment which, instead of seeing poverty-stricken female lawbreakers as candidates for non-custodial welfare intervention, interpreted their needs as being indicative of an increased risk of recidivism which could best be prevented by a custodial response (Hudson 2002). These changes in the *quantity* of imprisonment experienced by female populations, together with the related concept of *actuarialism* in criminal justice will be discussed again and in greater detail in Chapter 5 when possible answers to the question 'Why do relatively few women go to prison?' are discussed.

The legacy of Karl Marx (1818–1883)

Marx did not write in any detailed way about crime and punishment, though many political and social theorists have been influenced by Marx's analysis of capitalism (Marx 1956/1847) when they have examined the nature of criminal law and penality. Nor have many analysts of women's imprisonment taken an explicitly Marxist framework. But several of the criminologists whose work on women is discussed in this book have inevitably been influenced by Marxist work on the nature of factory discipline and social discipline in general, as well as by Marxist formulations about the private property and family relationships under capitalism. As Dario Melossi has pointed out, the concept of

> *discipline* is ... the key concept that links Marx's analysis of capitalist social relationships to the emergence of imprisonment (Melossi and Pavarini 1977: 9–95). Discipline (and the training for discipline) is essential, for Marx, to the creation of surplus-value which, in turn, is a question of life and death for capitalist accumulation. Marx sees discipline as *constitutive* of capitalist accumulation ... Furthermore, the key concept of discipline is what links Marxian analysis to Foucault's.
>
> (Melossi 1998b: xiii–xiv)

Before we examine how Foucauldian analysis has influenced feminist approaches to the study of female imprisonment, we must examine the theoretical debates which were provoked by what might be called the 'first wave studies' of women's crime and women's imprisonment, many of which were themselves influenced by Foucault and the growth of postmodern scholarship.

Feminist approaches

In this section a very diffuse range of feminist concerns is touched upon as the early and influential terrain for feminist debate about women's prisons is set out.

From 1980 there were many more studies of women's crime and women's imprisonment than there had been previously. But not all of those working on the topic explicitly claimed that their work was informed by feminist theories and concepts. And though they all focused (either theoretically or empirically) on the ways in which the social control of women, and especially of lawbreaking women, is different to the social control of men, not all of the authors explicitly styled themselves as feminists. However, insofar as authors writing on women's imprisonment have been concerned to remedy the gender-related wrongs done to women by criminologists, police, courts and prisons, together they have constituted a sociology of imprisonment which might loosely be called 'feminist' – albeit, strictly speaking, from a variety of theoretical perspectives and using several different methodologies. It is that disparate band of 'feminist' criminologists (and their feminist critics!) which we discuss in this section.

The studies of women, crime and imprisonment conducted in the 1980s and 1990s made five major contributions to the theoretical understandings of the meanings of women's imprisonment. Study after study revealed: first, that women's crimes are committed in different circumstances to men's, that women's crimes are the crimes of the powerless; second, that the profile of women prisoners is different to that of their male counterparts – fewer tend to have been in paid employment than male prisoners, higher proportions come from the non-manual classes and more have suffered physical and sexual abuse prior to imprisonment (Home Office 1992a; Carlen 1998); and third, that the penal response to women's lawbreaking is constituted within typifications of femininity and womanhood which further add to women's oppression (Carlen 1983, 1998; Edwards 1984; Eaton 1986; Worrall 1990).

The fourth contribution was made by authors who often (but not always) explicitly eschewing policy-oriented work, asked (variously) (a) whether the development of a feminist criminology is a possible theoretical project (Cousins 1980; Carlen et al., 1985); (b) whether the focus on 'women' lawbreakers is a proper concern of feminism; and (c) whether a 'feminist' jurisprudence is desirable and/or possible (see Adelberg and Currie 1987, for Canada; Dahl 1987, for Norway; MacKinnen 1987 for the USA; and Smart 1989a for England).

Fifth, and conversely, some writers did not disdain an explicit policy orientation and joined with campaigning groups for a better deal for women in trouble, before the courts or in prison (Carlen et al., 1985; Carlen and Tchaikovsky 1996; Seear and Player 1986; Padell and Stevenson 1988; Casale 1989; Cook and Davies 1999; Hannah-Moffat and Shaw 2000; Hannah-Moffatt 2001).

As will be apparent from the foregoing, the 'feminist' enterprise in relation to criminology and penology rise has been characterised by debates and disagreement not only about how it should proceed, but, indeed, about whether it should proceed at all! Three early contributors to these debates were Maureen Cain (1989) Carol Smart (1990) and Pat Carlen (1992).

Maureen Cain has made numerous contributions to the theoretical and methodological debates in the sociology of law and crime but the focus here is on her Introduction to *Growing Up Good,* an edited collection of research about the social control of young women in Europe (Cain 1989). It was here that Cain developed a concept which has become central to the methodology of feminist research in criminology and penal analysis – the concept of *transgression* – the notion that a feminist criminology and penal analysis should break out of the traditional subject boundaries of criminology and *deconstruct* all of the taken-for-granted assumptions about what it is to be female, and all of the official categories for defining women who break the law, whilst at the same time being *reflexive* about (that is, constantly calling into question) the process of deconstruction itself. More specifically, and very practically, Cain listed a number of questions which feminists might ask when analysing the discursive sites wherein the deviance of young women is officially constituted:

> how is gender constituted in these sites? how do these sites and modes of constitution of gender connect with other sites and modes? what are the effects of these practices for women and for human fulfilment?
>
> (Cain 1989: 6)

Carol Smart, in her seminal article, 'Feminist approaches to criminology or postmodern woman meets atavistic man' (1990) was more sceptical than Cain about the possibilities of criminology being a 'feminist' project, arguing that, logically, criminology must by definition be about the causes of crime, rather than being able to transcend or deconstruct them via the wider and transformative concerns of feminist critique. In other words, she was claiming that because the word 'criminology' denoted a set of real-world phenomena, any study done under the sign of 'criminology' must itself be a realist study, always tied down to its institutional site of origin and unable to 'transgress' by producing entirely new knowledge.

Pat Carlen (1992) was more reluctant than either Cain or Smart to abandon criminology. She agreed that it was difficult to attribute any meaning to the term 'feminist criminology' which could be considered either desirable or possible. It was not *desirable* because any universalising theories about a taken-for-granted criminality inhering in biological female subjects must be as reductionist and essentialising as the much maligned biological ones. It was not *possible* for three reasons: first, that knowledge about criminal women and criminal justice had not developed via explanatory concepts which could be called 'feminist' – unless one counted as explanatory the usually descriptive use of the word 'patriarchy' (see Cousins 1980); second, that once the historically and socially specific discourses and practices within which women's lawbreaking and criminalisation occurs in Britain, Europe, the USA and Australia are investigated, a concern with gender constructions rapidly merges with questions concerning class, race and imperialism; and third, that no single theory (feminist or otherwise) can explain three major features of women's imprisonment: that women in prison have committed relatively minor crimes; that disproportionate numbers of women in prison are from ethnic minority groups; and that a majority of female prisoners have been in poverty at some time in their lives.

Nonetheless, in reply to Smart's strictures about criminology being a peculiarly ideologically-burdened discipline, Carlen argued that the tension between the 'naming' of a site of knowledge (with its attendant ideological assumptions) and the capacity of critique to transcend its institutional and nominalist origins has been of perennial concern to philosophers and scientists. The anti-realist (but idealist) quest for an end to ideology was therefore neither a new issue nor one which had more critical implications for criminology than for any other science – social or otherwise. The problematics of the relationships between thought and experience are integral to all human knowledges – whether they be called sciences, ideologies or disciplines.

Broadly speaking, and to sum up this 'first wave' of 'feminist' studies of women's imprisonment, it could be argued that throughout the 1980s and 1990s there were two major approaches to questions about why and how women's prisons and women's imprisonment should be studied. Some writers took a modernist and structural approach, usually emphasising both the social structural determinants of the prison's capacity to coerce, and the social demographic characteristics of prisoners (for example, Carlen 1983, 1998). Others emphasised the postmodern and existential capacity of women (as social beings) to resist total domination by constant reinvention of the self and its repertoire of meanings (Worrall 1990; Bosworth 1999). Cross-cutting both broad groupings was a range of motives for studying women's prisons, as well as a range of epistemological (or anti-epistemological) positions; though all major writers on the subject explicitly claimed an interest in either feminist or prison politics, rather than in any traditional and positivistic penological objective of reforming or 'saving' female criminals.

Throughout the period, the work of Michel Foucault had an influence on writers on women's imprisonment – either implicitly or explicitly. Indeed, as the influence of Foucault and various critiques of modernism gained ground within criminology in the 1990s, it could be seen that, from the beginning of the 1980s, the bulk of writing on women's imprisonment had been undertaken by authors whose intellectual interests had been much more rooted in the debates between modernism and postmodernism than had those of the predominantly male authors of traditional criminology. Next, we examine the work of three authors who have claimed Foucault as an explicit influence – though it should be noted that the methodological and textual manifestations of his influence have been both extremely varied and of varying quality. (For the work of other writers on women's imprisonment who make an explicit acknowledgement of Foucault's influence see Zedner 1991 and Bosworth 1999.)

Foucauldian feminist approaches

In this section we examine some of the feminist work which has been more consistently and explicitly influenced by the work of Michel Foucault.

R.P. Dobash, R.E. Dobash and S. Gutteridge, *The Imprisonment of Women*. Oxford: Blackwell, 1986
In 1986, Dobash et al. published their account of the history of women's imprisonment in Scotland, informing their analysis of fieldwork which they had conducted in the Scottish women's prison in the early 1980s (just prior to the period when Carlen conducted the research for *Women's Imprisonment* 1983) with a historical and analytic account of past penal practices and ideologies in relation to women's imprisonment in Scotland. Thus, whereas Carlen had attempted to transgress the 'moment' of prison with a synchronic analysis which contextualised that 'moment' within its constitutive institutions (such as the family), ideologies (for example, of gender), and practices (for example, of social work) in contemporary Scotland, Dobash et al., attempted a diachronic analysis which, by demonstrating how past ideologies and policies in relation to women's imprisonment in Scotland had been constantly modified, amended and atrophied in practice, provided an enlightening account of how women's imprisonment in Scotland came to take the form it did in the early 1980s.

Adrian Howe, *Punish and Critique: Towards a Feminist Analysis of Penality*. London: Routledge, 1994
According to its author, the goal of this book was 'to pursue the critical project by pressing it into the service of those moving towards a theoretically-grounded feminist analysis of penality' (p. 3). Yet, although Howe's main focus was on the punishment of women in all its aspects, rather than on imprisonment in particular, she does provide a feminist (and appreciative) critique of Foucault's *Discipline and Punish*,

at the same time as arguing, and illustrating at some length, the way in which Foucault's analysis, and his followers' interpretations of it, have ignored the differential forms which the social control of women have always taken – forms which cannot be grasped by analyses which focus solely on state forms of penality. (See Chapter 5 of this volume for more discussion of how the informal control of women impacts on their formal control by the criminal justice system.)

Howe's book is actually one of the most sophisticated, comprehensive and detailed analyses of penality and women in the literature, and the questions which she raises about the complexity of the possible relationships between postmodern theorizing and politics are also those which link the 'first wave' of research on women and imprisonment (with its emphasis on exposing the hitherto 'invisible' women's prisons to both the analytic and the public gaze), to the concerns and critiques of the more explicitly Foucauldian or postmodern analysts. For, insofar as postmodernism is a term loosely used to denote all those perspectives which question the dualities (such as objective and subjective) of modernist rational thinking, and which argue that no methods of investigation can guarantee the production of any universalisable truths, a central question which has to be confronted by postmodern theorists who also want to engage in political action is this: if a postmodernist approach to theorizing requires all meanings to be constantly deconstructed, how can a postmodern critique of women's imprisonment be utilised as a basis for sentencing campaigns or policy changes which should themselves also be constantly open to deconstruction and critique? As Howe herself put it:

> [W]e must avoid the absurdity of infinite relativism: we must not forget that incarcerated women are more coerced than those outside the prison walls and that some women, notably black and other minority women, suffer from the coercion and oppression of institutionalised racism within Western criminal justice systems. The challenge ahead, then, for feminist analysts, is to address the difficult questions – such as whether or not to effect a disengagement of crime and punishment, or whether a consideration of the specificities of the punishment of women demands a fundamentally different kind of theoretical approach ... [A]nother challenge is that presented by the postmodern attacks on the analytical category of 'women'. How can a feminist who is informed by a postmodern sensibility that women no longer exist, speak for women prisoners?
>
> (Howe 1994: 164)

In an already long and complex book, Howe had no space to answer these questions, but they were questions which, in slightly different form, were to become of central concern to Kelly Hannah-Moffat (2001) in her book, *Punishment in Disguise.*

Kelly Hannah-Moffat, *Punishment in Disguise: Penal Governance and Federal Control of Women in Canada.* Toronto: University of Toronto Press, 2001

Punishment in Disguise (hereafter referenced as *PD*) tells a story about class, race, gender and 'the logics and strategies of governing that perpetuate long-established patterns' (*PD*:5) of incarceration. The place is Canada and ostensibly the tale begins in 1990 with the publication of *The Report of the Task Force on Federally Sentenced Women: Creating Choices* (Ottowa, Ministry of the Solicitor General) which 'set out a new philosophy and set of principles for the construction and operation of five new women-centred prisons'.

Writing from a Foucauldian 'governmentality' perspective, the author charts the ways in which the *Creating Choices* reforms were implemented, at the same time as she analytically details the conjunctions, disjunctions and transformations of the multiple logics implicit in their historical formations. The book thus provides a rich and thick description of the ideological and political conjunctures which produced the present state of women's imprisonment in Canada. Most originally, however, the main focus is not on the role of government departments, but on the part played by non-state agents (including feminists and Aboriginal activists) in the forging of 'neo-liberal techniques of penal discipline which stress "responsibilisation" and the production of self-governing prisoners'. (p. 18).

It is not a tale with a happy ending, as Kelly Hannah-Moffat fore-warns at the beginning:

> Over ten years have passed since the project began and, during which the government has committed itself financially and politically to a new vision, and during which five new archi-tecturally beautiful regional facilities (prisons) have been built with the goal of replacing the antiquated Prison For Women. The language describing women's imprisonment now speaks of empowerment, choice and healing; yet many argue that little about the regime has changed and that few lessons have been learned. (*PD*:4)

But *we* can learn much from Hannah-Moffat's book. *Punishment in*

Disguise has been chosen as the last book for mention in this chapter on theories of women's imprisonment because in our opinion it is simply the very best exemplifier of the state of the art at the beginning of the twenty-first century. It encapsulates all the tensions between writing about 'real women' and 'real political process' (see also Daly 1997; Snider 2003 – both are discussed in Chapter 6) at the same time as attempting to deconstruct the political processes which have constituted those 'real women' as significant to criminology and penality. Relatedly, it raises a range of questions about the desirable and possible relationships between theories and politics which will comprise the central theoretical concern of Chapter 6.

Conclusion

In this chapter we have examined a range of political, penological, sociological and criminological literature in order to see how the two questions: Why do women's prisons take the form they do? and, What are women's prisons for? might be answered. The ever-changing story of the theoretical and political struggles for justice for imprisoned women which we have begun to describe at the end of this chapter will now be continued in Chapter 5, where the politics of the alternatives to custody for women are unfolded and deconstructed, and where discussion will focus in more detail upon how the politics of campaigning on behalf of women prisoners have been theorized by feminists writing from a variety of theoretical perspectives.

Concepts to know

empirical: refers to the initial sensory awareness of social phenomena. However, research projects involving empirical investigation do not necessarily have to make *empiricist* assumptions about the meanings of the data thus collected (see the definition of empiricism below).

empiricism: an empiricist approach to knowledge makes the assumption that empirical data have pregiven or contingent meanings which are either immediately apparent via the 'common sense' with which all humans are supposed to be endowed, or discoverable via recognised scientific procedures for ascertaining probable causal relationships between phenomena.

stigma: as used in criminology, this term usually refers to the negative identities socially attributed to people perceived to be deviant in some way, and the ways in which such stigmatisation marks out the stigmatised for further exclusion or negative discrimination. For the classic sociological statement on stigma see Erving Goffman, *Stigma* (1961). For a history of the concept, see the definition in the excellent *Sage Dictionary of Criminology* (McLaughlin and Muncie 2001: 292).

Further reading

All books listed at the end of Chapter 1 are relevant, together with the references in the main body of the text of this chapter (according to students' interests). More specifically, the Durkheim extracts listed below should be read because Durkheimian perspectives on social control continue to inform many analyses of punishment. Melossi's *Sociology of Punishment* contains key extracts from all the major theoretical writings on imprisonment in general, though writings specifically on women's imprisonment are under-represented.

Durkheim, E. (1969 first published 1895) *Rules of Sociological Method.* New York, NY: Free Press

Durkheim, E. (1900) 'Two laws of penal evolution', in D. Melossi (1998a) *The Sociology of Punishment.* Aldershot: Ashgate, pp. 2–31

Freedman, E. (1981) *Their Sisters' Keepers: Women's Prison Reform in America 1830–1930.* Ann Arbor, MI: University of Michigan Press

Gelsthorpe, L. and Morris, M. (1990a) *Feminist Perspectives in Criminology.* Buckingham: Open University Press (an excellent collection of articles including those by Cain (1989) and Smart (1990) referred to in this chapter.)

Howe, A. (1994) *Towards a Feminist Analysis of Penality.* London: Routledge

Hudson, B. (1996) *Understanding Justice.* Buckingham: Open University Press (for an excellent and very accessible exposition and critiques of the penological justifications for punishment).

Marx, K. (1847/1956) *Capital Vol. 1.* London: Dent.

Melossi, D. (ed.)(1998a) *The Sociology of Punishment: Socio-Structural Perspectives.* Aldershot: Ashgate (this comprehensive Reader contains extracts from all the main theorists and perspectives in the sociology of punishment.)

Topics for discussion

1 Can the imprisonment of women ever be justified? If so, on what grounds?
2 Why are women's prisons different to men's?

Essay questions

1 'Explaining women's crimes, does not explain women's imprisonment.' Explain and discuss.
2 Why do women's prisons take the forms they do?
3 Is a 'feminist' theory of women's imprisonment either desirable or possible?
4 What are women's prisons for?
5 Which concepts have you found most useful in explaining women's imprisonment? Why?
6 'The penological justifications for imprisonment are difficult to operationalise separately; and it is logically and practically impossible to operationalise them all at the same time.' Explain and discuss.
7 Does women's imprisonment work? How could we know?

Chapter 5

Alternatives to custody

Introduction

'If men behaved like women, the courts would be idle and the prisons empty' – or so said Barbara Wootton (Heidensohn 1991). If men behaved like women, crime would be at a level that could be tolerated in a civilised society. 'Women are on the whole a law-abiding lot' (Carlen 1988: 3) and the inescapable fact is that female crime, as a social phenomenon and despite media hyperbole, still poses few challenges to the organisation of contemporary society. If the rate of female crime were to become the 'norm' then the problems of the criminal justice system would be resolved 'at a stroke' and criminologists would probably be out of work! That is not to argue that female crime is not 'real crime' or that a handful of individual female criminals are not dangerous or greedy or both. Rather it is to make the point that if all women's prisons were closed tomorrow, except for one wing in a closed prison, it is quite possible that no one would notice (see Carlen 1990 and Chapter 6).

Every year the Home Office produces its *Statistics on Women and the Criminal Justice System* (available from the Home Office website). At first glance, the statistics for 2001 may appear reassuring. Only 19 per cent of known offenders are women and most of those will be cautioned or conditionally discharged. This is partly because women are more likely than men to admit their offences and to be arrested for less serious offences. Only 13 per cent of offenders given community penalties (under the supervision of the National Probation Service) are women and, as we have seen, only just over 5 per cent of the prison population are women. Women commit fewer crimes than men, their offences tend to be less serious and their criminal careers shorter. So what is the problem? Do we need to explain (theorize) why women are relatively infrequently criminalised and imprisoned? Can we not just leave it to common sense? Well, no, because unless we begin to understand why women are not criminalised and imprisoned as frequently as men, we cannot properly understand what is happening when, as in the past decade, the common-sense view that 'women don't commit crime' is challenged, and women start to be criminalised and imprisoned at a disproportionate rate.

In this chapter we will examine first those criminological theories that seek to explain why women are not criminalised to the same extent as men. Then we will consider why the criminal justice system often appears to treat criminalised women leniently by *not* sending them to prison. Finally, we will discuss the advantages and disadvantages for women of the range of non-custodial provision that is now available to sentencers and the extent to which women offenders *resist* the transcarceralism of these so-called *alternatives* to custody.

Why aren't women criminalised as much as men?

An obvious answer to the question 'why aren't women criminalised as much as men?' is 'because they don't commit as much crime' and this answer is supported by every criminal statistic produced around the world. As Heidensohn puts it:

> Gender appears to be the single most crucial variable associated with criminality. Put more bluntly, most crime is committed by men; relatively little crime is committed by women.
>
> (1987: 22)

Theories of women's criminality (or lack of it) were traditionally confined to psychological and psychiatric texts and hardly featured in sociological theories of deviance before the 1970s. Frances Heidensohn was one of the first sociologists to draw attention to this neglect in an article in 1968, in which she suggested that both the neglect of women's deviance in sociological literature *and* the absence of evidence that women's deviance (unlike men's) was increasing should be topics of interest in their own rights. In saying this, she was implicitly supporting the symbolic interactionist argument that criminality inheres not in the 'act' but in the reaction to it. Women's *criminality* only exists to the extent that it is recognised as such. She suggested that women's (lack of) deviance could only be understood in the context of the structures and reactions of society to the role of women. She challenged the tendency to sexualise female crime and to make the false assumption that most female crime was related to prostitution when, in reality, theft was (and remains) the most common offence committed by both men and women. She called for 'a crash programme of research which telescopes decades of comparable studies of males' (1968: 171) in order to advance the study of female deviance.

Broadly speaking, there are two traditional positivistic explanations for women's apparent lack of criminality: those involving biology and those involving socialisation. Carol Smart sets out these theories very clearly in Chapter 2 of her book *Law, Crime and Sexuality* (1995), though it must be remembered that she writes from a feminist perspective and is therefore very critical of these theories. (For a fuller exposition, see Smart's (1976) pioneering book, *Women, Crime and Criminology.*) These theories argue either that women are genetically less inclined towards aggressive behaviour, being natural nurturers and protectors, or that they are socialised into greater conformity by internalising gender role expectations – they are taught what being a woman means in a particular society. Girls tend to be brought up to be more conforming and to behave in ways that will not get them into trouble with the law. Adolescent girls are seen to be more likely to be in 'moral danger' because of sexual promiscuity than to become involved in criminal activity. When they are adult, women have less *opportunity* to commit crimes because they are looking after their homes and children. If they cannot cope with these responsibilities, they are more likely to seek medical or psychiatric help than to turn to crime.

An alternative theory is offered by Otto Pollak whose book *The Criminality of Women* (1950) is concerned largely with the hidden or masked nature of female criminality. He argues that women are equally as criminal as men but that the type of offences they commit and their social roles protect them from detection. His analysis of the nature of women is a mixture of biological determinism and socialisation. He maintains that women are more cunning and deceitful than men and that these characteristics have a physiological basis. Unlike a man, a woman can hide her 'lack of positive emotion' because a 'woman's body permits such pretense to a certain degree and lack of orgasm does not prevent her ability to participate in the sex act' (1950:8 cited in Smart 1995). Because of their traditional domestic role, he argues that women are also able to enact their crimes in relative privacy. For example, as preparers of meals women are able to administer poisons to their victims without fear of detection, while as mothers or childminders they are able to mistreat or neglect their children (Smart 1995: 24).

As Smart points out, one of the implications of Pollak's theory is the extent to which he has perpetuated the belief that women are treated more leniently by the legal and penal systems than men are:

> One of the outstanding concomitants of the existing inequality between the sexes is chivalry and the general protective attitude of man towards woman ... Men hate to accuse women and thus indirectly to send them to their punishment, police officers dislike to arrest them, district attorneys to prosecute them, judges and juries to find them guilty and so on.
>
> (1950: 151 cited in Smart 1995)

A more scholarly and contemporary challenge (than Pollak) to the belief that most women are incapable of serious violent crime can be found in Anna Motz's (2001) book *The Psychology of Female Violence*, which adopts a psycho-dynamic approach to the links between childhood experience and adult behaviour. In a thought-provoking and highly informative discussion of female violence against children, against self and against male partners, Motz argues we do women a disservice by denying their capacity for violence through a sentimentality that causes us to lurch from idealisation to denigration. Instead, she argues, we should regard a violent act by women 'as a solution to a psychological difficulty and a bodily expression or communication of distress and anger' (2001: 7). Viewed in this way, violent and sexual crimes (particularly sexual abuse against children) by women are no longer acts which women 'don't do' (because of their sexual passivity and maternal instincts) but are acts which all women are capable of and which increasing numbers choose 'to do' (Worrall 2002b). Thus it is argued that the reason women aren't criminalised as much as men is that we choose not to see their criminal behaviour. In this way, we both protect ourselves from acknowledging their capacity for serious criminal acts and we control women by failing to respond to what they are communicating. As Hilary Allen has said (1987b) they are 'rendered harmless'.

Many writers (Ardener 1978; Feeley and Little 1991; see also Chapter 1) make the point that women are subject to greater informal social control than men through both family responsibilities and the associated, but separate (and increasingly absent), control imposed on them by male family members (husbands, partners, brothers, fathers, even sons). Such supposedly benign control is considered sufficient to sustain most women in social conformity without recourse to formal mechanisms of social control such as police, courts and prisons. It is only when these mechanisms appear to break down that formal criminal justice has to be invoked and, even then, the tendency is to seek to restore that informal control wherever possible.

But is this form of control as benign as is often assumed? Pat Carlen (1995) argues that it is not and suggests that it would be better described as 'antisocial control'. She defines the distinction thus:

- Social control: a generic term for a variety of benign institutionalised practices designed to set limits to individual action in the interests of the collectivity's proclaimed ideals of social and criminal justice as instanced in law and dominant ideologies.

- Antisocial control: a generic term for a variety of malign institutionalised practices that may *either* set limits to individual action by favouring one set of citizens at the expense of another so as to subvert equal opportunities ideologies in relation to gender, race and class (or other social groupings); or (in societies without equal opportunities ideologies) set limits to individual action in ways that are antisocial because they atrophy an individual's social contribution and do so on the grounds of either biological attributes or exploitative social relations. (Carlen 1995: 213-214)

Carlen argues that this distinction is helpful because it avoids the trap of assuming that social control (which is itself a notoriously ill-defined term) is always either a 'good thing' (in governmental terms) or a 'bad thing' (in libertarian terms). It enables policies and practices to be analysed from both perspectives and for their contradictory effects to be both explained and anticipated. She goes on to identify four forms of antisocial control that sets limits to women's actions before there is any perceived need to invoke formal criminal justice control. Women, she argues, are controlled by the discourses of femininity, which require them to be both 'in control' (coping and caring) and 'out of control' (fragile and dependent) of themselves; by the conflicting demands of the family (responsible for, but also regulated by it); by the contradictory messages about their place in the economy (for example, the alternating vilification of working mothers and welfare scroungers); and by the explicit and implicit violence of men (physical and sexual violence, restrictions in the use of public space and encouragement to resort to medication if they are unable to 'cope'). Given the complexities of exclusion and inclusion which routinely confront women, it is perhaps unsurprising that relatively few of them require formal social control. As Carlen puts it:

For women then, the Kafkaesque anterooms of the criminal courts are to be found in the simultaneity of the inclusionary and exclusionary devices of the antisocial family, the antisocial state, and the antisocial practice and discourses of men's violence, *mens rea*, men's rule and male menace.

(Carlen 1995: 215)

Why are some women treated leniently by the criminal courts (or are they)?

What 'being a woman' means has been the subject of many studies but we are concerned here with the relationship between 'being a woman' and 'being criminalised'. In the introduction to their book, *Gender, Crime and Justice,* Carlen and Worrall (1987: 2–3) describe 'being a normal woman' as itself an ambiguous state, characterised by both 'self-control and independence' and 'lack of control and dependence'. They describe femininity as being constructed within discourses of *domesticity, sexuality and pathological 'otherness'*. The impact for women who *do* break the law is summarised thus by Worrall:

> The female lawbreaker is routinely offered the opportunity to neutralise the effects of her lawbreaking activity by implicitly entering into a contract whereby she permits her life to be re-presented primarily in terms of its domestic, sexual and pathological dimensions. The effects of this 'gender contract' is to strip her lawbreaking of its social, economic and ideological dimensions in order to minimise its punitive consequences.
>
> (Worrall 1990: 31)

When a woman appears to step outside of the gender contract by committing a crime, the criminal justice system goes to considerable lengths to restore her to it. In her book *Offending Women*, Anne Worrall argues that this is a process of subtlety and complexity, involving the bringing together of a range of 'expert scripts' within the courtroom setting – in particular the discourses within which the scripts of magistrates, solicitors, psychiatrists and probation officers are constructed. Each of these 'experts' is authorised in law to construct the woman criminal as being either 'not woman' or 'not criminal' in order to re-present her as being suitable (or not) for punishment. Worrall asks two questions:

1 Under what conditions do certain people claim to possess knowledge about female lawbreakers?

2 What is the process whereby such claims are translated into practices which have particular consequences for female lawbreakers?

(Worrall 1990: 5)

In order to answer the first question Worrall proposes that courtroom personnel are obliged to 'make sense' of the relatively infrequent presence of women as offenders by describing them variously as invisible (as being too few in number to warrant serious attention), as guilty (of being failed women as well as criminals), as treatable (having a low-level mental disorder that lends itself to benign and relatively simple psychiatric intervention) and as manageable (within the community). While this construction is taking place, the women themselves are 'muted' – they play no part in writing the scripts of their own lives. Ardener's definition of 'muting' (see Chapter 2) 'does not require that the muted be actually silent. They may speak a great deal. The important issue is whether they are able to say all that they would wish to say, where and when they wish to say it' (Ardener 1978: 21, cited in Worrall 1990: 11).

Women who can be restored to the gender contract in this way may be dealt with more leniently than those who cannot and, as Worrall has argued more recently (2000a), increasing numbers of women are being excluded from restoration to the gender contract. Among them are those who are categorised as female sex abusers, female drug offenders, female perpetrators of domestic violence and the 'new breed' of 'liberated' violent girls. Whether or not such offenders exist in any quantity in reality, the construction of such categories creates new spaces and, like the building of new prisons, the vacuum of vacant spaces sucks matter in.

But some women resist this construction and Worrall terms these 'nondescript women'. They are the women who will not allow themselves to be fitted into stereotypical categories. Their resistance is rarely overt or obvious. But they show themselves to be deeply unimpressed by the notion of 'contract' and find ways of challenging the demands of supervision and exploiting the contradictions in official discourses. They are elusive, demanding, manipulative and, occasionally, outrightly resistant to 'advice' but in ways which constantly draw the helper back, regardless of their frustration. Precisely because the poverty and abuse in their backgrounds *is* recognised, the obligation on 'experts' is keenly felt but hard to execute:

As a result, the 'experts' find such women impossible to define and they appear to be beyond definition both as women and as criminals. Yet, while much of the women's resistance is individualistic, inconsistent, and, in some senses, self-destructive, it has the important effect of undermining the authority of official discourses and keeping open the possibility of the creation of new knowledge about them – both as women and as law-breakers.

(Worrall 1990: 163)

Alternatives to prison for women

In her book *Punishment in the Community*, Anne Worrall argues that non-custodial sentences should not be viewed merely as 'alternatives' to prison but that they should be understood as representing a different sphere of penal regulation which is based on self-government and normalising instruction. She points out that there is no generic term for such punishment that is not 'ineluctably hitched up to incarceration' and that means that 'our analysis is conceptually impoverished' (1997: 3). The most commonly used terms are 'alternatives to custody' or 'non-custodial sentences', but 'community punishment', 'community corrections' and 'community-based sentences' are now widely recognised terms, though the word 'community' in this context means little more than 'not-in-prison'. The extent to which the 'community' is involved in these sentences in practice is generally very limited and the implication that such sentences enhance social inclusion, rather than exacerbating social exclusion, is also debatable.

As we have seen in Chapter 4, some of the strongest theorizing (explaining) literature on prisons has not been gender-specific. Similarly, the literature on alternatives to custody, decarceration and trans-carceralism has not focused on women, although its insights have gendered implications for women. In this section we consider the theoretical assumptions behind each of these terms, using Cohen's analysis of the history of 'social control talk' (1983) which juxtaposes three different models of correctional change: 'uneven progress', 'benevolence gone wrong' and 'it's all a con' (1983: 104–106). We then consider the different non-custodial sentences and their implications for women.

Three models of correctional change (Cohen 1983)

Uneven progress – alternatives to custody, official rhetoric and administrative criminology

Accepting that, in an imperfect world, progress will never be unimpeded, Cohen describes, first, an optimistic conservative rhetoric which argues that penal reform has been steady and that alternatives to custody represent the enlightened values of an ever more civilised society. Before the end of the nineteenth century, the only non-custodial sentences (apart from the death penalty) used regularly by courts were fines and release on recognisances (the equivalent of cautions, binding over and discharges). Police Court Missionaries, founded in 1876 by the Church of England Temperance Society, often 'vouched' for released offenders and are generally regarded as the forerunners of the modern probation service. Most histories of the probation service place it within the humanitarian considerations of Victorian and Edwardian penal reformers but Raynor and Vanstone (2002) provide a more critical summary which emphasises the dimension of 'moral training'. An increasing confidence in both their material wealth and their scientific knowledge led reformers to believe that crime was a social disease for which a cure was possible through 'specific practices of normalisation, classification, categorisation and discrimination between criminal types' (Garland 1985: 32). Social control could now be achieved 'through attention to the material, social and psychological welfare of criminals' (Worrall 1997: 8) without the need for physical incarceration. This rehabilitative approach dominated work with offenders in the first half of the twentieth century and alternatives to custody were justified on the grounds that:

1 Prisons are ineffective and may strengthen criminal commitment by bringing offenders into close association with each other.

2 The stigma attached to imprisonment and the loosening of family and community ties may make it harder for the criminal to return to a normal life after prison.

3 Most offenders can be dealt with in the community safely, effectively, humanely and (crucially) more cheaply than in prison.

4 Since the causes of crime lie in the relationship between the offender and the community, that is where the cure for crime also lies.

Benevolence gone wrong – the demise of rehabilitation and the decarceration debate

The rehabilitative ideal came increasingly under attack in the 1960s and 1970s for both ideological and pragmatic reasons. Ideologically, attempts at offender rehabilitation were regarded as, on the one hand, intrusive and an infringement of civil liberties and, on the other hand, as a 'soft option' – an indulgence of middle-class liberals out of touch with the 'real' world of crime victimisation. Pragmatically, it seemed that rehabilitation just did not 'work' and, in some cases, made matters worse (Worrall 1997: 22).

Cohen's second account of penal change reflects this disillusion with rehabilitation which characterised much of the symbolic interactionist literature on the sociology of deviance and the 'nothing works' approach to punishment. Rather than seeking reform, we should be looking for ways to manage – both the system and individual criminal careers – so as to cause the least damage, cost and inconvenience to the rest of society. However, after a decade of defensiveness and soul-searching in the 1980s, advocates of rehabilitation slowly regained confidence with the discovery of what is now termed the 'what works' – or 'evidence-based' approach, which we will consider in more detail later in this chapter. For Cohen, however, these developments (though he wrote before the term 'what works' was coined) represented a process of official mystification.

It's all a con – intensive supervision, monitoring and transcarceralism

Cohen's third model presents a conspiracy of the powerful to mystify and obfuscate:

> Humanism, good intentions, professional knowledge and reform rhetoric are neither in the idealist sense the producers of change, nor in the materialist sense the mere products of changes in the political economy ... [T]he exercise of power itself creates and causes to emerge new objects of knowledge and accumulates new bodies of information.
>
> (Cohen 1983 cited in Worrall 1997: 25)

The decarcerated criminal is one such new object of knowledge about whom new bodies of information must be accumulated. Community programmes, far from reducing the restrictions on criminals who might otherwise have been sent to prison, create a new clientele of criminals who are controlled or disciplined by other mechanisms. The boundaries between freedom and confinement become blurred. The 'net' of social control is thus thrown ever wider into the community, its thinner mesh designed to trap ever smaller 'fish'. Once caught in the net, the penetration of disciplinary intervention is ever deeper, reaching every aspect of the criminal's life. This is sometimes referred to as 'transcarceralism', defined by Matthews (1989: 135) as the diversion of people from 'formal penal institutions ... into other segregative institutions which operate with more benign labels'.

Insightful as this 'vision of social control' is, however, it does not fully capture the experiences of women offenders because, as we have seen, women are already subject to much greater informal social control than men. Therefore, and rather perversely, the argument for subjecting them to greater formal social control within the community is not as persuasive as one might expect. It tends to be regarded by sentencers as being inappropriate *either* because (in the case of minor offences) there is already sufficient informal social control to rehabilitate the woman *or* because (in the case of more serious or repeat offending) it has already failed and what is now needed is more drastic action in the form of imprisonment. So the 'alternatives to custody' debate has been constructed in such a way as to ensure that it both ignores and is irrelevant to women. This is not because women are not sent to prison; clearly they are – and in increasing numbers – but the debate ignores the complexities of the route that leads them there. It does this in two ways. First, it renders the majority of women offenders invisible by constructing them as 'not recidivists'. Second, it renders a minority highly visible by assuming that their presence in prison demonstrates either their dangerousness or their incorrigibility, rather than demonstrating the inadequacy of the discourses within which they are so constructed (Worrall 1990: 115).

This policy of 'bifurcation' (separating out the 'minor' from the 'dangerous' criminals) has been a feature of the politicisation of crime in the past two decades and has allowed successive governments to sustain a paradoxical rhetoric of supporting alternatives to prison while arguing that there are many 'dangerous' criminals for whom alternatives are simply not 'suitable'. Since 'dangerousness' (as politically defined) is very much 'in the eye of the beholder', this line of official rhetoric has given rise to the concept of 'populist punitiveness', which has resulted in the chronic under-use and under-resourcing of alternatives to custody. Raynor and Vanstone (2002) discuss populist punitiveness and its impact on the use of community sentences. They argue that 'crime-related issues [are] defined by political elites as problems of insufficient punishment or as being "soft" on criminals' (2002: 69). By playing on understandable public concerns about crime, supporting biased media coverage and fuelling moral panics, politicians use crime-related issues to manipulate public opinion. Within this discourse, the only acceptable kind of community sentence is a 'tough' one, the implication being that most community sentences are far from 'tough'. The dialogue between probation or community corrections officers and governments (for a detailed account of one such dialogue, see Worrall 1997) has been one centred on the so-called 'strengthening' of community sentences by means of increasingly unrealistic 'conditions' that have to be met by offenders. Carlen (1989) has referred to this process as being one which disregards 'sentencing feasibility'. Practitioners often refer to it as 'setting an offender up to fail'.

This 'toughness' has resulted in a range of penalties known in the USA as 'intermediate sanctions' – penalties that 'fit' between traditional probation orders and prison. Intermediate sanctions involve a greater intensity of supervision, coupled with greater monitoring or surveillance (Byrne et al., 1992). Although intermediate sanctions take many different forms, we now describe the evolution of their key principles.

Three generations of intensive supervision

In England and Wales and the USA it is possible to identify three 'generations' of intensive supervision initiatives for adult offenders – those which developed in the 1960s and 1970s, those which were a feature of the 1980s and early 1990s but which continue in various forms to the present time, and those which have emerged in the late 1990s and are proliferating in the early years of the twenty-first century. Intensive supervision has been a more integral and continuous part of work with juvenile offenders but the interest here is in the extent to which this concept has been deemed appropriate for work with adult offenders.

First generation – 'the search for the magic number'
(Clear and Hardyman 1992: 355)

In England and Wales, four probation services participated in the now infamous Intensive Matched Probation and After-care Treatment (IMPACT) experiment from 1972 to 1974 (Folkard 1974, 1976). Based on the traditional 'treatment model' of probation, IMPACT sought to provide 'more social work, more counselling, more help' (Mair 1997: 65) to a small and select caseload of offenders, in the belief that greater frequency of treatment contact would rehabilitate offenders and reduce their criminal activity. The focus was on 'matching' offenders with different personality and social problems to different kinds of probation intervention and there was virtually no mention within the model of involving any other agencies. The evaluation reports were damning, apparently demonstrating that IMPACT participants were more, rather than less, likely to re-offend than non-participants, and providing evidence in the UK to support Martinson's claim (1974) in the USA (also based on evaluation of similar intensive supervision interventions) that 'nothing works'. As Lurigio and Petersilia (1992) report, smaller caseloads did not produce more contacts, failure rates appeared to increase and the wrong type of offender ended up on the projects as a result of 'net-widening'.

Second generation – 'institutional overcrowding and lack of respect for community penalties' (Clear 1997: 130)

In the 1980s, intensive supervision probation (ISP) was one of the most widely adopted intermediate sanctions in the USA, being implemented in at least 40 states (Will 1995). Its two-fold aim was to 'represent a response to pressures created by a demand for incarceration which exceeds prison capacity' while also offering 'one cost-effective option, satisfying demands for punishment, public safety and treatment objectives' (US Department of Justice 1988: 7). In England and Wales, the government's Green Paper *Punishment, Custody and the Community* (Home Office 1988a) and subsequent Action Plan for dealing with young adult offenders, *Tackling Offending* (1988b) led to eight pilot Intensive Probation schemes which ran between 1990 and 1992 and were evaluated by the Home Office (Mair *et al* 1994; Mair 1997). Unlike the first-generation projects, these projects made many more demands on offenders and included the concept of surveillance. Underpinned by the penal philosophies of specific deterrence and incapacitation, rather than rehabilitation (Lurigio and Petersilia 1992), the second-generation schemes involved targeted 'serious' offenders in multiple weekly contacts with their probation officers, and – in the USA – random home visits, curfews (sometimes electronically monitored), unscheduled drug tests, compulsory vocational education and victim restitution (Police Executive Research Forum 1990). They might be 'front-end' (alternatives to prison) or 'back-end' (early release from prison) programmes (Lurigio and Petersilia 1992) and involved, at least in theory, a multi-agency approach. Although the police were not directly involved in projects, the USA schemes often involved a pair of officers – a traditional probation officer and a surveillance officer – 'usually a former police officer or prison guard' (Police Executive Research Forum 1990: 58). In terms of embryonic information-exchange, it was also noted that:

> As part of their daily routine, ISP officers can be expected to collect information about the associates, hangouts and habits of their charges, saving police much time in developing offender dossiers.
> (Police Executive Research Forum 1990: 59)

Evaluations of ISP projects in the USA and in England and Wales were consistently discouraging in terms of their impact on recidivism. In the USA, it was found that they did not alleviate prison overcrowding and in some states exacerbated it as a result of increased revocations of orders for technical violations. They were more expensive than expected and they were no more effective than routine probation in reducing recidivism (Petersilia and Turner 1995). Programmes also varied greatly in terms of frequency of contact, size of caseload, extent of surveillance, type of offender accepted, practices of supervision and responses to violations (Lurigio and Petersilia 1992). The picture was similar in England and Wales (Mair et al., 1994) and the evaluators bemoaned the 'lack of innovation' in the schemes. In their favour, it was clear that offenders themselves spoke very positively of the projects, enjoying the additional attention. The projects were also successful in providing greater control or structure for offenders and thus making it more likely that they would persevere with – and possibly benefit from – treatment programmes.

Although ISP projects failed to meet their stated goals, it has been noted that they achieved a 'series of latent goals' (Mair 1997: 67) – organisational, professional and psycho-political. They enhanced the credibility of probation by appearing to demonstrate a 'change of culture' and a 'reduced tolerance of crime and disorder'. This, in turn, attracted more resources to probation and raised the esteem – and self-esteem – of probation officers. As Clear (1997: 130) puts it, succinctly: 'the very fact that ISPs proliferate is the evidence of their success'.

Third generation – 'an arrest and revocation should be seen as an arrest and not a failure' (Clear 1997:120)

ISPs have continued in the USA in a variety of forms (Fabelo 2001a) but they have been overtaken by Enhanced Supervision Partnerships (Parent and Snyder 1999) involving police and corrections personnel as equal partners. As we have seen, embryonic police-probation

Table 5.1 Three models of intensive supervision for adult offenders

Generation	First	Second	Third
Era	1960s–1970s	1980s–1990s	Late 1990s– present
England and Wales examples	IMPACT	Intensive Probation	Prolific Offender Projects
US examples	Intensive Supervision Probation	Intensive Supervision Probation	Enhanced Supervision Partnerships
Penal philosophy	Rehabilitation	Specific deterrence/ incapacitation/ restitution	Specific deterrence/ incapacitation/ rehabilitation
Lead agency	Probation	Probation	Police and Probation
Multi-agency approach?	No	Yes	Yes
Targeted offenders	'High-risk', but relaxed by 'net-widening'	'Serious'	'Prolific' (acquisitive crime, moving to acquisitive crime/ violent crime)
Predominant practice concern	Frequent contact + treatment	Frequent contact + surveillance	Frequent contact + surveillance + treatment
Goals	Reduce re-offending through rehabilitation	Reduce re-offending through surveillance; save money; increase public safety; reduce prison crowding	Reduce re-offending *and/or* increase arrests and breaches; save money; increase public safety

Source: Mawby et al., (2002)

partnerships existed during the 'second generation' era, and Conrad (1982) urged such an innovation as early as 1982 as a humane way of controlling persistently violent offenders on release from prison. Enhanced supervision partnerships in the USA and prolific (or persistent) offender projects in England and Wales represent an amalgam of the theoretical underpinnings, policy objectives and multi-agency practices of previous generations of intensive supervision. Combining penal philosophies of deterrence, incapacitation and rehabilitation, they seek to provide a mix of frequent contact, access to treatment (particularly drugs treatment) and community facilities, and constant monitoring. They also seek to demonstrate cost-effectiveness and increased public safety.

The major departure from previous projects, however, is their avoidance of the pitfall of relying on offenders to reduce their own rates of re-offending. This was always the weakest link in the chain and the one which consistently undermined claims of success. Instead, it is now accepted that prompt re-arrest (resulting from increased intelligence and monitoring) is also a measure of success. There is, however, a serious flaw in this logic. As Clear (1997: 120) points out, 'the idea that revocation is a good thing, taken to its logical extreme, is absurd'. And taking it to its logical extreme is precisely what Fabelo (2001b) does, using actual data from one project site. He demonstrates that, in order to meet targets for the reduction of particular crimes, increased order revocations (breaches) *and* increased arrests, there would need to be a huge increase in a range of other crimes. The possibility that a project could claim success entirely on the basis of arrests and order breaches does seem to be somewhat at odds with the spirit of the exercise (for specific examples of this conundrum, see Mawby et al., 2002; Worrall et al., 2003).

Women and community punishment

As Harris (1992:98) says, 'part of the problem is that it is unclear what the "better treatment of women" actually means'. There are no gender-specific sentences and all sentences available to men are, in theory, available also to women. These can be organised conceptually around three themes: self-regulatory, financial and supervisory penalties.

Self-regulatory penalties (such as police cautions and conditional discharges) assume that being identified as a wrong-doer is sufficient to prevent further misbehaviour. Denunciation of an otherwise upright citizen (or good wife and mother) is seen to be enough to shame and reintegrate her with that community. She admits her guilt, apologises and promises never to do it again. Women are more likely than men to receive a caution or conditional discharge and are more likely to receive such a sentence than any other sentence, even after taking account of the severity of the offence (Hedderman and Hough 1994).

One of the reasons that women are more likely to receive self-regulatory penalties is that sentencers are reluctant to impose financial penalties on women who have children to care for or who do not have 'independent' incomes (Hedderman and Gelsthorpe 1997). Although the fine remains the most popular sentence imposed by courts and is regarded by many as the most flexible of sentences since courts can, in theory, match its amount both to the seriousness of the offence and to the offender's ability to pay, in practice these two principles often conflict, especially where women are concerned. This may result in women receiving a sentence that may be perceived to be more 'lenient', such as a conditional discharge. Alternatively, it may result in the imposition of a more intrusive supervisory sentence.

The assumption underlying all punishments which involve an element of supervision is that the offender lacks the motivation or personal resources to repair their breach of contract with the community unaided. For a variety of rehabilitative, reparative and deterrent reasons, offenders are viewed as being in need of help, advice, treatment and/or monitoring which can only be provided by criminal justice professionals – predominantly probation officers, psychologists and psychiatrists. Historically, this assistance has taken the form of a probation order (now called a community rehabilitation order) but, since the 1970s, it has included a community service order (now called a community punishment order) and, since the 1990s, electronic monitoring (although this is used mainly to enable prisoners to be released early on Home Detention Curfew).

Women and fines

Allen (1989) identified four interrelated tendencies likely to influence the distribution of fines for female offenders:

1 Direct reluctance to fine women (because of their economic incapacity).

2 A readiness to use low-tariff sentences (because of their perceived limited culpability).

3   A relative preference for probation (because of a concern for their welfare).

4   A relative disfavour for high-tariff sentences (because of their perceived amenability to informal social controls).

The word 'tariff' was used widely in sentencing literature prior to the 1991 Criminal Justice Act. It represented the concept of a sentencing 'ladder', with an assumption that offenders would work their way up the ladder, step by step, with each new court appearance, until they reached the 'top' which was, of course, prison. The lowest steps were absolute and conditional discharges, followed by fines, then probation, community service and prison. It was often argued that the 'tariff' was, in practice, shorter for women because sentencers were reluctant to fine women and also (as we shall see below) reluctant to give women community service. This meant that, even though women tended to stay on the bottom step for longer than men, once they started to climb the ladder, they climbed it more quickly and were often sent to prison at earlier stages in their criminal careers than men.

The 1991 Criminal Justice Act effectively abolished the concept of the 'tariff' and replaced it with the two 'seriousness' thresholds. Under the Act, most offences were to be dealt with by means of discharges or fines. However, an offence could be 'serious enough' to warrant a form of supervision or 'so serious' that prison was the only option. The definition of 'seriousness', however, has always been contested and this aspect of the Act ran into difficulties almost immediately (Worrall 1997).

Apart from the introduction into legislation of the concept of 'seriousness', another (ill-fated) innovation of the Act was the *unit fine*. The purpose of the unit fine was to address the problem of the disproportionate number of people being sent to prison for fine default (failing to pay their fines) when their original offences were not particularly serious. Two examples affected women in particular. In the early 1980s the sentence of imprisonment for soliciting for prostitution was abolished. However, women were still ending up in prison because they were unable to pay the fines that were being imposed instead (and, ironically, were having to continue in prostitution in order to earn the money to pay their fines!). Matthews (1989: 136) refers to this as 'double tracking' – the retention of prison 'at the hub of the system' as a means of enforcing non-custodial measures. The second example relates to the disproportionate numbers of women charged and fined for television licence evasion (see Worrall 1990) because women were more likely than men to be at home watching television during the day when detector vans were operating. Failure to pay those fines resulted in some women being sent to prison for the offence of having no television licence – an offence whose very existence rightly astounds those not familiar with UK television legislation. The introduction of the unit fine enabled sentencers to make more appropriate links between the seriousness of offences and the ability of offenders to pay fines. An offender would be fined a certain number of 'units' which would then be translated into a sum of money, taking account of the offender's disposable income. In theory, such a measure should have benefited women and other offenders on low incomes, but it met with strong opposition from sentencers who ensured that it was brought into disrepute (Worrall 1997) and unit fines were abolished within two years.

As we have seen in Chapter 2, the numbers of women in prison at any one time for fine default have fallen over the past decade but it must be remembered that fine defaulters normally spend only a few days in prison so far more of them are *received* into prison than will appear in the snapshot average daily prison population.

Trends in supervisory community sentences for women

Every year the Home Office produces *Probation Statistics for England and Wales* and these are now available on the Home Office web site www.homeoffice.gov.uk/rds/pdfs2/probation). Table 5.2 shows the trends in these sentences over the past decade.

The first thing to notice is the change of terminology:

- Probation Orders are now called Community Rehabilitation Orders (CRO)

- Community Service Orders are now called Community Punishment Orders (CPO)

- Combination Orders (probation and community service combined) are now called Community Punishment and Rehabilitation Orders (CPRO)

The increase in all orders for men has been steady, with over 100,000 starting an order during 2001. On a much smaller scale, the same pattern can be seen in CPOs and CPROs for women. The ratio of male to female orders has also narrowed:

Table 5.2 Persons starting court supervision by sex

Year	Males	Females
CRO		
1991	36,994	8,399
1992	35,043	7,475
1993	35,757	7,104
1994	40,692	8,812
1995	39,443	8,828
1996	39,735	9,370
1997	41,258	10,251
1998	44,016	11,498
1999	43,837	12,066
2000	42,101	11,829
2001	43,094	11,376
CPO		
1991	39,462	2,330
1992	41,342	2,656
1993	45,147	3,032
1994	46,599	3,613
1995	45,352	3,828
1996	42,573	3,928
1997	43,401	4,469
1998	44,579	4,891
1999	44,951	5,531
2000	46,088	5,920
2001	45,899	6,287
CPRO		
1992 (new sentence)	1,262	125
1993	8,538	698
1994	11,551	1,055
1995	13,549	1,282
1996	15,463	1,541
1997	17,185	1,902
1998	18,968	2,202
1999	18,352	2,176
2000	16,607	1,963
2001	13,849	1,654

Source: *Probation Statistics England and Wales 2001*: Table 3.3.
http://www.homeoffice.gov.uk/rds/pdfs2
probation2001.pdf

There was an average of 18 men with a CS order for each woman
with a CS order in 1989. This ratio has fallen to 8 men for each
woman with a CS order in 1999. Sentencers have become more
ready to give a sentence of CS to a woman over the period 1989–
1999.

(Home Office 2001a)

But the trend is slightly different for CROs for women. The lowest figure
of 7,104 comes in 1993 and this represents a decline from nearly 12,000
probation orders a decade previously. At that time (1981) probation
orders on women represented 33 per cent of all such orders compared
with 16 per cent in 1993. Despite an increase since then, they still
represent only 18 per cent of all probation orders. The implication is that
sentencers have shifted from placing women on probation orders (with
their welfare connotations) to placing them on community service
orders, combination orders and, of course, prison. Overall, just under
20,000 women were given community sentences in 2001.

Women and community rehabilitation orders (formerly probation orders)

The probation order has a long history dating back to 1907 in the UK. Its
traditional purpose was to offer advice, assistance and friendship to
offenders, in the belief that they could thus be reformed or rehabilitated.
More emphasis is now placed on restricting offenders' liberty, protecting
the public and preventing re-offending. Offenders have to agree that,
while on probation (which may last from six months to three years) they
will keep in touch with their probation officer through regular office
appointments and receiving visits at home. They must notify their
probation officer of any change of address or employment and if they
fail to meet all these requirements, they may be subject to breach
proceedings, which means that they are taken back to court and
resentenced. It is also possible for courts to add conditions to a basic
order requiring an offender to live at an approved residence or to
undergo psychiatric treatment. More recently, courts have been able to
require an offender to attend treatment programmes or other activities.
Since 1991, it has been possible for courts to combine probation orders
with community service orders (see below) to produce combination
orders which are intended to fulfil both rehabilitative and reparative
penal purposes.

Traditionally, the probation order was the sentence 'of choice' for women. They were considered ideally suited to being 'advised, assisted and befriended' (to adapt the former mission statement of the probation service). In the early 1980s, while women represented between 15 and 17 per cent of known offenders, 33 per cent of probation orders were on women and many of those (36 per cent compared with 17 per cent of men) were first offenders. But the influence of feminist perspectives on criminal justice led many probation officers to be concerned that too many women were being placed on probation and, more significantly, too early in their criminal careers. The good intentions of probation officers in recommending supervisory sentences for women appeared to result in 'net-widening' and ultimately accelerating a woman's journey to custody. There was an assumption (informed by theories of labelling and deviancy amplification) that diverting women from probation would automatically reduce the numbers in prison. The theory worked for juvenile crime in the 1980s but it failed spectacularly for women (although it has to be said that juvenile justice workers demonstrated a much greater commitment to keeping young people out of custody, even at the risk of incurring magistrates' wrath, than probation officers have ever done to keeping women out of prison). As Eaton (1986) and Worrall (1990) demonstrated, probation officers' court reports (known then as social inquiry reports, now pre-sentence reports) constructed women within the ideological constraints of the family and inadvertently reinforced sentencers' stereotyped views on 'good' and 'bad' women. This emerging gender awareness among probation officer resulted in a concerted effort to write non- or anti-discriminatory reports which strove to avoid collusion with such stereotyping.

The effort was partially successful in that fewer women were placed on probation for minor offences, and for a while in the early 1990s, there was some cause for optimism. The Criminal Justice Act 1991, based on the principle of 'just deserts', *should* have resulted in a fairer deal for women criminals. If sentencing was to depend predominantly on the seriousness of the current offence, the implication *should* have been that fewer women would go to prison for relatively minor offences, however frequently committed. It did not automatically follow that women who commit serious offences would be dealt with by community disposals – probation centre programmes and community service orders. Nevertheless, it did enable such sentences to be argued for on the basis of a different logic – namely, that refusal to give such opportunities amounted to discrimination as defined in Section 95(1)(b). Given that the government had also tentatively suggested in its preceding White Paper, *Crime, Justice and Protecting the Public*, (Home Office 1990) that it might be possible to abolish custodial detention for young women under the age of 18 years, it was not unreasonable to think that someone, somewhere, at some time, was hoping that courts would send fewer women – and certainly fewer young women – to prison.

In her book, *Alternatives to Women's Imprisonment*, Pat Carlen (1990) researched both the ways in which prisons prepared women for release and the non-custodial alternatives that were available for women. At that time, there were 57 different probation service areas and Carlen found only 19 that claimed to be making specific provision for women offenders. Among those that did not make such provision, two justifications were offered: first, that the area was too small to make separate provision for women viable in terms of numbers and resources; and second, that there were too few women 'at risk' of imprisonment. One of the concerns of these latter areas was that of 'net-widening' – that making special provision for women encourages sentencers to make use of it for minor offenders, while still sending more serious offenders to prison. Nevertheless, those areas that *did* run women-only groups found them to be extremely worthwhile for the following reasons:

- women who have been victims of child abuse or domestic violence need a space where they can recover their confidence away from men;

- women on probation are often seen as a 'problem' and therefore women-only groups provide a positive resource for all officers;

- the material and psychological conditions conducive to women's offending (and, by implication, desistance from offending) are different to those conducive to men's offending and desistance – and require different approaches;

- women's groups can supplement the gaps in 'throughcare' provision and provide additional (or sometimes sole) support for women with drug, alcohol or mental health problems;

- women's groups can help prevent re-offending by focusing on offending behaviour, teaching women how to deal with stressful situations and generally offering advice and support;

- women's groups can promote solidarity amongst previously isolated women and enable them to campaign for better living conditions.

(Carlen 1990: 76–81)

But women-only groups faced prejudice from within the probation service, especially from some male probation officers who could not understand why women would want (or should be allowed!) to do things without the presence of men. Male probation officers often felt ambivalent about women clients. On the one hand, they were viewed as something of a 'problem' because they could not be treated in the standardised way that men clients were. On the other hand, women would sometimes say that they preferred the paternalistic approach of male officers and the officers would argue that it was good for the women to see 'normal' men providing positive role models. Then (as now) a mixture of hurt male pride and sheer atavism frequently put obstacles in the way of innovation.

More problematic, however, were the obstacles of social and criminal justice policy which demanded, on the one hand, that non-custodial penalties should be punitive and 'tough' yet, on the other, ensured that women offenders would find it impossible to break out of the poverty trap to secure the housing, employment and income that would enable them to desist from offending. Carlen concluded that:

> although some excellent non-custodial rehabilitative schemes for women already exist, they are by and large rendered ineffective in reducing women's imprisonment: first, because they are too few and far between; and, second, because government legislation in other spheres systematically subverts the welfare, housing, employment and education provision which *must* provide reliable backup to all non-custodial penalties.
>
> (1990: 9)

Women and community punishment orders (formerly community service)

Community service was introduced in the UK in 1973 (although its predecessor, hard labour, has a very long history) and requires offenders to undertake unpaid work in the community for a period ranging from 60 to 240 hours. It was introduced because of concern about rising prison populations and the apparent ineffectiveness of probation orders to reduce re-offending. It has a chameleon-like ability to adapt its aims and objectives to fit almost every traditional justification of punishment – retribution (visible hard work), reparation (unpaid work for the community), deterrence (working for no reward), incapacitation (restriction of liberty) and rehabilitation (learning skills and/or achieving something of worth). This has made it very popular with sentencers, who see it as having the flexibility of a fine but without its disadvantages. It has been described as a fine on time. Offenders typically work in groups on projects involving land restoration, painting, decorating and woodwork, or in individual placements with charity shops, voluntary organisations, and so on.

There is nothing in theory or in law to debar women from doing community service but sentencers have always had ambivalent feelings about giving such orders to women (Worrall 1997: 95). Research has suggested that there is greater inconsistency in the use of community service for women than for men and that women are more likely than men to receive such orders for their first offence (Hine and Thomas 1995). It has always been viewed by courts as not quite an appropriate sentence for women and the practicalities have always been an obstacle – the absence of childcare facilities being the main problem. (As will be argued in Chapter 6, even formal recognition of 'gender difference' does not itself entail any specific type of sentence or prison regime.) There is debate about what constitutes appropriate work for women on such orders. Should they be encouraged to broaden their horizons and do 'male' work or should they stick to what they know in order to get through the hours? In Western Australia, for example, one project enables women to collect large bags of old clothes from a central point and take them home to unpick all the buttons and zips. At first glance, this appears to be a soul-destroying and discriminatory project, but it enables women to do the work in their own homes at times of their own choosing and to complete their hours with the least possible disruption to their normal lives.

Despite an increase in the number of orders being made on women in recent years, none of the six community service 'pathfinder' programmes (funded by the Home Office) is aimed exclusively at women offenders (Home Office 2000a: 19). As the Howard League discovered:

> Across the country, the picture which emerges is of community service units dealing with women sent to them but on a case-by-case basis ... [I]f women continue to be regarded as an anomaly, then it is unlikely to engender sentencer confidence.
>
> (Howard League 1999: 18)

The Howard League's call for a national initiative to promote and develop community service for women seems to have fallen on stony ground, though the Director of the National Probation Service appears to accept the existence of a problem of discrimination against women in relation to community service (Roberts 2001). The problems surrounding community service for women are well-known but by no means unresolvable. What is required is a change in the attitude that regards community service as predominantly a punishment for 'fit, young men' (Worrall 1997: 98). Better child-care arrangements, more female supervisors and consideration for the kind of working environments most suitable for women would also result in greater use. Whatever the perceived disadvantages to women of doing community service, they cannot possibly outweigh the disadvantages of imprisoning those same women. Indeed, with the introduction of the Human Rights Act , it might be possible for women denied community sentences and given short prison sentences to claim violation of their right to respect for their private and family life (under Article 8), especially if that involves separation from small children and imprisonment at an unreasonable distance from home (Prison Reform Trust 2000a).

Women and drugs treatment

As we saw in Chapter 2, Hedderman and Gelsthorpe (1997) discovered that, although many women offenders were, statistically, still being dealt with more leniently than men offenders by magistrates, the two groups for whom this was no longer true were women who were first-time violent offenders and women who were recidivist drug offenders. The increase in the number of women charged with drug and drug-related offences is undeniable, though this is also true for men, and women still constitute only 21 per cent of drug offenders (Home Office 2001b).

Drug Treatment and Testing Orders (DTTOs) were introduced with the Crime and Disorder Act 1998 in three pilot areas. Since 2000 they have been available nationally and 4,400 orders were made in 2001, of which 83 per cent were made on men (Home Office 2002a). They constitute a government response to the increasing number of offenders who appear to commit crimes to finance their drug addictions and they are aimed at those offenders who are willing to co-operate with treatment, supervision and urine testing (Turnbull et al., 2000). DTTOs have been criticised for making drug treatment compulsory and for over-simplifying the link between drug use and crime. As with other penal innovations, they have also been criticised for being used for 'petty' offenders (net-widening), for not taking sufficient account of the needs of women and ethnic minority offenders, and for not providing sufficient social support to ensure that rehabilitation is sustained (Fowler 2002). A briefing paper from the Howard League (2000) argues that the introduction of DTTOs could provide a promising diversion from custody for women, if probation officers are willing to give special attention to the needs of women who misuse drugs. But if from the outset no attention is given to women's practical difficulties (suitable accommodation, pregnancy issues and child care) the DTTO will become yet one more male-centred provision which will be only half-heartedly 'adapted' for women (Fowler 2002).

Women and electronic monitoring

Electronic monitoring was introduced on an experimental basis in England and Wales in the 1980s for a number of reasons. It was seen as a way to reduce prison overcrowding and prison costs. It was also seen as a way to strengthen community punishment and to introduce privatisation to community punishment as well as to prisons. Finally, it was seen as a sophisticated way to subject offenders to some of the restrictions of prison without inflicting on them the damage of being removed from their home environment.

Electronic monitoring requires offenders to be fitted with a special bracelet or anklet which is connected electronically to a telephone which is, in turn, connected to a call centre, from whence regular checks are made on the offender's whereabouts. Offenders have individualised schedules requiring them to be at home between certain hours. There are now two distinct ways in which electronic monitoring is used to enable offenders to live in the community. First, courts can sentence offenders to curfew orders with electronic monitoring. Second, prisoners may be released several weeks before the end of their sentence, on condition that they are monitored. Both measures have been available nationally since 1999 and are likely to be incorporated increasingly into a number of community sentences in order to provide a stronger element of surveillance (Nellis 2003). In 2001, around 6,000 curfew orders with electronic monitoring were made. In the same year, around 14,000 prisoners were released on home detention curfew (HDC) and over 90 per cent successfully completed their curfew (Home Office 2002).

According to official statistics (Home Office 2003a) women are proportionately more likely than men to be eligible for HDC and are even more likely to be granted HDC. In 2001, 41 per cent of women eligible for HDC were granted it, compared with 24 per cent of eligible men. This is likely to be connected with the fact that women tend to have lower reconviction rates, which will be reflected in the HDC risk assessment.

Women and hostels

Access to adequate housing is one of the essential preconditions for women to escape the revolving door of short prison sentences (Eaton 1993) yet, in England and Wales, there is very little supported accommodation provided with the needs of women in mind. In 1990, Carlen reviewed Probation Service and voluntary sector hostel accommodation for women and found a picture of contradictions. Despite the apparent demand, those few hostels designed specifically for women were underused. Women, it seems, were reluctant to move away from their home area to take up places in hostels some distance away. Some women were prejudiced against the notion of living in hostels at all, regarding them as heavily rule-governed and authoritarian. On the other hand, hostels tended to exclude precisely the women most in need of them – those with histories of drug or alcohol misuse or with records of violence or arson. Most significantly, very few hostels were able to accommodate women with children. More hostels catering predominantly for men are willing to offer places to women but many women consider these unsuitable, either because of past abusive relationships with men or simply because they don't want to be a lone woman living with a group of men.

Arguably, an opportunity was lost in the early 1990s when, following the Woolf Report, the possibility of 'community prisons' for women was rejected by groups campaigning for women in prison, on the grounds of net-widening – the fear that establishing small semi-secure houses in the community would invite sentencers to send more women to prison (see Chapter 3). With hindsight, one might argue that, not only has the female prison population risen anyway, but there has subsequently been no investment in any alternative types of accommodation for female offenders, such as now exist in other countries. Australia provides examples of the imaginative use of 'Transitional Centres' – supervised houses for groups of women and children which serve as half-way measures both after a prison sentence and as a 'last chance' alternative to prison (see Carlen (2002h) for a description of one such centre in New South Wales – others exist in Queensland and Victoria).

Women and intensive supervision

Earlier in this chapter we discussed the emergence of a range of intensive supervision initiatives designed for repeat and prolific offenders. Such schemes provide a combination of intensive support, including drug treatment, housing, employment and constructive leisure activities, alongside intensive monitoring and police surveillance. Evaluations of these programmes in England and Wales (Worrall et al., 2003) suggest that, while they have a positive impact on offenders by reducing their offending while they are on the programme, this progress cannot always be sustained once they have left the programme. The programmes were also found to be very labour-intensive for those running them. What is clear, additionally, is that participants in such programmes are overwhelmingly male. The reason for this is simply that very few women qualify in terms of the frequency and severity of their offending. Where they do qualify, the programmes can be very beneficial because they are based on individually designed packages which can take account of the specific needs of each participant. They do not normally involve groupwork, nor are they committed to male-oriented activities.

Women and restorative justice

In response to the perceived failures of the formal criminal justice system to either satisfy victims or deter/rehabilitate offenders, the concept of restorative justice proposes a new approach to repairing the harm caused by criminal activity within communities. Although the term is now used to describe a very wide variety of informal and semi-formal measures, the generally accepted 'umbrella' defi-nition is that it is a 'process whereby parties with a stake in a specific offence resolve collectively how to deal with the aftermath of the offence and its implica-tions for the future' (Marshall 1999). The underlying principles are concerned with healing, rather than with punishment, and with restoring the real or metaphorical relationship between the offender, the victim and the community through 'moral learning, community participation and community caring, respectful dialogue, forgiveness, responsibility, apology and making amends' (Braithwaite 1999: 6).

At first sight, such a 'holistic' approach may appear rather suitable for women offenders, emphasising as it does mediation and negotiation. The widespread mechanism of 'family group conferencing' in which offender, victim and their respective families and supporters come together in a structured but private and relatively informal setting, seems to have the potential to benefit women. However, Christine Alder (2002) expresses some reservations. What such an apparently en-lightened approach fails to take sufficient account of is that many young women's experiences of informal control may have been physically, sexually or emotionally abusive. The victimisation of young women in the home at the hands of other participants in the conferencing process may become an excluded discourse, and entrenched attitudes about appropriate female behaviour may become reinforced rather than challenged.

Alder (2002) also points out that the concept of 'shame', which is integral to restorative justice, has particular connotations and risks for young women. Worrall (1990) has argued that women who commit crimes sometimes have difficulty in distinguishing between the strict legal concept of 'guilt' and their own subjective feelings of guilt (and, by implication, feelings of shame). This all-pervading sense of failure and lack of self-esteem is often cited as the underlying cause of the self-harming behaviour that is endemic in women's prisons and Alder is right to counsel caution in relation to situations where remorse and self-blame are encouraged too enthusiastically. Restorative justice and other informal mechanisms of conflict resolution such as family group conferencing may be dangerous for young women. The gender bias of the formal criminal justice system may be reproduced in informal practices but without even the minimal checks and balances afforded by the formal system. The informal is not necessarily benign or neutral.

What works for women offenders?

As previously indicated, the last decade of the twentieth century was dominated by the doctrine of What Works (Vanstone 2000). In North America, Canada, Australia and the UK, probation and community corrections have been preoccupied with a model of focused, accountable, standardised intervention in the lives of offenders, based on the actuarial concept of risk assessment, the science of cognitive behavioural psychology, the morality of individual responsibility and the politics of restorative justice. Offenders increasingly receive sentencing packages that involve time spent under supervision both inside and outside prison, and technology now makes it possible for many of the restrictions of imprisonment to be visited on offenders in their own homes and communities.

Worrall (2004b: 340–1) has suggested that one should approach the What Works agenda with a level of *political awareness* that involves asking why the simple phrase 'What Works' has become so invested with meaning? Or is it precisely because it *lacks* meaning that it has become so ubiquitous? There are at least four interest groups whose purposes might be served by the What Works agenda and whether those interests are to be viewed positively or negatively will depend entirely on one's standpoint:

- the interests of *governance* are served to the extent that the What Works agenda demonstrates to a sceptical public that community sentences can be tough, demanding and based on scientific premises which can be tested and evaluated;

- the interests of *management* are served to the extent that the agenda demonstrates accountability - showing that resources are being used efficiently, effectively and, above all, economically – and giving managers confidence that they know exactly what their workers are doing and why;

- the interests of *professionalism* are served to the extent that the agenda reassures individual workers that they are doing something worthwhile with the minimum of risk to their own status – that the areas in which they have to exercise their own judgement are limited and consequently so is the potential for error, thus reducing the otherwise stressful nature of the job;

- finally, the interests of *restorative justice* are served to the extent that the offender, victim and, possibly, the wider community believe that the agenda delivers on its promises. Whatever the content of any particular intervention, it can be argued that What Works aims to instil in the offender a sense of responsibility towards the community in general and empathy for the victim in particular. But in return, the offender has the right to expect to be *reintegrated* into that community and unless that right is respected, What Works becomes little more than a sophisticated form of the stocks – as indeed it is for many sex offenders who, no matter what programmes they have co-operated with, remain irredeemable and non-reintegratable in the eyes of the community (Worrall 1997).

To the question, 'What works for women offenders?' the official response is 'What works for men offenders with a few adjustments', judging by the reports of the Joint Prison/Probation Accreditation Panel in England and Wales. There are now a number of accredited offending behaviour programmes which can be used with either men or women and probation areas may tailor these to all-women groups if they wish – and if they have sufficient numbers of women with whom to work. However, programmes designed specifically for women are having greater difficulty in obtaining accreditation. The Hereford and Worcester (Probation Service) Women's Programme (Roberts, 2002), chosen as an original 'pathfinder' and much praised by the Wedderburn Report (Prison Reform Trust 2000a), was considered to lack focus on factors linked to offending (in particular, drug misuse) and on offending behaviour itself (despite the inclusion of a specific module for persistent offenders). It was deemed 'unlikely ever to be an accreditable ... approach' (Home Office 2000c: 9). Slightly more hopeful was a programme for women involved in acquisitive crime designed by South Glamorgan Probation Service and described by the panel as 'encouraging' (2000c: 14). This has been superseded by developmental work on a programme designed by the Canadian owners of the Reasoning and Rehabilitation programmes (T3 Associates) due to be piloted in several Probation areas from 2002. The failure of the Hereford and Worcester programme to obtain accreditation throws into sharp relief the conflict between criminal and social justice. In order to be accredited, programmes are required to meet eleven very specific criteria which demand clarity in respect of evidence-based models of change, targeting of risk factors, use of effective (for which read 'cognitive behavioural') methods, programme integrity (consistency of delivery), monitoring and evaluation. Such criteria, proponents argue, 'eliminate subjective, arbitrary decision-making, bias and prejudice' with issues of gender and race being 'added in' without undermining the basic model (Shaw and Hannah-Moffat 2000: 164). In line with the new penology (Feeley and Simon 1992) they ensure that offenders are classified objectively, using actuarial tools of risk assessment, and dealt with in the most efficient, effective and economical way. This programme operates on rather different (though, arguably, not incompatible) assumptions about the lives of women who offend:

> The aim is to help women avoid further offending by increasing their abilities to solve complex problems legitimately, by holding in balance the demands made upon them, the external resources and legitimate opportunities available to them, and their own capacities and abilities.
>
> (Prison Reform Trust 2000a: 70–71)

The programme designers would argue that it does, in fact, meet the criteria for accreditation. For example, evaluation appears to demonstrate that, while the reconviction rates of completers and non-completers were similar after six months, differences began to appear between the two groups after a year and were considerable after two years. However, two 'conceptual strands' that guided the development of the programme appear to have proved unacceptable to the Accreditation Panel:

One of these was 'normalisation', which encouraged an effort to reduce female offenders' isolation from community based networks of support. The second, complementary strand was to reduce the emphasis on the probation service as a focal resource for women who were seen to have social and personal needs in common with many non-offending women.

(Rumgay 1999, cited in Prison Reform Trust 2000a: 71)

The Wedderburn Report's recommendation for the setting up of a network of Women's Supervision, Rehabilitation and Support Centres (Prison Reform Trust 2000a: 70), giving women better access to a range of community agencies under one roof, was based on this Probation Service experiment but appears to have met with little response from the Service as a whole.

Hannah-Moffat (1999) warns about the danger of redefining women offenders' 'needs' as 'predictive risk factors'. When policy makers start talking about 'adapting' programmes and risk assessment tools for use by women, they rightly adopt the language of 'need'. However, rather than analysing and seeking to meet those needs through better access to community resources, 'needs talk' may merely replace 'risk talk' and 'high need' women become 'high risk' women who can then be subjected to the same programming as 'high risk' men. The main difference, according to Stewart is that women are more 'responsive' (which means they talk more), so 'the overall structure of the courses did not need to be changed; rather the emphasis was on providing additional, more appropriate role-play scenarios' (2000: 42). Approached in this way, women present only a minor challenge to the delivery of programmes.

Some prison psychologists (King and Brosnan 1998) are prepared to go further in recognising the difficulties in running programmes for women by acknowledging that women find it very difficult to leave 'at the door' the distress they experience from histories of abuse and domestic violence. Unless this distress is addressed outside the programme, it is accepted that women may be unable or unwilling to engage constructively in programmes. But underlying this response is a resistance to any suggestion that women's crime may have different causes from men's crime. To use the correct parlance, it is argued that women have broadly the same 'criminogenic needs' as men. But evidence for these assumed similarities is not conclusive and there is much evidence to 'confirm differences between the social circumstances, needs and possible motivations of male and female offenders' (Gelsthorpe 2001: 155).

Women-wise penology

At the end of her book, *Alternatives to Women's Imprisonment*, Carlen introduces the concept of a 'women-wise penology' which would have two fundamental aims:

1 That the penal regulation of female law-breakers does not increase their oppression *as women* still further.

2 That the penal regulation of law-breaking men does not brutalise them and make them even more violently and ideologically oppressive towards women in the future.

(Carlen 1990: 114)

As an aside to the main argument of this chapter, it is interesting that Carlen makes a link between the treatment of male and female offenders, arguing that the solution to women's abusive domestic backgrounds may not necessarily be found in the harsher treatment of male perpetrators. But that is a discussion for another book!

Central to Carlen's vision of a women-wise penology was a five-year experiment in the abolition of imprisonment for all but the most serious of women offenders. She argued that, because of their crime profiles, women in prison constituted a class of prisoners that was suitable for radical experimentation and that there should be a concerted effort to resource supportive alternative accommodation and treatment/ activities for all but a handful of women offenders. At that time, the female prison population was around 1,800 and Carlen's proposal seemed more feasible than it did ten years later. Indeed, between 1989 and 1993, the female prison population *did* decline temporarily to around 1,500. It has since tripled.

Although there has been a steady increase in the use of supervisory community sentences in the past decade, they have made no impact on the female prison population. Women are still being sent to prison sooner than their male counterparts. Statistical purists may insist that, since women offenders have much shorter criminal careers than men anyway, *all* sentencing disposals will show women to have fewer previous convictions than men and my argument here, they will say, is disingenuous. But *if* women have short criminal careers regardless of sentence, it should not be necessary to increase the numbers being sent to prison. If women have shorter and less serious criminal careers than men, the safety of society will not be threatened by a greater and more imaginative use of community sentences. If women's rates of recidivism are lower than those of men, *regardless of the sentence they receive*, then we can draw one of the following conclusions:

- whatever punishment women receive they are more likely than men to desist from offending subsequently, and/or
- a woman's recidivism is likely to be influenced less (even than a man's) by the sentence she receives and more by other factors.

If we accept this line of argument then it follows that a) we may as well give women the least costly punishment – economically and socially – that we have available, and b) we cannot expect any punishment to 'work' unless we have also addressed the other factors, which might be called, collectively, factors of 'social justice' – housing, income, health, education and employment.

In the early 1990s Eaton (1993) identified the factors that enabled women ex-prisoners to turn their lives around. Women offenders, she argued, will only change their lives when they have access to the structural preconditions of social justice – housing, employment and health facilities. None of these things has changed at the millennium (Gray 2000; Kendall 2002; Lowthian 2000). But structural factors alone are insufficient. Eaton also argued that women offenders need to feel that they are people of worth who can sustain and be sustained in reciprocal, rather than subordinate or exploitative, relationships. Maruna (2000), who included women in his study of desistance from offending, makes a similar point using different language. He talks about the need for a 'redemption script' ... The offender needs to 'construct a coherent personal narrative' out of a disorderly and contradictory past. Central to that narrative has to be the belief that the offender is in control of their life, has put their past behind them and has the ability to succeed in mainstream society. Sometimes this optimism is itself a 'cognitive distortion' and an inaccurate assessment of reality, but this will to succeed, or motivation, appears to be a vital prerequisite for desistance. Within this perspective, cognitive programming may well be the catalyst that starts the generation of what has been called a 'redemption script' but it is a means to an end rather than an end in itself, and there may be many other experiences that act as similar catalysts. The life-course approach would argue that what is crucial here is the ability to inspire prisoners to believe in themselves, rather than the specific content or delivery of the programme. Such inspiration may also come from other experiences – education, creativity, recreation, employment, religion and, above all, relationships.

Concepts to know

alternatives to custody: one of several terms used officially by criminal justice professionals to refer to sentences that do not involve imprisonment. A key debate about the term is whether an 'alternative' means a measure which seeks to avoid the constraints and privations of imprisonment or whether it means a different method of inflicting very similar constraints and privations.

decarceration: the movement (and debate) to remove deviant populations (primarily mentally ill people and criminals) from institutional care, treatment and control to supervision and monitoring within the community. The movement and the debate can be traced back to the early twentieth century but gained momentum with the demise of the rehabilitative ideal in the 1960s, when the rehabilitative role of institutions was challenged by writers such as Erving Goffman (1961).

transcarceralism: the blurring of the boundaries between freedom and custody; transferring the control of imprisonment into the community by such means as intensive supervision, surveillance and electronic tagging; constructing what Cohen (1979) refers to as the 'punitive city'. However, the reverse may also happen. With the closure of many psychiatric hospitals, it is often argued that mentally ill people have been abandoned to a misnamed 'care in the community' which frequently fails to support them (Scull 1984), with the result that those who commit crimes associated (directly or indirectly) with their mental disorder end up in prison. Carlen (1988) has also demonstrated the disproportionate number of young women in prison who have histories of spending time in children's homes or foster care.

Further reading

Home Office (annually) *Statistics on Women and the Criminal Justice System*. London: The Stationery Office (available from the Home Office website at www.homeoffice.gov.uk/rds/pdfs2/s95women02.pdf)

Maruna, S. (2000) *Making Good: How Ex-Convicts Reform and Rebuild their Lives*. Washington and American Psychological Association

Raynor, P. and Vanstone, M. (2002) *Understanding Community Penalties: Probation, Policy and Social Change*. Buckingham: Open University Press

Roberts, J. (2002) 'Women-centred: The West Mercia community-based programme for women offenders', in P. Carlen (ed.) *Women and Punishment*. Collumpton: Willan

Worrall, A. (2002b) 'Missed opportunities? The probation service and women offenders', in D. Ward, J. Scott and M. Lacey (eds) *Probation: Working for Justice* 2nd edn. Oxford: Oxford University Press, pp. 134–8

Topics for discussion

1   What works with women offenders and how can we know?
2   Is community service an appropriate sentence for women?
3   Should women offenders with small children to care for always be given non-custodial sentences?

Essay questions

1   Under what ideological and material conditions do criminal justice 'experts' claim to possess knowledge about women offenders and how is that claim to expertise translated into practices which have particular consequences for those women?
2   Despite the increase in their use, why have community penalties made so little impact on the rise of the female prison population?
3   What do we know about the factors that influence women's desistance from offending?

Chapter 6

Feminist theories of imprisonment and penal politics

Introduction

Explaining and campaigning are separate and distinct activities. Feminist academics who become involved in women's prison reform or abolition campaigns have therefore been especially exercised by questions about the relevance of their feminist politics to the types of research they should do and, conversely, about the relevance of their theories to political campaigning for either the reform or abolition of women's imprisonment. This chapter outlines and examines the issues raised by feminist theorizing and feminist campaigning on women's imprisonment and related issues. First it outlines four key perspectives on punishment which may inform changes in penal policies or campaigning. There then follows a description of some of the strategy dilemmas facing the English ex-prisoners' campaigning group *Women in Prison* during its first 12 years. Third, there is consideration of how feminist politics can or should inform research design and practice. Fourth, there is an examination of the possible relationships between theorizing and reforming (or even abolishing) women's imprisonment.

Administrative, critical, abolitionist and feminist perspectives on punishment

Administrative Penology

Administrative penology has the following characteristics:

- it is research carried out, or sponsored, by official departments in order to assess the operation of troublesome aspects of the penal system;

- it may be critical of the operation of some aspects of the penal system and even call into question their efficiency and their efficacy, but it does not call into question the legitimacy of the system itself;

- research publication is usually dependent upon permission of a government department which will not publish any research likely to embarrass the government of the day;

- nowadays, it is usually 'evidenced-based' (that is, research acceptable to policy makers who want statistics and empirically verifiable facts on which to base their policies) rather than 'blue sky' theorizing (that is, theorizing which calls into question all existing knowledge in the attempt to produce something new).

The term 'administrative penology' as used here is an adaptation of the term which Jock Young coined in the 1980s to refer to the revival of 'establishment criminology' in the UK and the USA after a period when positivist criminology had appeared to be on the wane and the new, radical criminology, with its emphasis on the social causes of crime, appeared to be gaining ground (Young 1986; McLaughlin 2001).

Like administrative criminology, administrative penology is less concerned with the systemic causes of lawbreaking, and more concerned with how to reduce crime via the fashioning of penal responses which can be proven either to deter lawbreakers or to reduce recidivism. Insofar as administrative penology *is* concerned with the social causes of crime, it is concerned with them only as they affect individual offenders' reintegration into society, and unlike critical penology, does not routinely see the more common forms of social deprivation (for example, poverty, parental neglect or abuse) as mitigating circumstances which, in part, might explain or excuse the initial lawbreaking.

The beginning of the twenty-first century has seen a series of critiques of contemporary research funding and sponsorship which argue that since the final decade of the last century there has been increasing official and university-based pressure on academics to engage in administrative penology rather than radical (or even scientific) critique, and that the claimed academic independence of the government financed research funding councils, as well as those funded by non-government organisations have to some extent been affected by government demands that all research should be 'evidence based'. The complaint has been that the demand for 'evidence' is not only based upon an erroneous and inappropriate conception of what constitutes 'evidence' in conventional science, but also upon a rhetorical and self-serving populism that by definition must rule out all the speculative and theoretical critique which often, as it happens, questions the legitimacy of punishment in grossly unequal societies.

Additionally, of course, an insistence on the facticity of the here and now cleverly pre-empts all claims that the criminal justice and penal systems could (or should) be otherwise than they are (Carlen 2002f; Hillyard et al 2002; Walters 2003).

Critical perspectives

There are many critical perspectives on punishment – Marxist, postmodern, feminist, socialist-feminist, abolitionist and combinations of all five. They share the following characteristics:

- critical perspectives on punishment define their research agenda within theories which do not take for granted the meanings of criminal and penal systems as defined either by governments or by 'common sense'. Relatedly, they constantly refuse to accept that the significance of any crime-related phenomenon is already known for all time and all places;

- they do not take for granted the legitimacy of penal systems and constantly call into question the right of states to punish;

- one of the most frequent questions posed by critical penal theorists asks, 'What are the relationships between social and criminal justice?'

- critical theorists adhere to the liberal, classical ideal of science: that science should be: open; constantly recognising, questioning, and, if necessary, denying, the conditions of its own existence; and neither 'trimming' its questions to make them politically correct or ex-pedient, nor 'clubbing', that is, pulling its punches, either to conform with contemporary academic fashions or political prejudices, or in response to downright bullying by either political or academic powers-that-be;

- critical theorists try not only to think the unthinkable about crime and punishment, but also to speak the unspeakable about the conditions *in which* and *by which* it is known. (For discussion of the main critical perspectives see Taylor, et al. (1985); Carrington and Hogg (2002.))

Abolitionist perspectives

Abolitionism also comes in several varieties, and a good, short overview of them is given by Sim (2001: 2) in the *Sage Dictionary of Criminology*. They share many of the same assumptions as 'critical perspectives', but all, to a greater or lesser degree, are committed to the two following tenets which, if acted upon, would logically lead to the abolition of imprisonment – at least as we have known it – in societies committed to democracy and justice under the rule of law:

1 That a penal system which operates to the detriment of the poorer sections of society and to the advantage of the rich, cannot claim to be a legitimate arm of democratic government.

2 That the way in which penal systems operate in unequal societies actually increases inequality and thereby aggravates the problems of crime which penal systems purport to address.

However, abolitionists do not deny that crime is a problem, especially crimes of violence and exploitation of all kinds which, again, hit the poor and the otherwise vulnerable (especially poor women and ethnic minorities) harder than they do the better-off who are much better protected by money and status.

Abolitionists take lawbreaking seriously, but they do not see exclusion by imprisonment as the answer. Instead, abolitionists work on alternative visions of justice, and, as Sim has pointed out,

> have increasingly connected with the emerging discourses and debates around human rights and social justice which they see as mechanisms for developing negative reforms, thereby promoting a response to social harm that is very different from the destructive prison and punishment systems that currently exist.
>
> (Sim 2001: 4)

Feminist perspectives

Feminist critiques of penal ideologies and penal systems as they have operated in patriarchal and capitalist societies have already been discussed in Chapter 4. Like all the other critical perspectives, feminist critiques of crime and punishment come in various forms and combinations of other critical perspectives, the main feminist perspectives on punishment having been influenced by:

- liberal critiques of gender-discriminatory practices in the criminal justice and penal systems which disadvantage women;

- feminist, Marxist-feminist and socialist-feminist critiques of patriarchal penal relations in capitalist societies;

- Foucault's and postmodernist critiques which deny to classical epistemologies their guarantees of truth;

- postmodernist critiques of law which, in contrast to systemic modernism's project of the progressive rationalisation of both knowledge and society, reject the notion that any master-narrative (such as law) can guarantee truth and, instead, insist that all discourses require a constant deconstruction in search of their conditions of existence, and, concomitantly, the secrets of their power (Carlen 2003).

However, as the admixtures of critical, Marxist, abolitionist, Foucauldian and postmodern perspectives have become more and more intertwined and complex, it has seemed to many feminists that getting their radical critiques in such a twist has not been too helpful at the level of political action (see Snider 2003). Feminists who originally set out to engage in the more modest project of reducing the numbers of women sent to prison and achieving greater substantive justice for them (and concomitantly reducing the pains of imprisonment through recognition that women's in-prison and rehabilitative needs are different to those of male prisoners) have become increasingly concerned that after 20 years or so of campaigning they have not achieved very much by way of ameliorative changes in the penal responses of the state to female lawbreakers. Instead, since the late 1990s, women's prison populations have been characterised by steep increases in North America, Australia, the UK and the rest of Europe. In England, more prisons have opened for women, and, as was discussed in Chapter 5, some of the rehabilitative programmes which employ psychologistic models to explain crime appear to be retrogressive rather than progressive. Indeed, their mode of theorizing, which implies that the main problems of women criminals are to be explained more by reference to their states of mind than to the state of their financial circumstances outside prison, suggests that they have more in common with early twentieth-century aetiologies of crime than with the sociological and welfarist models that gained sway later in the century and to which most campaigners and reformers adhere.

Yet even as feminist prison reformers and activists have pondered the disjunction between the immense energy and effort which have gone into their theoretical endeavours and the paucity of progressive and sustainable changes which they witness in courtroom and prison responses to female lawbreakers, the campaigning work has continued, often spearheaded by ex-prisoners, and with the active collaboration of criminologists, lawyers, and other committed academics from the sciences and the arts.

Campaigns for abolition of women's imprisonment

This section will look at the first twelve years of the English campaigning group, Women in Prison (WIP). Since the nineteenth century, there have been many compassionate people who have worked in various capacities to alleviate the misery of women in prison. Many of them have been religiously motivated to improve the morality of the labouring or indigent classes. Others have set out to reduce the risks attendant upon the existence of a potentially mutinous army of unemployed (or otherwise pauperised) women who, though excluded from citizenship benefits, have not been excused paying their penal dues. And at the same time, and as we saw in Chapter 4, there have been the political and academic critics of imprisonment whose focus has been less on the crimes of the incarcerated and more on questions about whether the penal system itself can be reformed; whether, indeed, any penal system can be reformed independently of the specific social formation – in the case of the UK, a social formation shaped by capitalism – which make penal relations take the forms they do.

By and large, the academic and political critiques did not inform the practical work of the nineteenth- and early twentieth-century moral and pragmatic reformers. Their gaze, like that of their famous forerunner, Elizabeth Fry, was more directed at the behaviour of women prisoners than at the systems and people responsible for the forms, functions and social effects of women's incarceration, and although there were perennial attempts by both campaigners and administrators to improve general conditions in prisons the social needs of women were treated with ambivalence (see Chapter 1). It was not until the 1980s that campaigning began specifically for better conditions for women prisoners in particular and all women in the criminal justice system in general. In England, the group which put the needs of women in prison firmly on the penal politics agenda was the campaigning group Women in Prison.

Women in Prison (WIP) was founded in 1983. An ex-prisoner Chris Tchaikovsky gathered together a group of women perturbed by the numbers of disturbed petty offenders held in Holloway and concerned, too, about the standards of safety and care maintained in the prison. Ten years later, the only academic founder member of that group, Pat Carlen, wrote a retrospective analysis of the theoretical and political issues which the group had had to face as it tried to carve out a rationale for its existence, for the types of interventions it had been making, for the way it responded to official proposals for reform and the reason why in some ways it could be argued that WIP had achieved so little.

As a founder member, Carlen had drawn up WIP's first manifesto and she had been privy to most of WIP's policy debates and arguments of those first 12 years. As an academic sociologist engaged in writing and research on women's prisons at the same time as actively campaigning against their existence, the probity of her own position was one that she had little time to ponder. When she did think about it she came to very few firm conclusions. The following account is based on the Carlen and Tchaikovsky (1996) review of WIP's first 12 years. It is presented here as a case study in the relationships between politics and research to demonstrate how these issues never present themselves in real life as the 'either/or issues' which they are often represented as being in either methods textbooks, blueprints for political action or feminist, radical, (and other brands of) propaganda.

Right from the beginning, WIP had to consider what is *special* about *women's* imprisonment. After all, there were already plenty of organisations in the UK which *claimed* to campaign for better conditions for *all* prisoners, though only one of them, *Radical Alternatives to Prison*, had seriously campaigned against the rebuilding of Holloway Prison in the early 1970s. WIP's *raison d'être* therefore was based initially on the following claims:

- that women's imprisonment is different to men's, and that the special and distinct pains of women's imprisonment had, in the main, been ignored by writers, campaigners and prison administrators;

- that women in prison suffer from discriminatory practices by administrators that result in their receiving fewer education, work and leisure opportunities than male prisoners serving comparable sentences;

- that women prisoners suffer from discriminatory practices by prison officers – as instanced by their being subjected to closer disciplinary surveillance and regulation than male prisoners with similar criminal records;

- that women in prison do not receive adequate medical care for gynaecological conditions and that their special needs during menstruation, pregnancy and menopause are often not catered for;

- that mothers in prison do not receive adequate support and counselling in relation to their children outside prison;

- that, because there are relatively few of them, women in custody in the UK are more likely than men to be held in institutions a long way from their homes;

- that *certain* women are sent to prison on the basis of a judicial logic that sentences them as *flawed women* rather than as lawbreaking citizens.

On the basis of these domain assumptions about the special nature of *women's* imprisonment, WIP's early campaigns centred on:

- increasing the public awareness of the debilitating regimes characteristic of the women's prisons;

- the plight of women held in extremely close confinement or under brutally harsh disciplinary regimes, for example, the inmates of Durham Prison H-Wing, kept under extremes of surveillance because of the one person confined there who had been (wrongly, as the courts later decided) convicted of a bombing offence; and the behaviourally disturbed women of Holloway's notorious C1 Unit;

- the daily pains of imprisonment, and especially those specific to women and/or exacerbated by the particular regimes or practices of the different women's prisons;

- the difficulties facing women upon their release from prison.

From the outset, WIP was also very aware of the disproportionate numbers of women prisoners from ethnic minority groups, and the need for liaison with organisations catering for black and foreign women in prison. Additionally, and in order to pursue strategies directed at achieving both a reduction in the prison population and an amelioration of existing unsatisfactory conditions in *all* prisons, WIP joined with a variety of other penal reform organisations to campaign against the all-pervasive secrecy, non-accountability to the public, censorship, and other undemocratic practices which have characterised the British prison system from the nineteenth century onwards. Around the same time, two specialist organisations catering for two of the most neglected groups of incarcerated women were founded: Hibiscus, founded by Olga Heaven for foreign national women prisoners; and WISH (Women in Special Hospitals) founded by Prue Stevenson.

At the end of its first 12 years, WIP could certainly claim with justification that its work had been central to the increase in public awareness of the pains of women in penal custody. (Whether or not there had been a concomitant diminution of those pains was, of course, a much thornier question.) Since 1983, many other non-statutory groups had been campaigning or caring specifically for female prisoners. In addition to Hibiscus and WISH two other organisations began to work on women's prisons issues: WPRC (Nacro's Women Prisoners' Resource Centre) and the Black Female Prisoners Scheme. Each of them had a slightly different task-emphasis, but their very existence constituted an early recognition by campaigners that the category 'woman prisoner' has no global application to women prisoners' needs, all of which require analysis in the contexts of individual women's socio-biographies, as well as in the light of prevailing penal politics. Innumerable policy documents and books relating to women in the criminal justice and penal systems had also been published (Seear and Player, 1986; NACRO 1991; Women's National Commission, 1991, to name but three), and since the founding of WIP the media had been continually seizing on (and feeding on) 'women in prison' stories whenever they could. But what had actually been achieved for women in prison? At the institutional level there had been formal recognition that the needs of women prisoners are different to those of men. In terms of radical and fundamental improvement in women prisoners' regimes the two remaining founder members, Carlen and Tchaikovsky (1996) were constantly discussing the lack of headway that was being made in effecting any real and long lasting change for the better in any of the areas where WIP had been putting so much of its effort. Take, for instance, the outcome of the 'Holloway C1 Unit' and 'Durham H-Wing' campaigns.

In the 1980s Holloway's C1 Unit was for women prisoners who manifested a variety of mental and behavioural abnormalities, though from time to time it had been used to house women who had been sent there as punishment, or merely because prison overcrowding meant that there was nowhere else to put them. In 1985 CI prisoners were kept permanently locked in small cells, received their food and medication through a hatch in the cell-door, and reports of incidents of self-mutilation were horrific (see O'Dwyer et al. 1987). Campaigning by WIP (and others) against conditions in the Unit was followed by the publication of two reports (Clare and Thompson 1985; Home Office 1985) recommending far-reaching changes, and on 17 July 1985 the then Home Secretary Leon Brittan acknowledged the desirability of relocating C1 in purpose-built accommodation in a different part of the prison (O'Dwyer et al. 1987: 190). But C1 was not relocated; and in 1995 although the women in C1 Unit were no longer locked in their cells all day, there had been no fundamental improvement in the situation of mentally disturbed women in prison, with many still engaging in self-mutilation as imprisonment worsened their already fragile emotional states (see Liebling 1994).

Durham Prison's H-Wing had already housed top-security women prisoners for 15 years when in 1989 the Lester and Taylor Report concluded that inmates were treated less favourably than they would have been if they had been male prisoners, and that without radical improvement H-Wing should be closed as soon as possible (Lester and Taylor 1989: 11).

Changes *were* made – in sanitation, association (time allowed out of their cells in association with other prisoners) and facilities. But prisoners still complained about the claustrophobia occasioned by confinement to just one wing of a *men's* prison, as well as about the Prison Department's seeming use of the unit as a penal warehouse for prisoners whom they could not quite decide what to do with, and who, for a variety of reasons, were seen to pose a problem to prison management.

And elsewhere in the women's prison system? Female prisoners were *still* imprisoned far from their homes, they *still* were subject to more petty restrictions than men, they *still* complained about the quality of the medical treatment they received, and they *still* had fewer educational, work and leisure opportunities than male prisoners. (All of which is *still* true of conditions in the women's prisons at the beginning of the twenty-first century.) Horror stories (like, for instance, the 1993 one about the woman at Styal Prison who, at the insistence of prison officers had remained handcuffed both during labour and while giving birth in an outside hospital) *still* regularly surfaced in the newspapers and were confirmed by the Prison Department (and most recently were endorsed in Wyner 2003). As for the female prison population: in 1981 the average daily population in the women's establishments in England and Wales was 1,407 (Home Office 1982); in June 2003 it was 4,542. Moreover, despite the massive increase in publicity given to women's prison issues since 1983, it could be argued that, as in 1983 (the year when WIP was founded) women's imprisonment in the UK has remained as marginalised in serious penal debate as it ever was. Now, in the first decade of the twentieth-first century the reform wheel seems to have turned full circle. Governments and the administrative criminologists who serve them see women's prison reform more in terms of making 'prison programmes' fit women's 'criminogenic needs' (Social Exclusion Unit 2002:140) than in terms of an 'abolitionist', and 'women-wise' penal politics committed to assessing all penal innovations according to their potential to redress criminal harms without increasing class, racist and gender injustices still further (see Carlen 1989). Hannah-Moffat (2001), Carlen (2002g) and Snider (2003) have all demonstrated how the knowledges of feminist theorists have unwittingly contributed to official characterisation of women prisoners and women's prisons today! It is not surprising therefore to find that feminists are much more hesitant about claiming they have anything to offer prison campaigners and women prisoners in terms of analyses which might help inform their attempts to make a difference via campaigns aiming to reduce the numbers of women who go to prison at the same time as reducing the pain of imprisonment for women who are already inside (see Carlen 1994, 2002g; Hannah-Moffat and Shaw 2000b; Hannah-Moffat 2001, 2002).

Feminist politics and prisoner research ethics

Feminists researchers working in the social sciences have debated at length how feminist research methods might differ from other methods. Many of the precepts developed have not been specific to feminist criminologists and some have really been little more than reminders that good manners and consideration for others' time, privacy and safety are ethical concerns that should inform all human relationships, including the research relationship. Many of these more general research protocols will be addressed in Chapter 7 when the practical problems of researching women's prisons are discussed. The questions left for discussion in this section relate to the relationships between substantive feminist theorizing and its implications for research protocols and possibilities. They either stem therefore from the epistemological positions and deconstructive precepts of postmodernism, or concern the ways in which feminist researchers should behave differently in the research setting to non-feminist researchers. They are explained and debated below as a number of questionable precepts and propositions.

Feminists should not be studying women prisoners at all

From a *postmodern rationale* the arguments are several:

- that a postmodernist feminist cannot study 'real women prisoners' without being theoretically compromised by an apparent acceptance of the ideological state baggage that must come with the already givenness of what it is to be a 'woman prisoner' (Smart 1990);

- that as postmodernism is committed to deconstructing social phenomena, to study women already defined as 'women prisoners' is to be politically compromised by apparent collusion in, and worse, the further exploitation of, the powerlessness of already-exploited women (Howe 1994);

- that to study 'real women' is to engage in a positivism which does not accept that women have multiple selves, and erroneously implies that their histories are unitary. Instead, it should be recognised that the concept 'woman' is a cultural artefact that does not encompass the varying life experiences of women of different ages, cultures and classes (see especially Daly 1997).

Critical criminologists would agree with several of the propositions above (all of them, if they subscribe to a postmodern perspective) , but they might also argue that, instead of studying the 'powerless' (women prisoners), prison research should be directed more at the powerful, the prison administrators, government penal policies and sentencing which, in part, make women's imprisonment take the form it does. However, other critical criminologists might reply that the main rationale for doing research *with* (rather than *into*) women prisoners is because they suffer; and also because it is important that the voices of the powerless be heard.

Feminists must allow women prisoners to speak for themselves

Some feminists have also argued that one of the ways in which feminist research should differ from conventional social research is that the world-view of the women themselves should always be probed and represented. This argument is rooted in the belief that as patriarchal societies are characterised by representations of the world as seen through a male lens, it is the duty of feminist researchers to give women a voice in representing their own world-view. Others, however, have pointed out that, important though it is to take into account how people experience and understand their world, no one has privileged knowledge of their own conditions of existence. For example, a black female prisoner may know that she has been racially abused by the police who call her racist names, but may not also know that her sentence of imprisonment was disproportionately severe when compared with white women with similar crime profiles sentenced for the same crimes. (See Gelsthorpe 1990 for a detailed discussion of the different positions feminist researchers have taken on these issues of representation.)

Theorizing the relationships between theory, penal politics and campaigning for change

Questions about the relationships between explanations of the forms and functions of women's imprisonment and prescriptions for change in the ways in which lawbreaking women are responded to by the courts and the prisons have been questions which have perennially engrossed feminist criminologists – not least because explanations which provide adequate (or 'as-far-as-they-go' adequate) explanations for social responses to deviant women can only provide pointers to, rather than prescriptions for, campaigning action or remedial policy making. Theorizing women's imprisonment and theorizing the likely conditions for changing it, involve entirely different objects of knowledge. For, whereas theories of penal relationships explain why those relationships currently take the form they do, political theorizing involves calculation about the likely effects of different changes in the balance of power among the competing groups and ideologies which constitute penal politics. For example, prescriptions for changes in sentencing policy cannot just be 'read off' from research which, say, finds that women who are without men are more likely to be imprisoned than those in a relationship of male-related domesticity. Even if the finding is explained by a theory which relates it to the position of women in a patriarchal society where the assumption is that women should, in the first instance, be controlled by men, this in itself requires further conceptual elaboration (sometimes through invocation of concepts torn from entirely disparate discourses) before an argument for changes in sentencing can be presented. If the formal principle of parity-in-sentencing (from a justice-as-fairness discourse) were to be invoked to argue effectively that such discrimination against women without men should cease, the practical outcome could still not be predicted. For parity could be achieved either by sending all women and men to prison for similar crimes and crime profiles, or by sending none, and knowing that a theorist who rejoices in the label of 'feminist' would not tell you whether or not she would be pleased with the 'parity' outcome. If she were a so-called liberal feminist content with achieving formal parity between men and women she might accept the former solution; but if she were a more radical feminist intent on reforming penal systems by forging change based on a recognition that women's difference makes them more vulnerable within a penal system developed and run primarily for *men*, she might not. Moreover, a feminist who is also a prison abolitionist might reject campaigning on either the 'parity' or the 'women's difference' ticket, and instead query the legitimacy of all imprisonment of certain categories of women on the basis of failure by governments to fulfil their obligations to provide for the basic citizenship needs of women in poverty, women battered or sexually abused by men or women excluded from other human or social rights.

To make things even more complicated, all campaigners for reform and change in penal policy must, as well as theorizing their own policy positions, theorize the likely responses of their opponents, and especially the responses of state governments and officials who, for a variety of reasons, may find it in their interest to incorporate the rhetoric of feminist (and other) reforms into policy statements which are either never implemented or, during their implementation, transformed in such ways that the intent of the reforming logic is negated, even though its language may be retained. (For examples of this, see the instances of the incorporation of radical discourses by official discourses at the end of Chapter 1 and in Burton and Carlen 1979). Additionally, sociological theorists engaged in penal politics often attempt to calculate the likely range of unintended consequences of otherwise seemingly well-intentioned reform (for example, when publicity about more benign prison regimes or programmes for women might unintentionally and tacitly suggest to sentencers that even more women might benefit from a prison sentence – see Carlen 2002e).

As well as being especially concerned either to make a specific theorization of women's imprisonment which gives primacy to the role of gender relations in explaining the forms and functions of women's imprisonment or to improve the general situation of women prisoners as a group, many of the feminist theorists engaged in penal politics have been influenced either by critical criminology or prison abolitionism. Both perspectives can, in their ideal-type form, be distinguished from the administrative criminology practised as a support service for the implementation and monitoring of the state's official penology. Thus, although several different competing and/or overlapping paradigms can be identified in the practice and rhetoric of penal politics, for the purposes of our discussions here, four ideal-types (one penology and three penal critiques) have been distinguished: administrative, critical, abolitionist and feminist. In the remainder of this chapter the relationships between theorizing and politics are discussed with reference to the constantly changing dynamics of power between these four key perspectives on punishment.

Four main issues of theories and politics in feminist campaigns for the reduction of both women's prison populations and the pains of women's imprisonment have been raised in recent years: first, the extent to which the reform of women's imprisonment can or should be theorized independently of the reform of men's; second, concern about the incorporation of feminist reform strategies and penal rhetoric into state justifications for imprisonment aimed at buttressing the legitimacy of rising female prison populations; third, the issue of reform versus the virtual abolition of women's imprisonment; fourth, the possible and desirable relationships between theorizing and politics.

Can, indeed should, the reform of women's imprisonment be theorized separately from that of men's?

A difficult theoretical question confronting analysts of women's prison issues is: how can penal justice for women be theorized as having distinct conditions and effects which are different to those currently attendant upon penal justice for men? The problem here is not that there is insufficient evidence to support, at the most general level of abstraction, the claims most frequently advanced to justify the separate theorizing of women's imprisonment. The following claims have been well-supported by argument and empirical evidence:

- that the economic, ideological and political conditions in which women break the law are different to those in which men do (Messerschmidt 1986);

- that female prisoners have, both nowadays and previously, been treated differently to their male counterparts (Rafter 1985; Dobash et al. 1986; Howe 1994);

- that, overall, (and still giving primacy to the very general category 'women'), women are primarily coerced not by the state's criminal justice and penal systems but, as we saw in Chapter 5, by innumerable 'anti-social' and informal controls that, for the time being, atrophy women's opportunities for full citizenship.

Now, admittedly, once it is recognised that 'real women' (of different races, sexual orientation and ages) may have opposed interests, it is difficult even to justify campaigning for a better deal for 'women'! Why not therefore just campaign for 'prisoners'? First, because empirically it can be demonstrated that there is absolutely no doubt that, for many reasons and in many of its characteristics, women's imprisonment in general *is* different to men's; and second, because there is no doubt also that the differences can be theorized according to their distinct conditions of existence. They have meanings which exist independently of the meanings of men's imprisonment and cannot be known independently of the specific abstractions within which knowledge of women is constructed.

So yes, women's imprisonment certainly can be theorized independently of men's. But should it be? How useful is such a theorization to understanding penal politics? For what is at stake in this question is not so much whether women's imprisonment is different to men's, and can be theorized as such, but whether, in order to achieve changes in women's imprisonment, campaigners should take more seriously the nature of the penal system and the necessary logic of imprisonment which make all prisons have features in common and which have, as we saw in Chapter 1, always been both gender-specific and not gender-specific. Moreover, given that the penal system is, on some analyses, designed by men for men, and given too, that the legislation governing imprisonment is not formally gender-specific, just how far can gender-specific analyses go in providing explanations of women's imprisonment which can inform reform strategies independently of gender-neutral analyses of the prison's essential power to punish by keeping people securely locked up? It is a question which Pat Carlen (1994) raised in an article entitled, 'Why Study Women's Imprisonment or Anyone Else's?' In that article she argued that many prison reforms are based on erroneous assumptions about what prisons can and cannot be because they ignore the essential function of the prison: to punish people by keeping them securely under lock and key for a specified period:

> Sure: class, gender, race and racism should still be studied in relation to imprisonment. And the views of prisoners and prison officers should still be taken seriously. None the less, let us for a time, at least, give empirical research priority to the prison's overwhelming power to punish. For this punitive power has a specificity which exists and persists independently of the best

attempts of (some) prisoners to defeat it via strategies of resistance, and the best attempts of (some) prison officers to defeat it via humanistic zeal. It is a power which grinds both women and men and it grinds them independently of the gender-specific modes wherein it is activated.

(Carlen 1994:137)

Similarly, in her book, *Punishment in Disguise*, Kelly Hannah-Moffat (2001) put forward the view that one reason for the failure of the much-publicised reforms in the Canadian women's federal prison system during the last decade of the twentieth century was that the feminist campaigners who helped pilot the reforms were slow to realise that the very specific systems of governmental power relationships constitutive of prison legitimacy and governance are well-able to incorporate (i.e. absorb and change) feminist rhetoric and reform proposals without the nature of the prison regime being changed at all. It is because of the observable power of the prison to encroach upon and colonise all alternative power structures that Hannah-Moffat argued that a gender-centric focus on the specificity of women's imprisonment is insufficient for achieving sustainable prison reform. Unless gender-specificity is theorized within penal relations which also require either gender-neutral or male specific analyses, the best attempts of feminists to achieve radical change may be either atrophied by *encroachment* (Hannah-Moffat 2002) or destroyed by *carceral clawback* (Carlen 2002a). For instance, an emphasis on a rhetoric of women prisoners' re-habilitative needs within prison (as opposed to a more fundamental analysis of *all* prisons and prisoner oppression, both male and female), may even contribute to an increase, rather than a decrease in the women's prison population, especially if repeated official assurances that women are a 'suitable case for treatment' lead sentencers to believe that women's imprisonment is different to men's insofar as it is more benign – and not really an imprisonment at all (which was the view of a majority of judges interviewed in Carlen (1983).

Incorporation and administrative penology

Fear that the power of radical critique will be neutralised if incorporated into the prison's administrative machinery has always provoked debate among prison campaigners as to the extent to which they should become involved in issues relating to the day-to-day running of the prisons. The concern is threefold: first, that changes seemingly based on radical critique will become part of short-term reformist schemes which often lend a spurious appearance of legitimacy to prison regimes without diminishing their fundamentally debilitating effects; second, that reformers will become involved in in-prison programmes which, though experienced positively by women already in prison, are seen by sentencers to provide justification for sending even more women to prison; and third, that the participation of known campaigners in prison reform will lend legitimacy to reform packages which, though they might *in principle and in part* be radically progressive, are likely *in practice and overall* either to be perverted by perversely punitive sentencing and organisational practices, or subverted by lack of adequate funding and support. Take, for example, a 1990s proposal by the government-funded Nacro that women prisoners should serve their sentences in 'community houses'. The basic idea of the community house as put forward by Nacro (1991) was driven by the ideal of keeping women offenders in their home area, close to court, in houses set aside for the purpose. The women would reside there during custody and avail themselves of the community's services to supply the elements of their daily regime. This would be essential since it would be uneconomic for the Prison Service to provide full programmes in very small units. Contact with home and family would be maintained by proximity or by joint residence for young children, space permitting. This was an imaginative concept and could, in the best (utopian) scenario, lead to the abolition of women's imprisonment as it is has always been known. Yet once the proposal was assessed against the *backcloth of contemporary penal politics* in early-1990s UK, Carlen and Tchaikovsky were wary of supporting it. They thought that in the context of the new punitiveness towards young unmarried mothers as *the* folk-devils of late twentieth-century 'welfare', it was very likely that the existence of such houses would soon be perceived by sentencers as providing yet another excuse to lock up more and more young women seen to be in need of 'training' as 'mothers'. Similarly, some of the proposal's rosier assumptions about women's need for family under all circumstances began to fade when set against what was already known about either domestic violence, or the non-existent 'family lives' of many young women prisoners who had been state-reared in local authority care. And finally, although the suggestion that, 'Allowing women in this situation to use community facilities would be essential' (Nacro, 1991: 19) was, in itself, an excellent one, it was also known that for the previous ten years (at least) it had been the constant complaint of workers attempting to deliver 'alternatives to custody' that their best efforts had been repeatedly subverted by the scarcity of *any* resources in the 'community' – and especially those most relevant to women's needs, for example, nursery schools, further education grants, satisfying work, move-on accommodation, crisis loans for furniture, and affordable care for elderly relatives, to name but a few. In short, Carlen and Tchaikovsky concluded that if community houses for women prisoners were to be founded without stringent sentencing controls, and adequate funding and extensive community back-up facilities, they would soon deteriorate into latter day workhouses for the welfare state's 'undeserving' and poverty-stricken mothers.

So why take the concept of 'community houses' seriously in the first place? First, Carlen and Tchaikovsky argued, because any *intention* to reduce the pains of imprisonment for women is *good in itself*. Second, because while prisons exist, in any form, such a good can only be pursued if campaigners continue to engage in democratic discussion and co-operative enterprise with prisoners, prison staff, prison administrators and opinion leaders. Third, because it is essential to keep open to public view the inner workings of the whole carceral machinery, so that its endemic secrecy can be held in check, and its chronic tendency for periodic reversion from progressive to retrogressive practices constantly monitored.

A writer who has written insightfully and theoretically on the problem of confronting the possibilities of incorporation is Carol Smart (1989a). Although her work in the book *Feminism and the Power of Law* was primarily about civil law issues, it has provided continuing theoretical inspiration for feminists writing on criminal law. Most importantly, Smart emphasised the concept of *strategy*, action that is based on assessment of the balance of possibilities and probabilities at a particular historical conjuncture for short-term movement towards the long-term goal. Pointing out that what was correct strategy for nineteenth-century feminists might nowadays be fraught with dangers of neutralisation of reform through incorporation into a 'master discourse' such as law, Smart's analyses of the fate of some feminist campaigns based on the pursuit of the legal redress of discrimination, provided a timely reminder that because the conditions for change constantly change, the relationships between feminist theory and political action must be constantly open to review – a conclusion shared by most feminists writing in the same and related areas. However, reflexivity does not in itself solve the issue of strategy at times when it is thought that a very desirable and maybe compelling short-term strategy will inevitably obstruct progress towards the long-term goal. The dangers of 'short-termism' have been prominent in debates about prison reform versus prison abolition.

Short-term reform of prisons versus their abolition

The debates about whether feminist campaigners on prison issues should support short-term reforms rather than, or as well as, prison abolitionism (often nowadays modified as prison reductionism, or 'abolition of prisons as we have known them') have taken several directions, though all are concerned that short-term reforms are subversive of, or diversions from, the goal of abolition. Listed below are some of the concepts within which the reform versus abolition debate has been framed.

Incorporation of radical critique by the state's ideological apparatus which, in a democratic society, has constantly to renew its justifications for the use of force to enforce citizen compliance is, as we have already seen, one reason why some anti-prison campaigners argue that prison reform is impossible. For them, the only justifiable campaigns are those which focus on making those changes in society and the criminal justice system which would lead to the abandonment of imprisonment as a punishment in favour of less damaging or more reparative penalties.

Co-optation is a concept which describes a more modern neutralisation technique than *incorporation* and is used by Kelly Hannah-Moffat to describe the *co-optation* of feminists and aboriginals to the reforming programmes of the Canadian federal prisons for women during the 1990s. Pat Carlen (2002c) has also described how several groups working for women (but with little prior knowledge of prisons) were co-opted by the Prison Service for England and Wales at the end of the 1990s to act as partners in the delivery of new programmes for women prisoners.

In reviewing the Canadian reforms, Kelly Hannah-Moffat also developed the concept of *encroachment* to describe the process whereby the model of traditional corrections continually encroached upon the ideal of *women-centred prisons* until the ideal had been completely eroded and neutralised (Hannah-Moffatt 2002: 210–215).

Carceral clawback is a term coined by Carlen (2002a, 2002c, 2002d, 2002e, and defined fully in Chapter 4 pp. 90–1) to denote the prison's existential necessity to keep people in prison and therefore place security above all other considerations, is another reason for campaigners to argue that women's prisons can never justify their existence by claiming that they can help needy women (see Hudson 2002). For prison can never adequately address the needs of women within a secure environment where security has to be the first consideration. To illustrate the power of carceral clawback and the way it infuses all aspects of prison life – even those not immediately seen to be security-related – Carlen gave two examples:

One of the commonly described characteristics of women prisoners is 'low self-esteem'. Is it possible to believe that *any* person's self-esteem would be enhanced by the regular strip-searching which women in prison undergo in the name of security? Similarly, with programmes designed to help women be more assertive or manage their anger better. Prisoners are not expected to answer back or question rules ... so much for self assertion! And as for anger? Isn't it hypocritical to offer anger management techniques in a situation where strip-searching and innumerable petty rules are such that they would be likely to try the patience of a saint? So, what I am saying is that the only type of prison reform that is possible is that which remedies any abuses of human rights – but that any other type of reform in terms of legitimating programmes for prisoner rehabilitation is impossible.

(Carlen 2002e: 82)

Legitimacy issues in relation to women's imprisonment take two forms: the first queries any short-termism which implies that the position of women now is inevitable and eternal; the second argues from the demographic characteristics of female prison populations.

The legitimacy debate relating to positivistic conceptions of 'women now' can be illustrated by the following debate. Does the argument that, because they are more involved with childcare than fathers, mothers suffer more from the pains of imprisonment retrogressively collude with a state of things which feminists should be campaigning to change rather than taking for granted as the norm? The argument against feminists employing such a rationale to keep mothers out of prison is that such a short-term reformism though based upon recognition of the structurally and ideologically disadvantaged position of 'women now', may also imply that the condition of 'women now' cannot change. Instead of engaging in such short-term reformism say abolitionists, feminist campaigners should hold fast to a long-term abolitionism which would deny that the formal and substantive inequities attendant upon the position of 'women now' are inevitable and forever.

Yet both short-term reform and long-term abolitionism have much to recommend them. Reform of women's prison regimes on the grounds that women's family ties result in them experiencing greater pain when separated from their families would support the notion of a substantive equality for women prisoners by recognising that because, *as wives, daughters and mothers*, they currently are expected to invest more of themselves (both emotionally and psychologically) in their families, they may suffer more anxiety and guilt than men do when imprisonment separates them from their loved ones.

Arguments based on the concept of substantive equality have been employed to support reforms that would either exempt mothers from prison or allow them to have their babies with them in prison, halfway houses, or other non-custodial facilities. Some abolitionists, however, would deny that the present familial exploitation of women is either inevitable or desirable and therefore approach with caution any proposal which implies that it is desirable to reproduce uncritically contemporary 'family' conditions for women prisoners. Others would ask whether such conceptions of the claims of 'motherhood' might in any case discriminate against childless women, lesbian or very young women? And finally, all campaigners worry that any reforms which make prisons *appear* to be less oppressive places are likely to encourage sentencers to have fewer qualms about the legitimacy of imprisoning women.

The second type of argument about the illegitimacy of women's imprisonment as a form of punishment simply assumes that, until there is good reason to believe that lawbreaking is *not* distributed evenly across all classes and ethnic groupings, prison populations composed of disproportionate numbers of poverty-stricken and/or black people are *illegitimate* because they bear witness to the state's use of imprisonment as a tool for the containment of troublesome populations rather than for the furtherance of criminal justice via any of the classical penological justifications (as described in Chapter 4 of this volume).

What are the possible and desirable relationships between theory and politics?

In the previous sections of this chapter we have tried to elucidate the various difficulties, contradictions and asymmetrical dilemmas confronting feminists engaged in campaigning and research about women's imprisonment. As campaigners and theorists have grappled with these issues in the real world of penal politics and the human misery which penal systems embody, they have often reached entirely different conclusions. Analysis of their ruminations upon the relationships between theorizing and politics frequently appear to be based upon a hotchpotch of rationales which usually only make sense within the play of feminist and penal politics within which the theorist was framing her arguments. We therefore end this chapter with a chronological summary of the views of a range of feminist writers, to indicate how at different times the theory/politics debate has been confronted.

Law reform, de-centring law, and feminist politics (Smart 1989a)

Carol Smart's concern with the ways in which feminists can use law without their ideals being subverted in the process has already been described. Yet, she maintains, law can still be used by feminists, as long as it is informed by a postmodernism that does not see law as a totalising theory whose 'truth' is unitary in its intent and effects, the same for all women at all times and in all places.

Precisely because law is powerful and is, arguably, able to continue to

> extend its influence, it cannot go unchallenged. However, it is law's power to define and disqualify which should become the focus of feminist strategy rather than law reform as such. It is in its ability to redefine the truth of events that feminism offers political gains ... At the point at which law asserts its definition, feminism can assert its alternative ... This strategy does not preclude other forms of direct action or policy formation. For example, it is important to sustain an emphasis on non-legal strategies and local struggles.
>
> (Smart 1989a: 165)

Standpoint epistemologies, reflexivity and political action (Cain 1986, 1989, 1990)

Maureen Cain was one of the earliest feminist theorists writing on law and crime to set out the implications of her theoretical position for research and political action. Writing as a realist and from a feminist standpoint Cain is concerned that the knowledge she produces should be relevant and accountable to those whose world view (standpoint) she endorses and from which she writes. Consequently, Cain argues that:

> There can be no getting away from the fact (*sic*) that we all think (speak, work, create and distribute knowledge) from somewhere in our society, from some site or other. Putting it another way, we all have relationships. The particular intersection of these relationships in us is the site from which we produce knowledge and in that sense each site is unique, historical and changing.
>
> (Cain 1990: 131–2)

Standpoints are not given, they are chosen, but this also has implications for how a feminist writer should proceed:

Theoretical reflexivity is a key concept and a key practice in the identification of standpoints and in the production of knowledge from a feminist standpoint. Theoretical reflexivity means understanding theoretically how being a professional criminologist articulates both with personal and particular relationships as well as with relationships of more general scope such as class, race, age and gender. Such theoretical knowledge about oneself is what makes it possible to say that if I want to write from a feminist standpoint I must make connections with feminist struggle – join a women's group or get involved in feminist teaching, lobbying, advocacy, cooperative marketing or child minding.

(Cain 1990: 133)

Recognition, deconstruction and denial (Carlen and Tchaikovsky 1996)

It was in answer to debates about contradictions between: (a) holding a postmodernist approach to knowledge and taking 'real women prisoners' as a starting point for research; (b) studying the experiences of real women prisoners and yet denying that women's experience is unitary and universal; and (c) short-term reformism and long-term abolitionism that Carlen and Tchaikovsky (1996) insisted that both in theorizing and in politics there was no alternative but to work on the contradictions by recognition, deconstruction and denial of (the inevitability of) their force:

If campaigners are to make relevant and progressive policy interventions into the women's prison system, it is essential that they recognise the gender, race and class differences (as well as other differences) which shape individual women's experiences differently both in and out of prison. In other words, it is not only the different gender histories of men and women prisoners which need to be taken seriously, but also the differences between women themselves (including those between campaigners outside prison and women with first-hand experience of its cutting edge inside!). That acknowledged, it is none the less our contention that because official policy for the women's gaols is often based either on stereotypes of *all* women, or on society-wide gender relationships which dis-empower (in varying degrees) *all* women, it is important to investigate and describe the ideological discourses and material conditions that result in women's imprisonment taking the form that it does, before *analysing* it to explain *why* it does take that form. Then, once the present forms of women's imprisonment have been broken down into their constituent parts, the relationships between carceral and extra-carceral social and ideological conditions can be specified. And their inevitability denied! By both recognising present realities of women's imprisonment *and* denying that their existence pre-empts conceptions of utopian (and always un-finished) alternatives (Mathiesen 1974), campaigners can facilitate the setting up of 'worst scenario' and 'best scenario' models against which changes in penal policy can be evaluated.

(Carlen and Tchaikovsky 1996: 212–13)

The political and the practical (Howe 1994)

Towards the end of Chapter 4 we left the feminist theorist, Adrian Howe, asking, 'How can a feminist who is informed by a postmodern sensibility that women no longer exist, speak for women prisoners?' (Howe 1994: 164). But it was not a rhetorical question posed as excuse for political inaction. Though broadly agreeing with a claim made by Carol Smart in 1989 that ' the feminist desire to be political has been confused with the desire to be practical' (Smart 1989b), Adrian Howe nonetheless goes on to point up all the dilemmas inherent in *not* being concerned with practical policy issues, and her conclusion is that, despite the dangers of being implicated in policy making, feminists must continue to make political and policy interventions while at the same time engaging in a persistent self-critique.

How can postmodern feminism inform a radical practice in relation to the state's power to punish? It can, and must, in the same way that it informs all feminist politics – by engaging in a persistent critique of what one is up to when one calls on the state to punish women or men; by speaking for prisoners while simultaneously engaging in an interrogation of one's uni-versalising self-authorising moves; by constantly scrutinising what our representational politics authorises and who it erases; by always working to breach the self-evidence of 'women' *and* of coercive and disciplinary practices, and by seeking to overcome the disjunction between postmodern critique and feminist practice. And even as we refuse essentialist notions of already given groups, we will have to tackle the difficult penal questions, such as how to rethink punishment for violent offenders. This may seem a lot of work ... But these are the preconditions of a radical practice which does not fall into the universalising and essentialising traps which

have constrained feminist, socialist and progressive representational efforts on behalf of oppressed groups in the past.

(Howe 1994: 217)

'It is better to do something than nothing' (Hannah-Moffat 2002: 216)

Although aware of the ironies and contradictions of deconstructing the
meanings of women's imprisonment at the same time as becoming
involved in campaigning issues, both Kelly Hannah-Moffat and Pat
Carlen agreed at a Conference held in London in 2001 that, when
confronted with knowledge about the pains of women's imprisonment,
it is better to do something than nothing. By this they did not mean that
any intervention is better than none. Rather, the very failure of a number
of different campaigns with which each had separately been involved
had suggested to them that both official policies and political action
opposing them should be accompanied by continuous and rigorous
critique of how new policies and campaigns are actually impacting on
sentencing and prisons. Furthermore, both also came to the conclusion
that however more attractive reform rhetoric is than penological
discourse, the main purpose of prison is to punish, and that it is within
that context that all reform has to be thought:

> The first lesson is the importance of sustaining 'truth in
> punishment' – in other words, of not losing sight of the experiential
> 'reality' of prison and of prisoners being involuntary subjects in
> regimes whose legal authority is derived from the power to
> punish ... It reminds us of the context of reform and forces a
> discussion of what is possible 'within the context of imprison-
> ment' ... The second lesson is that change needs to be deeply
> embedded in the organisation structure – going beyond discourse
> and piecemeal practices. A reflexive approach to strategic reforms
> and advocacy is based on recognition of the involuntary and
> repressive nature of and awareness and acknowledgement of the
> past ... While we continue to live with the prison we ought not to
> accept its presence as inevitable ... Clearly, developments that
> appear more positive de-centre the prison and reduce the reliance
> on imprisonment while simultaneously acknowledging and
> addressing the plight of those who remain incarcerated.
>
> (Hannah-Moffat 2002: 215–216)

While this imperative to action involves compromises, the
contradictory and action-undermining imperative to monitor the

reform product of those compromises necessitates continuous and uncompromising critique ... Incorporation ... has to be resisted; not because ... constant criticism is morally superior to jumping off the fence and doing something; nor because 'critics' or academics know best; but because politicians, civil servants, practitioners, prisoners, campaigners and academics all know *differently* – and the conversation must go on.

(Carlen 2002g: 19)

Conclusion

In this chapter we have examined the relationships between feminist theorizing and political action and have seen that by the early twenty-first century many feminist writers and campaigners on women's prison issues were influenced by postmodern conceptions of knowledge. We saw that postmodernism is attractive to feminists because of the emphasis on the deconstruction of all authoritative modes of knowledge and essentialised categories such as women and gender. However, the postmodernist emphasis on denying authority to the already-known and official meanings attributed to women prisoners and women's prisons have posed dilemmas for feminist theorists and feminist campaigners: they continuously wonder to what extent their 'real world research' and campaigning actually fails to deny imprisonment's official meanings, and, instead, merely acknowledges, or even consolidates and increases, the prison's power to punish (see Snider 2003 for a strong version of this argument). The consensus among people working and writing in the area in the early part of this century is that campaigning and theorizing should continue, with campaigning being informed by both theoretical and historical knowledge, and change being also constantly monitored and reviewed. In the spirit of reflexive critique, however, and in the knowledge that the conditions for change constantly change, critical theorists of all persuasions (and all admixtures of persuasions – critical, abolitionist, feminist, postmodern and Marxist) are persuaded both by their theories and by 'events' that the relationships between theory and politics are always unfinished (cf Mathiesen 1974; Young 2002; Carlen 2002f).

Concepts to know

The following concepts are all defined in the main body of the chapter:

abolitionism; incorporation; co-optation; de-centring law; standpoint epistemology; reflexivity; de-centring the prison; encroachment.

Further reading

Carlen, P. (1994) 'Why study women's imprisonment or anyone else's?', *British Journal of Criminology*, 34: 131–40.
Gelsthorpe, L. and A. Morris (1990a) *Feminist Perspectives in Criminology*. Buckingham: Open University Press (especially articles by Gelsthorpe, Cain and Smart).
Hannah-Moffat, K. (2001) *Punishment in Disguise*. Toronto: University of Toronto Press.
Howe, A. (1994) *Punish and Critique*. London: Routledge, Chapters 5 and 6.
Smart, C. (1989a) *Feminism and the Power of Law*. London: Routledge.

Topics for discussion

1 What are the distinctive characteristics of 'feminist' perspectives on punishment?
2 Do feminist researchers into women's prisons have any obligation to engage in campaigns for reform of women's prisons? Why?
3 'Prison abolitionism – in either its literal or revised forms – is idealist nonsense.' Discuss.

Essay questions

Illustrate all answers with referenced illustrations from published works.

1 What, if anything, can campaigners for penal justice for women learn from feminist critiques of women's imprisonment?
2 Assess the arguments for and against studying women's imprisonment without studying men's?
3 What difficulties confront feminists campaigning for prison reform? How might they be resolved?
4 'Feminist researchers may be justified in studying women's imprisonment, but they can put forward few justifications for studying women prisoners.' Explain and discuss.

5 Briefly explain and critically discuss (in the context of the issues discussed in this chapter) *three* of the following concepts: abolitionism; incorporation; co-optation; de-centring law; standpoint epistemology; reflexivity; de-centring the prison; encroachment; carceral clawback.

Chapter 7

Investigating women's imprisonment: practical issues

Introduction

Women's imprisonment is a complex phenomenon, and the researcher who sets out to investigate it may well be spoilt for choice of focus as she considers the kaleidoscope of social processes which together constitute the subject of this book. Those processes range along the whole spectrum of social control from the informal to the formal, encompassing en route the range of relationships within which gender is differentiated, each and every stage of the criminal justice pathways that may or may not lead women to prison, as well as the labyrinthine modes, meanings and metaphors of the prison itself, and its transcarceral and non-transcarceral alternatives.

The authors of this book have conducted extensive research in relation to women's imprisonment, though not all of it within prisons. Indeed, that is one of the first points that we wish to make: that an understanding of women's imprisonment requires investigation of many more social processes than those which can be understood from inside the prison gate. And we make this point now, because, for reasons which should become apparent when we go on to discuss the necessarily high levels of security with which gaols operate, prison administrators understandably allow very little (if any) undergraduate research to be undertaken within the walls. Therefore, although much of this chapter will discuss the ethics and practicalities of in-prison research, it will suggest several women's imprisonment-related research projects which can be undertaken by undergraduates without benefit of prison access.

The second introductory point we wish to make is that the prison research site itself is also extraordinarily complex – and not like any other. First and foremost it is a mechanism of calibrated punishment for a society of captive lawbreakers, and this alone endows it with ethical dilemmas galore for the researcher who seeks to penetrate the secrets of its power. Yet, almost equally in importance, the prison is a multi-professional workplace for a miscellany of specialists working under several different, and often opposed, legal auspices and professional ideologies. This inter-professional dimension results in all prison personnel being acutely conscious of the multitude of ways in which their work within the prison puts them at risk of violating their own professional ethic or of falling foul of that of other professionals; and it can also make them wary of researchers, especially of any who fail to show their appreciation of prison staff priorities or institutional concerns. Then again, the prison is also a service provider of education, medical facilities, psychiatry, psychology, dentistry and social work; it is a long-term home (or even refuge) for some prisoners while simultaneously imposing harsh punishments and deprivations on others; and it is an institutional site governed by very specific legal provisions, violation of which puts transgressors themselves at risk of a prison sentence – as the cautionary notices outside prisons warn all entrants – whether inmates, staff, officials or visitors. Indeed, anyone entering a prison may be searched (even strip-searched) for contraband, and will almost certainly face prosecution if found with any once inside the prison. Finally, all the lawful activities of those who live, work or research within the prison have to be subjugated to the security demands deemed essential for keeping prisoners securely within penal custody at all times.

This final chapter of the book is not setting out to be a conventional chapter on methods. Rather, the authors merely wish to share some of their own experience of researching women's imprisonment, highlighting those issues which they themselves have found to be important, and providing students with a basic toolkit for 'getting started' on their own projects. For philosophical discussions of ontological and epistemological issues, and for philosophical and technical discussions of statistical technique, students should consult the many comprehensive 'methods' textbooks which are available.

Designing the project

Why careful project design is important

Project design is the most important step in any research, both for all the intrinsic reasons related to research efficiency, and all the extrinsic ones related to gaining access to the research site and competing for research funds. But above and beyond all the usual reasons for careful research design, the prison researcher has to be especially well-prepared: first, because the prison research-site houses people who are captives, and whose ensuing vulnerability entails an especial duty of care towards them (in terms of ensuring both the integrity and the publication of the research); and second because the secure nature of the prison means that once the research is finished it is usually impossible to return to the research-site and have a second bite at the cherry.

Project design checklist

Before you even begin to think of the project, do read C. Wright Mills's *Sociological Imagination*, (Mills 1970/1958). It has provided inspiration for several generations of sociologists since it was published in 1958, and its magic still works today. Then, before you begin the project, check that you have made the following plans:

- **You have formulated a research objective** either in terms of a question (or series of questions) to be answered, or in terms of specifying an 'object of knowledge' to be investigated via conceptual elaboration which will provide new knowledge.

- **You have decided on the most appropriate methods** for achieving the research objective.

- **You have a made a timetable** for the various stages of the research project, including gaining access at the beginning and writing-up and disseminating the results at the end.

- **You have fully costed the project** – remember that everything has to be paid for: stationery, equipment, travel, payments to interviewees, researcher time, office, office staff, computer time and any other items specific to a particular piece of research.

- **You have made plans to cover all foreseeable practical, ethical, methodological and personal research-related issues** (e.g. *practical*:

have you familiarised yourself with the tape recorder? *ethical*: what will you do if you see someone acting unlawfully in the prison? *methodological*: have you decided on whether or not you will sample? *personal*: have you prepared yourself for how distressing prison interviews can be?).

- **You have made plans for *dissemination* of your results**.

- **You have made plans for *leaving* the research site**.

Gaining access

In order to do research in relation to prisons, probation, social work and the courts it is necessary to make a formal approach to the relevant service or agency, and, additionally in the case of the courts and prisons, to each of the occupational groups to be included in the research. Because of the complexity of the process, it is usually best for students to make the initial contact through an academic supervisor. The same applies to access to specialist libraries or archives.

It is frequently possible for the researcher to make a direct approach to individuals, voluntary organisations and campaigning groups though, there again, when possible it is as well to employ an intermediary who can vouch for your character and authenticity during the initial approach. When making a direct approach to a research access provider, one tried and proven method is first to write a letter briefly introducing the researcher and her credentials, explaining the research and the facilities required, and stating that this letter will be followed by a phone call in ten days' time. This approach has the following advantages: the recipient is given both information and time to reflect before there is a direct approach; the recipient does not feel 'rushed' into making a decision there and then; the recipient is not put to the trouble of answering the letter; the researcher has prepared the ground before making the direct approach, and when she telephones can concentrate on forming a relationship with the 'access facilitator' rather than getting bogged down in the details of research credentials and protocols.

Even when formal permission has initially been obtained from a service headquarters or agency, whether or not research access is finally granted will more often than not depend upon the impression the would-be researcher makes on the staff 'on the ground', those to whom will fall the burden of responsibility for ensuring that the research runs smoothly within the institution. In sum, whatever the eventual outcome of access negotiations, getting access can be a long business, so make sure that you plan a realistic time scale for this stage of the research.

Do not, however, make the mistake of regarding the quest for research access as 'lost' research time. 'Gaining access' should be seen as an integral part of the investigation itself, and a research diary should be kept from the time that the first contact with the potential research-site is made. Access negotiations often reveal much about the research object, for example: power relations (including those involving gender, class and ethnicity; a range of (sometimes opposed) institutional and professional ideologies; and the most important institutional concerns in relation to, for example, security, professional competencies, working relationships. During this time the researcher has an excellent opportunity to learn the institution's research 'dos and don'ts' – a most important learning experience if she is to comport herself without offence during the lifetime of the project. In fact, 'gaining access' is such an important business that it merits a checklist of its own.

Gaining access checklist

- Make sure that the project you wish to do can be justified: theoretically (i.e. it will contribute new knowledge); and methodologically (i.e. the method is the most appropriate for pursuing the specified research objective).

- Find out as much as you can about the research site in advance: whatever, your 'ideal' research methods might involve, they have to be tailored to the operational exigencies of the particular research site. The degree of co-operation that even the most willing research-site host can provide will necessarily be constrained by, for instance, security concerns, professional ethical concerns, legal requirements, insurance requirements, and most importantly, working shifts. So be realistic and economical in your research requests.

- Make sure that both you and your research-site host are agreed on the research rules: that is, on the methods to be used (e.g. tape recorder or not?); on issues of confidentiality and anonymity; on sampling; on the research facilities to be provided; and on the timetable. Additionally, the researcher should explicitly ask that any particular legal or institutional requirements be brought to her attention before the research commences. (This is especially important in relation to in-prison research where the researcher may be asked by inmates to carry messages or engage in other activities which would be a contravention of Prison Regulations.) As regards dress: our impression is that both staff and prisoners in women's prisons expect researchers to be smartly dressed.

- Ascertain if there is any way you can repay the research hosts for their hospitality (often provided at great inconvenience in terms of increased workloads or rearranged timetables). Research payback is often difficult in prisons, though staff themselves sometimes provide an opportunity by asking for advice about the provision of, and entry requirements for, various academic courses. When this happens, researchers should gratefully provide as much assistance as they can. Outside prisons, voluntary organisations and campaigning groups can nearly always use an extra pair of hands (or an additional brain or two), and many researchers feel that they have an ethical duty to make some sort of return in kind for the research help they have received. (A special consideration is required in relation to how involved a researcher can/should become with women ex-prisoners, and that is addressed later in this chapter.)

- Draw up non-technical explanations of the research aims which will be suitable for all the different groups you wish to involve in the project.

Contacting the interviewees or research participants

Once the researcher has permission to do the research, she will need to contact the interviewees, or in the case of participant observation or an observational study, the other research participants. Whatever method of making contact is chosen, ensure that, where applicable, it has first been cleared with the research host.

If prisoners are to be interviewed, it is best to send them a letter detailing the purpose of the research, the ways in which respondents' anonymity and confidentiality will be protected, what will be required of them, and emphasising that participation is voluntary. The letter should also indicate that although participation in the research will not harm prisoners in any way, it also will not give them any benefits in terms of advantages within or beyond the prison. As the introductory letters will most probably be delivered by prison staff (and the recipients may well discuss them with staff too) it is essential that the researcher take time (where possible) to secure the interest of the relevant prison personnel.

When volunteers are to be interviewed they should always be given a document containing the following information prior to interview: a simple explanation of the sampling methods (if any) employed (i.e. why *they* have been chosen to take part in the research); a description of the research objectives and methods; the researcher's credentials and contact address; and the steps to be taken to safeguard respondent anonymity and confidentiality. Respondents' written permission to use the data from their participation in the research should also be sought prior to the commencement of interviewing or observation. However, in some organisations, different groups will wish to meet the researcher for further assurances, and in these cases the researcher should be prepared to be grilled about every aspect of the research (hence the checklists above). In these cases, too, prior understanding of the organisation should make the researcher better prepared for the specific organisational worries likely to be raised in the initial stages of access negotiations.

Finally, it is important that researchers assess the risks involved in any interview venues which they may set up. Interviewing women at home may involve contact with violent men, drugged or drunken companions, unruly children or fierce dogs. The interviewer may also receive invitations to partake in activities which she would rather avoid, such as drinking alcohol or smoking cigarettes or drugs. It is always advisable that the address you are visiting be known to an associate and that they also know when you are due back from the interview. You should also be prepared to abandon an interview if the setting is too noisy or in other ways unsuitable and if the respondent is less than coherent as a result of alcohol consumption or other drugs. Transcribing interviews is expensive, and there is no point in wasting time, money or labour on unusable tapes or recording schedules. We issue these dire warnings on the basis of some of the worst experiences which we have had over the years. However, we should also point out that the bad experiences have been the exception (and very few and far between). The vast majority of interviews which we have conducted in released prisoners' homes have been hosted by women who have gone out of their way to put us at our ease and whose generous hospitality has made the research experience quite life-enhancing.

Ethical issues

Most research institutions have their own codes of ethics for researchers and students and staff are required to submit their proposals for perusal by a research ethics committee prior to access approaches being made.

Professional associations also publish ethical codes, and in some applications for funding it is sufficient for an applicant to append the relevant ethical code and confirm that she will abide by its provisions. In other instances researchers are required to list the specific ethical issues which might arise in the research proposal under consideration. The most likely issues to arise in connection with women's imprisonment research are as follows:

Confidentiality of interview data

It is usual in social science research to guarantee that the confidentiality of all respondents' interview answers will be respected and protected. Yet a researcher who has been told by a prisoner that she is suicidal may find herself in a difficult ethical dilemma as to the proper course to take with this information, as may a researcher who is told by a prisoner (serving a sentence for child cruelty) that, unbeknownst to the prison authorities, she is pregnant, and intends to have the baby in a secret location to avoid having it taken away by social services. In fact, many situations can arise in a prison where the researcher is told things which burden her with knowledge which might have life-and-death signifi-cance and where the conventional rule of respecting the confidentiality of respondents can appear problematical. It is not possible to be prescriptive as to the right course of action for hypothetical situations, but here are some useful guidelines which can be followed when faced with a dilemma concerning confidentiality:

- seek advice from a research supervisor, mentor, colleague;

- outline the problem to the governor of the prison (or the head of any other organisation providing research facilities) as a hypothetical case and take her advice. It is especially important to check on the legal and ethical dimensions of the issue;

- remember that research should not proceed 'at all costs', and especially at risk to someone's life.

Anonymity of respondents

A major method for securing research co-operation is to promise respondents anonymity, to guarantee that nothing in the research report will lead to their identification. Two problems frequently arise: first, some respondents insist that they want to be named in the published work; the identity of other respondents is impossible to hide without damaging the report's authenticity by rendering everything about it totally anonymous. In both cases, it is essential to discuss the alternatives with the relevant respondents, in an attempt to come up with a solution acceptable to all parties.

Respondents who want to see their names in print can usually be satisfied by an agreement to include their names in the acknowledgments. Others, however, want to have their names attached to each quotation. Some researchers would argue that this is fair enough, that the wishes of the respondent should be paramount. We take a different view, what some might argue is a more 'maternalistic' approach. We do so because we know from experience that upon release from prison women often see things differently to how they did inside. For that reason we would always try to persuade interviewees in prison to agree only to having their interviews quoted anonymously, and would suggest that the following procedure be adopted. When, for instance, a woman talking about engaging in drugs, prostitution, theft or other crime insists that she is not ashamed of what she has done, and wants her name attached to all quotations from her interview, it may be enough for the researcher to tell her that she (the researcher) cannot take responsibility for publishing a respondent's name in a context where it might be detrimental to her future life chances. If the woman insists on having her name associated with her quotations, the researcher might well have a duty not to interview her on those terms.

Equally difficult in relation to anonymising data is the case of the respondent whose position is unique to an institution (e.g. a prison only has one governing governor) or even a national agency (e.g. there is only one Chief Inspector of Prisons). Many occupants of these senior positions are quite happy to have their words attributed to them and then, where that is so, there is no problem (not for the researcher, at any rate!). But where the respondent would prefer to remain anonymous the researcher may be able to disguise identity by generalising rank; for example, a governing governor becomes, 'one of the governor staff', a chief inspector becomes 'one of the inspectorate', and so on. Maybe in these cases there is a loss of quotation impact as the respondent is reduced in rank, but usually the loss is of minimal significance and the alternative, of certainly revealing identity, would make it impossible to quote the respondent at all. The most important point here is that issues of anonymity and confidentiality must be discussed in advance with all respondents and the agreed strategy recorded in writing; together with permission to conduct the interview/participant observation and use the resultant data for the purposes declared in the research proposal.

Witnessing unlawful activities

What should a researcher do if she sees either a prisoner or a prison employee behaving illegally? This is a question that often arises in discussions of ethical dilemmas in prison research, yet it is not a dilemma with which the authors have ever been faced, though it is a possibility that each has considered. The conclusion they have come to is that unless the illegal behaviour involved physical abuse of a prisoner or an attack on an officer (if, for instance, they inadvertently witnessed an act of pilfering by an officer or prisoner) they would mind their own business (unless subpoenaed to give evidence in court). In the case of abuse of a prisoner, they would feel obliged to report what they had seen; in the case of an attack on an officer they would bear witness for the officer as required. Ultimately, this is an issue which researchers must decide for themselves – though, as with all the other ethical questions discussed here, it is as well to be prepared!

Payments to respondents?

When research is being conducted in prisons, prisoners are not allowed to accept money in return for giving an interview. In some prisons researchers are allowed to offer a cigarette or to buy a cup of tea for an interviewee during the course of the interview. However, any researcher wishing to put an interviewee at ease by proffering a cigarette or other refreshment should have the written permission of the governor (or authorised deputy), otherwise she will be at risk of prosecution.

Whether payment should be made to interviewees outside prison is an ethical issue. The Research Councils and other funding bodies have been known to allow for payments to respondents but seem to vary in their approach. Some have been known to allow payments on the ethical grounds that unemployed respondents should be paid for their time. Others have refused to respond to an ethical case, arguing that payments will only be made if an instrumental case is made that failure to meet requests for payment from essential respondents could put the research at risk.

We ourselves have never found that ex-prisoners have required payment in return for an interview. Indeed, most women prisoners agree to be interviewed before ever knowing that payment is available. In the one 'instrumental case' which came to our attention some male corporate criminals refused to grant interviews without being wined and dined and sent home in chauffeur-driven cars afterwards. The funding body paid up! Even without this example to hand, it has always seemed to us that the practical (instrumental) approach to interviewee payment will usually operate to the benefit of the powerful and the detriment of the powerless.

We see no reason why professionals whose employers' agree to their being interviewed during work-time should be paid. However, lawyers and other self-employed persons may well argue that they incur financial loss while being interviewed. Many researchers, ourselves included, believe that poverty-stricken ex-prisoners should be paid for their time, while those who oppose paying ex-prisoners give the following reasons: that lawbreakers should not benefit from their crimes; that payments will be spent on illegal substances (researchers concerned about this often resolve the dilemma by making payment via food vouchers); that payments will result in respondents exaggerating their stories in order to be seen to earn their fee. In response, we would argue, first that any opportunity for an ex-prisoner to earn honest money is an unequivocal good. (After all, even the daftest explanations of female crime have never suggested that women break the law in order that they may some day have the chance to earn ten quid or so for a sociological interview!) Second, we hold that a person's right to be paid for her labour exists independently of how those earnings might possibly be spent. Lastly, although we have indeed found that there is some substance in the fear that paid respondents might assume an obligation to 'sex-up' their answers according to a mistaken idea that only thus will they earn their fee, we have also found that they usually make this assumption quite explicit by demurring when payment is first mentioned that they 'haven't anything very exciting to say. I'm just an ordinary prostitute, me'. Or, 'I just did cheque fraud for me habit. Then I just got nicked'. Demurrers such as these certainly provide opportunity for the interviewer to emphasise that 'ordinary' ex-prisoners are who she's interested in, that she's not a reporter, and that the 'boring bits' are what she wants to know about. Nonetheless, it is as well to stress to all respondents that you just want them to 'tell it how you remember it', that they will be paid however uneventful their stories are.

Whose side are we on?

The question 'Whose side are we on?' when we are engaged in empirical research was raised by the American sociologist Howard Becker (1967) in the 1960s in an article where he argued that sociologists researching contested situations should take the viewpoint of the less powerful because the world-view of the powerful is conventionally the dominant one. Becker's argument was opposed by fellow-American Alvin

Gouldner (1968), who argued that sociologists should not be taking sides at all, that they should be explaining the power structures wherein certain classes and ideologies become dominant. This latter position is most akin to that of the present authors, who hold to a belief that the task of a sociologist is either to explain empirical differences via theoretical constructs (rather than to determine 'truth' by judging between opposed accounts) or to produce new knowledge via the deconstruction and realignment of the already-known. Nonetheless, there are still research situations where the question 'whose side are we on?' is raised in one form or another, and where the answers are still seen as being contentious.

Women prison researchers should speak from the standpoint of women prisoners

We have already seen in Chapter 6 how some feminist criminologists have argued a position which is similar to that of Howard Becker – that feminist researchers should ensure that the voices of the women they study are heard when the research is written up. Others, like Maureen Cain have even argued that feminist sociologists should themselves engage in feminist struggles if they are to write from an authentic feminist standpoint (Cain 1986, 1989, 1990). Although these are political issues that each researcher must decide for herself, it does seem to us that whether or not the researcher speaks from the standpoint of her subject should depend upon the research objective. If the main objective of the research is to represent faithfully how women prisoners claim to experience their imprisonment, then anything the researcher can do to enhance her own (and her readers') understanding of that experience will further the research object. (The same would apply if the main object were to faithfully represent how either male or female prison officers see their jobs in the prison.) However, as soon as one goes beyond description to explaining, or even to examining the conditions of possibility in which experiences can be represented one way rather than another, *then*, speaking from the standpoint of the prisoners is not enough, and close adherence to standpoint logic will almost certainly be obstructive of new knowledge or insights.

Prison researchers should appreciate the viewpoint of prison officers

A recent concern of a minority of prison researchers has been rooted in their contention that, over the years, there has been a growing tendency for a majority of prison researchers to pay so little respect to the concerns of prison staff that prison research overall has suffered from a prison-officer suspicion and resentment of researchers that has been deleterious to prison studies in general. To remedy this state of affairs, Alison Liebling and her colleagues have argued for what they call a new mode of 'appreciative inquiry' in prison studies, a type of policy-oriented research which, instead of aiming at problem-oriented critique, 'appreciates' the best aspects of an institution and the work of its staff in order to get a more rounded picture ('truth') of institutional relationships (Liebling et al. 1999). 'Appreciative inquiry', they argue, is presented as a corrective to the overwhelmingly 'problem-oriented' approach of the last couple of decades. Yet, if the research object is clearly defined and the theoretical tools and protocols for achieving it plainly stated, neither 'problems' nor 'appreciation' should be uppermost in the mind of the designer of a research project. The aim of sociological research should not be to achieve as fully rounded a picture as possible of some empirical phenomenon. Rather, the aim should be to elucidate theoretically the relationships which make that empirical phenomenon take one or more of the forms it does. A sociological explanation, moreover, should in any case not only suggest why prison officers systematically do their job in the way they do, but why *any one of us* would be likely to do the job in that way if we were to do that same job under identical social and institutional conditions. In that sense, sociological inquiry has always been 'appreciative'. A fully sociological explanation or analysis, moreover, should never point the finger of blame towards individuals, but should, instead, indicate where structural change might be required. 'Appreciative inquiry', as defined by Liebling et al. (1999) is, by contrast, merely the flip side of 'problem-oriented' research. Both approaches imply an empiricist, policy-oriented approach rather than a commitment to theoretical critique untrammelled, at the moment of research, by consciously radical, feminist, official or any other political or policy concerns. This is unfortunate for the future of prison studies, as it cannot be denied that during the last decade there has been increased pressure on research grant applicants in general, and would-be prison researchers in particular, to make their projects more 'relevant' to the concerns of governments and/or prison authorities. How should researchers respond? Should they at least be on the same side as their potential funders?

Researchers should not 'trim' their questions or their findings to suit the policy agendas of governments or research funders
There is no reason at all, in theory, why a contract researcher should not produce work of integrity and originality. The concern about contract research in practice, however, is that too often the research questions are first of all trimmed to suit the interests of the official agency contracting

the research team, and that, thereafter, the results are further trimmed, or even totally suppressed, so as not to provoke any political embarrassment for the relevant authority, minister or party.

More insidious than the open partisanship of contract research, however, is the silent exclusion which many researchers today believe operates against any research which problematises powerful (or even conventional) interests. Pat Carlen (1994) has written forcefully about the effects of this on prison research during the last decades of the twentieth century, and more recent critiques of biased funding in the social sciences have been made by Carlen (2002f), Hillyard et al. (2002) and Walters (2003). Overall, we agree with all those who would exhort new researchers (and old ones too) to remember that constant confrontation is inherent in the nature of critique; and, moreover, that what we would call a 'critical' penology would be no more and no less than one which adheres to the liberal, classical ideal of science. That is that science should be: open; constantly recognising, questioning, and, if necessary, denying the conditions of its own existence; and neither 'trimming' its questions to make them politically correct or expedient, nor 'clubbing' – that is, pulling its punches – either to conform with contemporary academic fashions or political prejudices, or in response to downright bullying by either political or academic powers-that-be. For, above all, it seems to us that a critical penology must try not only to think the unthinkable about women's imprisonment, but also to speak the unspeakable about the conditions *in which* and *by which* it is known.

Leaving the research site

One of the surprises likely to be in store for the less experienced researcher into women's imprisonment is that leaving the research site can pose several new problems, most of them centring around 'feedback', dissemination and 'payback'.

Feedback

This is relatively easy, and refers to the researcher's obligation to provide feedback (where feasible) to research participants requiring it. Returning to the research-site to explain a research report may turn out to be a harrowing experience but the prospect of it should not affect the way in which the report is written. In our experience, research participants and funders are much more interested in the quality of the report than in whether its conclusions concur with their own political prejudices.

However, there are certainly known instances of the latter (prejudices) affecting assessments of the former (quality).

Dissemination

A researcher who has received public money to fund her research and/ or who has received public co-operation in the research endeavour, has an obligation to disseminate the results where possible: by publication, media work or public lecture. Even undergraduates should make sure that copies of their final project are available at their research site. Postgraduates should seek advice about publication from tutors, the British Criminology Society and journal editors.

Payback

We have left 'payback' till last because, in our experience, it is one of the most difficult ethical and practical issues to confront a researcher on women's imprisonment. By 'payback' we refer to the question of the extent of the obligations which researchers may or may not have to women in the criminal justice system and women prisoners or women ex-prisoners with whom they become involved during the research. 'Payback' obligations can suddenly and often unexpectedly pose a most acute problem for researchers in participant observation studies and William Whyte's (1943) account of his post-research relationship with 'Doc' of *Street Corner Society* fame is still essential reading for first-time researchers today who, though their technical preparation for research may have been elaborate, may still be unprepared for coping with the human and emotional costs of social research.

The majority of research relationships are brief and unproblematical, especially when they involve nothing more than one short interview. Most respondents in most types of research situation have no further interest in either the research or the researcher once the brief research encounter has ended. However, in research involving more than one interview, after interviews of a very personal kind (e.g. life stories) or informal social interaction over a period of time (participant observation) respondents or other research participants may wish to prolong the relationship with the researcher beyond the research period. Alternatively, the researcher herself may have become so involved with the problems of the participants that she finds it difficult to walk away from them at the end of the research (see Liebling 1992).

We have found that the desire to prolong the research encounter has been more prevalent among isolated young women in prison who have no family and few friends; and among isolated ex-prisoners caring for very young children. In the case of a young woman in prison, the sending of a card or letter may be sufficient to satisfy her desire for continued contact. Some cards will never be acknowledged, others may engender a correspondence that lasts for years. Some respondents may ask you to visit them in prison; ex-prisoners may ask you to visit them at home again. We would not presume to tell you how you ought to act if any of these situations should arise. Our purpose here is primarily to appraise you of what might happen so that you are not taken completely by surprise if it does. But we would suggest the following rules of thumb:

- Always inform the prison authorities if you intend to communicate with a serving prisoner after the empirical research period has ended;

- Before acceding to a request to continue to meet with a respondent after the research period has ended, assess whether or not it will be to her advantage, and try to answer the following questions:

  - What does she want from me? (companionship, money for drugs, legal advice, general support, financial assistance, sexual relationship);

  - Am I willing and able to supply what she wants?

  - Is it in her interest for me to supply what she wants?

  - Will I be able to end the relationship when I want to?

  - What risks, if any, are inherent in any continuation of this relationship?

  - What would be my motivations for acceding to this request?

Conclusion

In this chapter we have tried to discuss some of the most basic practical and ethical research issues, those which in our experience are often only touched on in research methods books but which, nonetheless, often preoccupy the empirical researcher for longer, and with a greater intensity, than all the other more cerebral research dilemmas put together. We have not dealt here specifically with the issues of doing research as 'women on women'. Those issues were addressed in Chapter 6. Nor have we dealt with the major ontological and epistemological questions which have to be addressed before any academic research whatever can be undertaken. For discussion of these we refer you to the standard methods texts. Our aim has been much more modest: to provide readers with some personally tried and tested practical tips about how best to address selected issues which routinely arise in empirical investigations relating to women's lawbreaking, prosecution and imprisonment.

All that remains now is for us to wish you good luck in your endeavours.

Further reading

Bell, J. (1996) *Doing Your Research Project*. Buckingham: Open University Press.

Becker, H. (1967) 'Whose side are we on?', *Social Problems*, 14: 239–47. Also reprinted in H. Becker (1970) *Sociological Work: Method and Substance*. London: Allen Lane/The Penguin Press.

Carlen, P. (2002f) 'Critical criminology: In praise of an oxymoron and its enemies', in K. Carrington and R. Hogg, *Critical Criminology: Issues Debates, Challenges*. Cullompton: Willan, pp. 243–50.

Carlen, P. (1994) 'Why study women's imprisonment? Or anyone else's?', in *British Journal of Criminology*.

Davies, P. (2000) 'Doing interviews with female offenders', in V. Jupp, P. Davies and P. Francis (eds) *Doing Criminological Research*. London: Sage.

Gouldner, A. (1968) 'The sociologist as partisan: Sociology and the welfare state', *American Sociologist*, 3: 103–16.

Liebling, A. (1992) *Suicides in Prison*. London: Routledge.

Liebling, A., Price, D. and Elliot, C. (1999) 'Appreciative inquiry and relationships in prison', *Punishment and Society*, 1(1): 71–98.

Mills, C. Wright (1970/58) *The Sociological Imagination*. London: Penguin.

Smith, C. and Wincup, E. (2000) 'Breaking in: Researching criminal justice institutions for women', in R. King and E. Wincup (eds) *Doing Research on Crime and Justice*. Oxford: Oxford University Press.

Whyte, W.F. (1943) *Street Corner Society* (esp. Appendix). Chicago, IL: University of Chicago Press.

Topics for discussion

1 Are there any conceivable situations where an interviewer would be justified in breaking the 'confidentiality' agreement with a respondent?

2 Are there any conceivable situations where a researcher should put a research project at risk by breaking the 'confidentiality' agreement with respondents?
3 Should all, or some, respondents be paid? Why?
4 A prisoner becomes very distressed during an interview. What should the interviewer do:
  • Stop the interview for good?
  • Stop the interview and fix another time?
  • Ignore the woman's distress unless she herself wishes to end the interview?
  • Suggest to the woman that the prison authorities be informed and counselling sought?
  • Inform the prison authorities whether or not the woman agrees?
  • Review all the interview questions to avoid this happening with other interviewees?
  • Other?
5 A prison officer asks an interviewer if a certain prisoner made any remarks about prison staff during the interview. What is the appropriate response of the interviewer?

Project areas and topics

Undergraduates

It is unlikely – and even undesirable – that undergraduates will be given permission to do in-prison research. However, there is still a great deal of research into women's imprisonment which can be conducted 'on the outside':

1 Library-based research into the historical conditions of women's imprisonment.
2 Archive-based research into representations of women prisoners in the newspapers (investigate the British Library Newspaper Library).
3 Statistical and cross-national comparisons of women's imprisonment rates.
4 Use of policy documents available from the Home Office and The Prison Service to chart the policy changes in relation to female lawbreakers.
5 Investigation of EU and Council of Europe websites to compare European directives and policies with national policies.
6 Research in a specific non-custodial project for female offenders.

Postgraduates

1 How does women's imprisonment affect prisoners' families?
2 What are the main determinants of women's post-prison careers?
3 Whose (or what) interests are paramount in the organisation and administration of women's prisons?
4 How do women inmates survive prison?
5 How do female prison officers make sense of their jobs in women's prisons?
6 How are women prisoners viewed by the many and varied professional staff who come into contact with them while they are serving their sentence?
7 Do women experience imprisonment differently to men?
8 Investigate the history (and evaluate their work in relation to women's imprisonment) of one of the many prison reform/prisoner aid groups (e.g. Women in Prison; Prison Reform Trust; Howard League; Nacro; Hibiscus; Black Prisoners' Support Scheme; Clean Break; CAST).
9 What were the main reasons for the soaring female prison populations at the beginning of the twenty-first century?
10 What effects does their imprisonment have on released women prisoners?
11 What have, historically, been the main determinants of female prison population size in England and Wales?
12 Investigate changing justifications for sending women to prison.

Sources and addresses

Organisations

Amnesty International
99–119 Rosebery Avenue
London EC1R 4RE
Website: www.amnesty.org.uk

British Library Newspaper Collection
The British Library
Newspaper Library
Colindale Avenue
London NW9 5HE
Website: http://www.bl.uk/collections/newspapers.html

British Society of Criminology
Room G05,
Duncan House,
University of East London,
High Street,
Stratford,
London, E15 2JB
Website: http://www.britsoccrim.org/index.htm

British Sociological Association
Unit 3F/G
Mountjoy Research Centre
Stockton Road
Durham DH1 3UR
Website: http://www.britsoc.org.uk/

Catholic Agency for Social Concern
39 Eccleston Square
London SWIV IBX
Website: http://www.faithworks.info/index.asp

Centre for Prison Studies
Institute of Criminology
University of Cambridge
7 West Road
Cambridge CB3
Website: www.law.cam.ac.uk/crim/index.htm

Churches Criminal Justice Forum
Catholic Agency for Social Concern
39 Eccleston Square
London SW1V 1BX
Website: www.ctbi.org.uk/chsoc/networks.htm

Criminal Policy Research Unit
South Bank University
103 Borough Road
London SE1 0AA
Website: http://www.lsbu.ac.uk/cpru/

HM Prisons Inspectorate for England and Wales
HM Inspectorate of Prisons
Room 1013
50 Queen Anne's Gate
London SW1H 9AT
Website: www.homeoffice.gov.uk/hmipris/hmipris.htm

HM Prison Service for England and Wales
Directorate of Resettlement
Women's Policy Group
316 Abell House
John Islip Street
London SW1 4PLH
Website: http://www.hmprisonservice.gov.uk/

Howard League for Penal Reform
1 Ardleigh Road
London N1 4HS
Email: howardleague@ukonline.co.uk
Website: www.howardleague.org

International Centre for Prison Studies
King's College London
School of Law
26–29 Drury Lane
London WC2B 5RL
Website: www.prisonstudies.org

Nacro
169 Clapham Road
London SW9 0PU
Website: http://www.nacro.org.uk/

National Probation Service
Home Office
Horseferry House
Dean Ryle Street
London SW1P 2AW
Website: http://www.probation.homeoffice.gov.uk/output/Page1.asp

Penal Reform International
Secretariat
Unit 450
The Bon Marche Centre
241–251 Ferndale Road
Brixton SW9 8BJ
Website: www.penalreform.org

Prison and Probation Ombudsman
Ashley House
2 Monck Street
London SW1P 2BQ
Website: http://www.ppo.gov.uk/

Prison Governors Association
Room 409
Horseferry House
Dean Ryle Street
London SW1P 2AW
Website: http://wavespace.waverider.co.uk/~prisgvuk/

Prison Reform Trust
15 Northburgh Street
London EC1V 0AH
Website: www.prisonreformtrust.org.uk

Quaker Prison Ministry Group
QPSW
Friends House
173 Euston Road
London NW1 2BJ
Website: www.quaker.org.uk/support/prison.html

Revolving Doors Agency
45-49 Leather Lane
London EC1N 7TJ
Website: http://www.revolving-doors.co.uk/home.asp

Social Exclusion Unit
35 Great Smith Street
London SW1P 3BQ
Website: www.socialexclusionunit.gov.uk

Women in Prison
22 Highbury Grove
London N5 2EA
Website: http://www.womeninprison.org.uk/

Women into Work SOVA
Unit 112, Aizlewoods Mill
Nursery Street
Sheffield S3 8GG
Website: http://www.sova.org.uk/

Web information on imprisonment and women's imprisonment

Council of Europe
http://www.coe.int/portalT.asp

European Journal of Social Work
http://www.tandf.co.uk/journals/titles/13691457.html.

European Reintegration Offenders Services Project
www.erosproject.org

The European Institute for Crime Prevention and Control, Human
Rights Internet
http://www.hri.ca/welcome.asp

International Labour Organisation
http://www.ilo.org/public/english/

Organisation for Security and Co-operation in Europe (OSCE)
www.osce.org/

University of London, International Centre for Prison Studies
http://www.kcl.ac.uk/depsta/rel/icps/prison_health.html

European Directives on Women in Prison
http://www.hri.ca/fortherecord2000/euro2000/vol1/women.htm

European Human Rights System
http://www.hri.ca/fortherecord2000/euro2000/vol1/women.htm

Parliamentary Assembly adopted recommendation/1450/(2000)
on the subject of violence against women in Council of Europe member
states.
http://www.hri.ca/fortherecord2000/euro2000/documentation/
parassembly/prec14502000.htm

Recommendation 1469 (2000) Mothers and babies in prison
Council of Europe, Parliamentary Assembly
http://assembly.coe.int/
http://www.hri.ca/fortherecord2000/euro2000/documentation/
parassembly/prec14692000.htm

Recommendation 1257 (1995) on the conditions of detention in Council
of Europe member states
Council of Europe, Parliamentary Assembly
http://assembly.coe.int/
http://assembly.coe.int/
Main.asp?link=http%3A%2F%2Fassembly.coe.int%2FDocuments%2F
AdoptedText%2Fta95%2FEREC1257.htm

European Directives on Social Exclusion
Recommendation 1582 (2002) Domestic violence against women
Council of Europe, Parliamentary Assembly
http://assembly.coe.int/
http://assembly.coe.int/
Main.asp?link=http%3A%2F%2Fassembly.coe.int%2FDocuments
%2FAdoptedText%2Fta02%2FEREC1582.htm

Domestic violence
Doc. 9563
23 September 2002
Council of Europe, Parliamentary Assembly
http://assembly.coe.int/
http://assembly.coe.int/
Main.asp?link=http%3A%2F%2Fassembly.coe.int%2FDocuments%
2FWorkingDocs%2FDoc02%2FEDOC9563.htm

Domestic violence
Doc. 9525
17 July 2002
Council of Europe, Parliamentary Assembly
http://assembly.coe.int/
http://assembly.coe.int/
Main.asp?link=http%3A%2F%2Fassembly.coe.int%2FDocuments%
2FWorkingDocs%2FDoc02%2FEDOC9525.htm

Recommendation 1450 (2000) Violence against women in Europe
Council of Europe, Parliamentary Assembly
http://assembly.coe.int/
http://assembly.coe.int/
Main.asp?link=http%3A%2F%2Fassembly.coe.int%2FDocuments%2
FAdoptedText%2Fta00%2FEREC1450.htm

Recommendation 1355 (1998) Fighting social exclusion and
strengthening social cohesion in Europe
Council of Europe, Parliamentary Assembly
http://assembly.coe.int/
http://assembly.coe.int/
Main.asp?link=http%3A%2F%2Fassembly.coe.int%2FDocuments%
2FAdoptedText%2Fta98%2FEREC1355.htm

Recommendation 1304 (1996) on the future of social policy
Council of Europe, Parliamentary Assembly
http://assembly.coe.int/
http://assembly.coe.int/
Main.asp?link=http%3A%2F%2Fassembly.coe.int%2FDocuments%
2FAdoptedText%2Fta96%2FEREC1304.htm

Recommendation 1269 (1995) on achieving real progress in women's
rights as from 1995
Council of Europe, Parliamentary Assembly
http://assembly.coe.int/
http://assembly.coe.int/
Main.asp?link=http%3A%2F%2Fassembly.coe.int%2FDocuments%
2FAdoptedText%2Fta95%2FEREC1269.htm

Recommendation 1261 (1995) on the situation of immigrant women in
Europe Council of Europe, Parliamentary Assembly
http://assembly.coe.int/
http://assembly.coe.int/
Main.asp?link=http%3A%2F%2Fassembly.coe.int%2FDocuments%2FAdopted
Text%2Fta95%2FEREC1261.htm

Recommendation 1229 (1994). Equality of rights between men and
women Council of Europe, Parliamentary Assembly
http://assembly.coe.int/
http://assembly.coe.int/
Main.asp?link=http%3A%2F%2Fassembly.coe.int%2FDocuments%2FAdopted
Text%2Fta94%2FEREC1229.htm

Recommendation 1146 (1991) Equal opportunities and equal treatment
for women and men on the labour market
Council of Europe, Parliamentary Assembly
http://assembly.coe.int/
http://assembly.coe.int/
Main.asp?link=http%3A%2F%2Fassembly.coe.int%2FDocuments%2FAdopted
Text%2Fta91%2FEREC1146.htm

Parliamentary Assembly of the Council of Europe Thirty-fifth
Ordinary Session Resolution 801 (1983)
The campaign of Amnesty International for a universal amnesty for all
prisoners of conscience
Council of Europe, Parliamentary Assembly
http://assembly.coe.int/
http://assembly.coe.int/
Main.asp?link=http%3A%2F%2Fassembly.coe.int%2FDocuments%2FAdopted
Text%2Fta83%2FBRES801.pdf

References and further reading

Adelberg, E. and Currie, D. (1987) *Too Few to Count*. Vancouver: Press Gang Publishers

Agozino, B. (1997) *Black Women and the Criminal Justice System*. Aldershot: Ashgate

Alder, C. (2002) 'Young women offenders and the challenge for restorative justice,' in H. Strang and J. Braithwaite (eds) *Restorative Justice: Philosophy to Practice*. Aldershot: Ashgate

Alemagno, S. and Dickie, J. (2002) 'Screening of women in jail for health risks and needs', *Women and Criminal Justice*, 13(4): 97–108

Allen, F. (1981) *The Decline of the Rehabilitative Ideal*. New Haven, CT: Yale University Press

Allen, H. (1987a) *Justice Unbalanced*. Buckingham: Open University Press

Allen, H. (1987b) 'Rendering them harmless: Professional portrayals of women charged with serious violent crimes', in P. Carlen and A. Worrall (eds) *Gender, Crime and Justice*. Buckingham: Open University Press

Allen, H. (1989) 'Fines for women: Paradoxes and paradigms', in P. Carlen and D. Cook (eds) *Paying for Crime*. Buckingham: Open University Press

Andrews, D. and Bonta, J. (1998) *The Psychology of Criminal Conduct*, rev. edn. Cincinnatti, OH: Anderson Publishing

Ardener, S. (1978) *Defining Women*. London: Croom Helm

Ballinger, A. (2000) *Dead Women Walking: Executed Women in England and Wales, 1900–1955*. Aldershot: Ashgate

Beck, U. (1992) *Risk Society: Towards a New Modernity*. London: Sage

Becker, H. (1963) *Outsiders: Studies in the Sociology of Deviance*. New York, NY: Free Press

Becker, H. (1967) 'Whose side are we on?', in *Social Problems* 14: 239–47; reprinted in H. Becker (1970) *Sociological Work: Method and Substance*. London: Allen Lane, The Penguin Press

Becket, K. and Sasson, T. (2000) *The Politics of Injustice: Crime and Punishment in America*. Beverly Hills, CA: Pine Forge Press

Bell, J. (1996) *Doing Your Research Project*. Buckingham: Open University Press

Bienek, H. (1972) (trans. Ursula Mahlendorf) *The Cell*. Santa Barbara, CA: Unicorn Press

Birch, H. (1995) 'A special kind of evil'. *The Independent*, 23 November

Blumstein, A. and Beck, A. (1999) 'Factors contributing to the growth in US prison population', in M. Tonry and J. Petersilia (eds) *Prisons*, vol. 25 *Crime and Justice: A Review of Research*. Chicago, IL: University of Chicago Press

Bosworth, M. (1999) *Engendering Resistance: Agency and Power in a Women's Prison*. Aldershot: Ashgate

Bottoms, A.E. (1977) 'Reflections on the renaissance of dangerousness', *Howard Journal of Penology and Crime Prevention*, 16(2): 70–96

Bottoms, A.E. (1983) 'Neglected features of contemporary penal systems', in D. Garland and P. Young (eds) *The Power to Punish: Contemporary Penality and Social Analysis*. London: Heinemann

Bottoms, A.E. (1995) ' The philosophy of punishment and sentencing ' in C.M.V. Clarkson and R. Morgan (eds) *The Politics of Sentencing Reform*. Oxford: Clarendon Press

Boyle, J. (1977) *A Sense of Freedom*. London: Pan

Boyle, J. (1985) *The Pain of Confinement: Prison Diaries*. London: Pan

Braithwaite, J. (1989) *Crime, Shame and Reintegration*. Cambridge: Cambridge University Press

Braithwaite, J. and Pettit, P. (1990) *Not Just Deserts: A Republican Theory of Criminal Justice*. Oxford: Clarendon Press

Braithwaite, J. (1999) 'Restorative justice: Assessing optimistic and pessimistic accounts', in M. Tonry (ed.) *Crime and Justice, A Review of Research*, 25: 1–126. Chicago, IL: University of Chicago Press

Bull, D. and Wilding, P. (eds) (1983) *Thatcherism and the Poor*. London: Child Poverty Action Group

Burton, F. and Carlen, P. (1979) *Official Discourse*. London: Routledge and Kegan Paul

Byrne, J.M., Lurigio, A.J., Petersilia, J. (1992) *Smart Sentencing: The Emergence of Intermediate Sanctions*. London: Sage

Caddle, D. (1998) *Age Limits for Babies in Prison: Some Lessons from Abroad*. Home Office Research Findings No. 80. London: Home Office

Caddle, D. and Crisp, D. (1997) *Imprisoned Women and Mothers*, Home Office Research Study 162. London: Home Office

Cain, M. (1986) 'Realism, feminism, methodology and law', *International Journal of the Sociology of Law*, 14(3/4): 255–67

Cain, M. (1989) 'Feminists transgress criminology,' Introduction to *Growing Up Good*. London: Sage

Cain, M. (1990) 'Realist philosophy and standpoint epistemologies or feminist criminology as a successor science', in L. Gelsthorpe and A. Morris (eds)

Feminist Perspectives in Criminology. Buckingham: Open University Press

Cameron, M. (2001) *Women Prisoners and Correctional Programs: Trends and Issues, no. 194*. Canberra: Australian Institute of Criminology

Cann, J., Falshaw, L., Nugent, F. and Friendship, C. (2003) *Understanding What Works: Accredited Cognitive Skills Programmes for Adult Men and Young Offenders*. Findings 226. London: Home Office

Carlen, P. (1983) *Women's Imprisonment*. London: Routledge

Carlen, P. (1985) 'Law, psychiatry and women's imprisonment: A sociological view' *British Journal of Psychiatry*, 146 (June): 618–21

Carlen, P. (1986) 'Psychiatry in prisons: Promises, premises, practices and politics', in P. Miller and N. Rose, *The Power of Psychiatry*. Cambridge: Cambridge University Press

Carlen, P. (1988) *Women, Crime and Poverty*. Buckingham: Open University Press

Carlen, P. (1989) 'Crime, inequality and sentencing', in P. Carlen and D. Cook, (eds) *Paying For Crime*. Buckingham: Open University Press

Carlen, P. (1990) *Alternatives to Women's Imprisonment*. Oxford: Open University Press

Carlen, P. (1992) 'Criminal women and criminal justice: The limits to, and potential of, left realist perspectives,' in R. Matthews and J. Young (eds) *Issues in Realist Criminology*. London: Sage

Carlen, P. (1994) 'Why study women's imprisonment? Or anyone else's?' in R. King and M. Maguire (eds) *Prisons In Context*. Oxford: Clarendon Press

Carlen, P. (1995) 'Virginia, criminology and the anti-social control of women', in T. Blumberg and S. Cohen (eds) *Punishment and Social Control*. New York, NY: Aldine de Gruyter.

Carlen, P. (1996) *Jigsaw: A Political Criminology of Youth Homelessness*. Buckingham: Open University Press

Carlen, P. (1998) *Sledgehammer: Women's Imprisonment at the Millennium*. Basingstoke: Macmillan

Carlen, P. (2000a) 'Against the politics of sex discrimination', in D. Nicolson and D. Bibbings, *Feminist Perspectives on Criminal Law*. Oxford: Clarendon Press

Carlen, P. (2000b) 'Youth Justice? Arguments for Holism and Democracy in Responses to Crime', in P. Green and A. Rutherford, *Criminal Policy in Transition*. Oxford: Hart Publishing

Carlen, P. (2001a) 'Death and the triumph of governance? Lessons from the Scottish women's prison', *Punishment and Society*, 3(4): 459–71

Carlen, P. (2001b) 'Questions of survival for gender-specific projects for women in the criminal justice system', *Women, Girls and Criminal Justice*, 2(4): 51–2, 64

Carlen, P. (2002a) 'Carceral clawback: The case of women's imprisonment in Canada', *Punishment and Society* 4(1)

Carlen, P. (2002b) 'Governing the governors', *Criminal Justice*, 2(1)

Carlen, P. (2002c) 'Controlling measures: The repackaging of common sense opposition to women's imprisonment in England and Canada', *Criminal Justice*, 2(2)

Carlen, P. (ed.) (2002d) *Women and Punishment: The Struggle for Justice*. Cullompton: Willan

213

Carlen, P. (2002e) 'Women's imprisonment: Models of reform and change,' in *Probation Journal* 49(2): 76–87

Carlen, P. (2002f) 'Critical criminology: In praise of an oxymoron and its Enemies', in K. Carrington and R. Hogg, *Critical Criminology*. Cullompton: Willan

Carlen, P. (2002g) 'New justifications and discourses of punishment and reform for women's imprisonment in England', in P. Carlen (ed.) *Women and Punishment: The Struggle for Justice*. Cullompton: Willan

Carlen, P. (2002h) 'Women's imprisonment: Cross-national lessons', in P. Carlen (ed.) *Women and Punishment: The Struggle for Justice*. Cullompton: Willan

Carlen, P. (2003) 'Official discourse and the play of governance', in G. Gilligan and J. Pratt (eds) *Crime, Truth and Justice: Official Inquiry, Discourse, Knowledge*. Cullompton: Willan

Carlen, P., Hicks, J., O'Dwyer, J., Christina, D. and Tchaikovsky, C. (1985) *Criminal Women*. Cambridge: Polity Press

Carlen, P. and Tchaikovsky, C. (1996) 'Women's imprisonment in England at the end of the twentieth century: Legitimacy, realities and utopias', in R. Matthews and P. Francis (eds) *Prisons 2000: An International Perspective on the Current State and Future of Imprisonment*. New York, NY: St Martin's Press

Carlen, P. and Worrall, A. (eds) (1987) *Gender, Crime and Justice*. Buckingham: Open University Press.

Carrabine, E., Lee, M. and South, N. (2000) 'Social wrongs and human rights in late modern Britain: Social exclusion, crime control and prospects for a public criminology', *Social Justice* 27(2): 193–251

Carrington, K. and Hogg, R. (2002) *Critical Criminology*. Cullompton: Willan

Carter, H., Klein, R. and Day, P. (1992) *How Organisations Measure Success: The Use of Performance Indicators*. London: Routledge

Casale, S. (1989) *Women Inside: The Experience of Women Remand Prisoners in Holloway*. London: Civil Liberties Trust

Castel, R. (1991) 'From dangerousness to risk' in G. Burchell, C. Gordon, and P. Miller *The Foucault Effect: Studies in Governmentality*. Chicago, IL: University of Chicago Press

Catan, L. (1992) 'Infants with mothers in prison', in R. Shaw (ed.) *Prisoners' Children – What Are the Issues?* London: Routledge

Cavadino, M. and Dignan, J. (2000) *The Penal System: An Introduction*. London: Sage

Chaudhuri, A. (2000) 'Twisted sisters', *The Guardian*, 15 August

Chesler, P. (1974) *Women and Madness*. London: Allen Lane

Chesney-Lind, M. (2000) *Program Assessment of Women at Risk Program of Western Carolinians for Criminal Justice, Ashville, North Carolina: Report Prepared for the National Institute of Corrections*. Ashville, NC: Women at Risk

Chesney-Lind, M. and Pasko, L. (2004) *The Female Offender: Girls, Women and Crime*, 2nd edn. London: Sage

Chesney-Lind, M. and Rodrigues, N. (2004) 'Women under lock and key', in M. Chesney-Lind and L. Pasko (eds) *Girls, Women and Crime: Selected Readings*. London: Sage

Chevigny, P. (2003) 'The Populism of Fear: Politics of Crime in the Americas', *Punishment and Society*, 5(1): 77–96

Chiqwada-Bailey, R. (1997) *Black Women's Experience of Criminal Justice: A Discourse on Disadvantage*. Sussex: Waterside Press

Cippolini, R., Faccioli, F. and Pitch, T. (1989) 'Gipsy girls in an Italian court', in M. Cain (ed.) *Growing Up Good*. London: Sage

Clare, A. and Thompson, J. (1985) *Report Made on Visits to C1Unit Holloway Prison, London*. London: National Council for Civil Liberties

Clark, D. and Howden-Windell, J. (1999) *A Retrospective Study of Criminogenic Factors in the Female Prison Population*. London: HMP Prison Service

Clear, T.R. (1997) 'Evaluating intensive probation: The American experience', in T.R. Clear and P.L. Hardyman *Intensive Supervision Probation: How and for Whom?* and in A. von Hirsch and A. Ashworth (eds) *Principled Sentencing*. Edinburgh: Edinburgh University Press

Clemmer, D. (1940) *The Prison Community*. New York, NY: Holt Rinehart and Winston

Cohen, S. (1979) 'The punitive city: Notes on the dispersal of social control', *Contemporary Crises*, 3: 339–63

Cohen, S. (1983) 'Social control talk: Telling stories about correctional change', in D. Garland and P. Young (eds) *The Power to Punish*. London: Heinemann

Cohen, S. (1985) *Visions of Social Control*. Oxford: Polity Press

Cohen, S. and Scull, A. (1983) *Social Control and the State*. Oxford: Basil Blackwell

Cohen, S. and Taylor, L. (1972) *Psychological Survival*. London: Penguin

Coker, J.B. and Martin, J.P. (1985) *Licensed to Live*. Oxford: Basil Blackwell

Conrad, J.P. (1982) 'The quandary of dangerousness: Towards the resolution of a persisting dilemma', *British Journal of Criminology*, 22(3): 255–67

Cook, D. (1997) *Poverty, Crime and Punishment*. London: Child Poverty Action Group

Cook, S. and Davies, S. (eds) (1999) *Harsh Punishment: International Experiences of Women's Imprisonment*. Boston, MA: Northeastern University Press

Cousins, M. (1980) 'Men's Rea: A note on sexual difference, criminology and the law', in P. Carlen and M. Collison (eds) *Radical Issues in Criminology*. Oxford: Martin Robertson

Crow, I. (2001) *The Treatment and Rehabilitation of Offenders*. London: Sage

Cullen, F. and Gilbert, K. (1982) *Reaffirming Rehabilitation*. Cincinatti, OH: Anderson

Dahl, T.S. (1987) *Women's Law: An Introduction to Feminist Jurisprudence*. Oslo: Norwegian University Press

Daly, K. (1994) *Gender, Crime and Punishment*. New Haven, CT: Yale University Press

Daly, K. (1997) 'Different ways of conceptualising sex/gender in feminist theory and their implications for criminology', *Theoretical Criminology*, 1(1): 25–51

Davies, I. (1990) *Writers in Prison*. Oxford: Blackwell

Davies, P. (2000) 'Doing interviews with female offenders', in V. Jupp, P. Davies and P. Francis (eds) *Doing Criminological Research*. London: Sage

Deane, H. (2000) 'The influence of pre-sentence reports on sentencing in a District Court in New Zealand', *The Australian and New Zealand Journal of Criminology*, 33(1): 91–106

Dennis, N. and Erdos, G. (1992) *Families Without Fatherhood*. London: IEA Health and Welfare Unit

Denton, B. (2001) *Dealing: Women in the Drug Economy*. Sydney: University of New South Wales Press

Denton, M. (1992) *Reports are Still Coming in: An Analysis of Offending Against Discipline in Three Women's Prisons*, Occasional Paper 5. Keele: University of Keele

Department of Health (1994) *Inspection of Facilities for Mothers and Babies in Prison*. London: Department of Health

Department of Health (1999) *Working Together to Safeguard Young Children*. London: HMSO

Department of Health (2002) *Women's Mental Health: Into the Mainstream*. London: Department of Health

Devlin, A. (1998) *Invisible Women. What's Wrong with Women's Prisons?* Winchester: Waterside Press

Dobash, R.E., Dobash, R. P. and Gutteridge, S. (1986) *The Imprisonment of Women*. Oxford: Blackwell

Dowden, C. and Andrews, D. (1999) 'What works for female offenders? A meta-analytical analytic review', *Crime and Delinquency*, 45(4): 438–52

Durkheim, E. (1969/1895) *Rules of Sociological Method*. New York, NY: Free Press

Durkheim, E. (1998/1900) 'Two laws of penal evolution', in D. Melossi *The Sociology of Punishment*. Ashgate: Aldershot

Eaton, M. (1986) *Justice for Women? Family, Court and Social Control*. Buckingham: Open University Press

Eaton, M. (1993) *Women After Prison*. Buckingham: Open University Press

Eaton, M. and Humphries, J. (1996) *Listening to Women in Special Hospitals*. Twickenham: St Mary's University College

Edwards, S. (1984) *Women on Trial*. Manchester: Manchester University Press

Fabelo, T. (2001a) *Project Spotlight: First Year Implementation Overview and Recommendations for Improvement*. Austin, TX: Criminal Justice Policy Council

Fabelo, T. (2001b) *Project Spotlight: Program Overview, Early Implementation Issues and Outcome Measures*. Austin, TX: Criminal Justice Policy Council

Fabiano, E. and Ross, R. (1983) *The Cognitive Model of Crime and Delinquency: Prevention and Rehabilitation*. Toronto: Planning and Research Branch of the Ontario Ministry of Correctional Services

Fabiano, E., Porporino, P. and Robinson, D. (1990) *Rehabilitation Through Clearer Thinking: A Cognitive Model of Correctional Intervention.* Research Brief no. B-04, Ottowa

Farrell, A. (1998) 'Policies for incarcerated mothers and their families in Australian corrections', *The Australian and New Zealand Journal of Criminology*, 31(2): 101–18

Farrington, D. and Morris, A. (1983) 'Sex, sentencing and reconviction', *British Journal of Criminology*, 30(4): 449–75

Feeley, M. and Little, D. (1991) 'The Vanishing Female: The decline of women in the criminal process, 1687-1912', *Law and Society Review*, 25(4)

Feeley, M. and Simon, J. (1992) 'The new penology: Notes on the emerging strategy of corrections and its implications', *Criminology* 30(4): 449–75

Folkard, M.S., Smith, D.E. and Smith, D.D. (1974 and 1976) *IMPACT. Intensive Matched Probation and After-Care Treatment, Vol.11.* Home Office Research Studies 24 and 36. London: HMSO

Forbes, J. (1992) 'Female sexual abusers: The contemporary search for equivalence', *Practice*, 6(2): 102–11

Foucault, M. (1972) *The Archaeology of Knowledge.* London: Tavistock Institute

Foucault, M. (1977) *Discipline and Punish.* London: Penguin

Foucault, M. (1978) 'Politics and the study of discourse', *Ideology and Consciousness*, Spring 1978

Foucault, M. (1981) *The History of Sexuality*, vol. 1. London: Penguin

Fowler, L. (2002) 'Drugs, Crime and the Drug Treatment and Testing Order,' *Issues in Community and Criminal Justice Monograph 2*, London: NAPO

Fowler, R. (1999) 'When girl power packs a punch', *The Guardian*, 12 July

Fox, K.J. (1999) 'Changing violent minds: Discursive correction and resistance in the cognitive treatment of violent offenders in prison', *Social Problems*, 46(1): 88–103

Freedman, E. (1981) *Their Sisters' Keepers: Women's Prison Reform in America, 1830-1930.* Ann Arbor, MI: The University of Michigan Press

Friendship, C., Blud, L., Erikson, M. and Travers, R. (2002) *An Evaluation of Cognitive Behavioural Treatment for Prisoners.* Findings 61, London: Home Office

Gadd, D., Farrall, S., Dallimore, D. and Lombard, N. (2002) *Domestic Abuse Against Men in Scotland.* Edinburgh: Scottish Executive Central Research Unit

Garland, D. (1985) *Punishment and Welfare: A History of Penal Strategies.* Aldershot: Gower

Garland, D. (1990) *Punishment and Modern Society.* Chicago, IL: University of Chicago Press

Garland, D. (1996) 'The limits of the sovereign state', *British Journal of Criminology*, 36(4): 445–71

Garland, D. (1997) 'Governmentality and the problem of crime', *Theoretical Criminology* 1(2): 196–7

Garland, D. (2000) 'The culture of high crime societies: Some preconditions of recent "law and order" policies', *British Journal of Criminology*, 40(3): 347–75

Garland, D. (2001) *The Culture of Control: Crime and Social Order in Contemporary Society.* Oxford: Oxford University Press

Garland, D. and Sparks, R. (2000) 'Criminology, social theory and the challenge of our times', *British Journal of Criminology*, 40(2): 189–204

Garland, D. and Young, P. (eds) (1983) *The Power to Punish.* London: Heinemann

Garrett, J. (1980) *Managing the Civil Service.* London: Heinemann

Gelsthorpe, L. (1990) 'Feminist methodologies in criminology: A new approach or old wine in new bottles?', in L. Gelsthorpe and A. Morris (eds) *Feminist Perspectives in Criminology.* Buckingham: Open University Press

Gelsthorpe, L. (2001) 'Accountability, difference and diversity in the delivery of community penalties', in A. Bottoms, L. Gelsthorpe, and S. Rex, (eds) *Community Penalties: Change and Challenges.* Collumpton: Willan

Gelsthorpe, L. and Morris, A. (eds) (1990a) *Feminist Perspectives in Criminology.* Buckingham: Open University Press

Gelsthorpe, L. and Morris, A. (1990b) 'Women's imprisonment in England and Wales: A penal paradox', *Criminal Justice*, 2(3): 277–301

Giallombardo, R. (1966) *Society of Women.* New York, NY: Wiley

Giallombardo, R. (1974) *The Social World of Imprisoned Girls.* New York, NY: Wiley

Gibbens, T. (1971) 'Female offenders', *British Journal of Hospital Medicine*, September

Giddens, A. (1990) *The Consequences of Modernity.* Cambridge: Polity Press

Girshick, L. (1999) *No Safe Haven: Stories of Women in Prison.* Boston, MA: Northeastern University Press

Glendinning, C. and Millar, J. (1988) *Women and Poverty in Britain.* Brighton: Harvester Wheatsheaf

Glendinning, C. and Millar, J. (1992) *Women and Poverty in Britain: The 1990s.* Brighton: Harvester Wheatsheaf

Goffman, E. (1961) *Asylums.* London: Penguin

Gorman, K. (2001) 'Cognitive behaviourism and the Holy Grail: The quest for a universal means of managing offender risk', *Probation Journal*, 48(1): 3–39

Gouldner, A. (1968) 'The sociologist as partisan: Sociology and the welfare state', *American Sociologist*, 3: 103–16

Gray, B. (2000) 'Helping women into jobs', *Prison Service Journal*, 132: 54–6

Greig, D. (2002) *Neither bad nor mad: The Competing Discourses of Psychiatry, Law and Politics.* London: Jessica Kingsley

Hale, C. (1998) 'The labour market and post war crime trends in England and Wales', in P. Carlen and R. Morgan (eds) *Crime Unlimited? Questions for the 21st Century.* Basingstoke: Macmillan

Hamlyn, B. and Lewis, D. (2000) *Women Prisoners: A Survey of Their Work and Training Experiences in Custody and on Release.* Home Office Research Study no. 208. London: Home Office

Hampton, B. (1993) *Prisons and Women.* Kensington, NSW: NSW University Press

Hannah-Moffat, K. (1999) 'Moral agent or actuarial subject: Risk and Canadian women's imprisonment', *Theoretical Criminology*, 3(1): 71–94

Hannah-Moffat, K. (2000) 'Prisons that empower: Neoliberal governance in Canadian women's prisons', *British Journal of Criminology*, 40(3): 510–31

Hannah-Moffat, K. (2001) *Punishment in Disguise: Penal Governance and Federal Imprisonment of Women in Canada*. Toronto: University of Toronto Press

Hannah-Moffat, K. (2002) 'Creating choices, reflecting on choices', in P. Carlen (ed.) *Women and Punishment: The Struggle for Justice*. Cullompton: Willan

Hannah-Moffat, K. and Shaw, M. (2000a) 'Thinking about cognitive skills? Think again!', *Criminal Justice Matters*, 39: 8–9

Hannah-Moffat, K. and Shaw, M. (eds) (2000b) *An Ideal Prison? Critical Essays on Women's Imprisonment in Canada*. Halifax, Nova Scotia: Fernwood Publishing Press

Hannah-Moffat, K and Shaw, M. (2001) *Taking Risks: Incorporating Gender and Culture into the Classification and Assessment of Federally Sentenced Women in Canada*. Ottowa: Status of Women. www.swc-cfc.gc.ca

Harris, R. (1992) *Crime, Criminal Justice and the Probation Service*. London: Routledge

Hayman, S. (1996) *Community Prisons for Women*. London: Prison Reform Trust

Hedderman, C. (1995) 'Gender, crime and the criminal justice system', in M. Walker (ed.) *Interpreting Crime Statistics*. Oxford: Clarendon Press

Hedderman. C. and Gelsthorpe, L. (1997) *Understanding the Sentencing of Women*, Home Office Research Study 170. London: HMSO

Hedderman, C. and Hough, M. (1994) 'Does the criminal justice system treat men and women differently?', *Research Findings* 10. London: Home Office Research and Statistics Department

Heidensohn, F. (1968) 'The deviance of women: A critique and an enquiry', *British Journal of Sociology* 19(2): 160–73

Heidensohn, F. (1985/1996) *Women and Crime*. Basingstoke: Macmillan

Heidensohn, F. (1986) 'Models of justice? Portia or Persephone? Some thoughts on equality, fairness and gender in the field of criminal justice', *International Journal of the Sociology of Law*, 14(3–4): 287–98

Heidensohn, F. (1987) 'Women and crime: Questions for criminology,' in P. Carlen and A. Worrall (eds) *Gender, Crime and Justice*. Buckingham: Open University Press

Heidensohn, F. (1991) 'The crimes of women', *Criminal Justice Matters*, 5: 9

Henriques, Z.W. and Manatu-Rupert, N. (2004) 'Living on the outside: African-American women before, during and after imprisonment', in M. Chesney-Lind and L. Pasko (eds) *Girls, Women and Crime: Selected Readings*. London: Sage

Hillyard, P., Sim, J. and Tombs, S. (2002) 'Power, politics and the state of criminology', Crossing Borders, British Criminology Conference 2002, Keele University, 17–20 July.

Hine, J. and Thomas, N. (1995) 'Evaluating work with offenders: Community service orders', in G. McIvor (ed.) *Working with Offenders. Research Highlights in Social Work 26*. London: Jessica Kingsley

HM Chief Inspector of Prisons (1997) *Women in Prison: A Thematic Review.* London: Home Office

HM Inspectorate of Prisons (1999a) *Suicide is Everyone's Concern: A Thematic Review.* London: Home Office

HM Inspectorate of Prisons (1999b) *Lifers: A Joint Thematic Review.* London: Home Office

HM Inspectorate of Prisons (2001) *Follow up to Women in Prison: A Thematic Review.* London: Home Office

HM Inspectorate of Prisons and Probation (2001) *Through the Prison Gate.* London: Home Office

HM Inspectorate of Probation (1991 *Women Offenders and Probation Service Provision.* London: HMSO

HM Prison Service (1999) *Report of a Review of Principles, Policies and Procedures on Mothers and Babies/Children in Prison.* London: HM Prison Service

Hobbes, (1968/1651) *Leviathan.* London: Penguin

Home Office (1982) *Prison Statistics for England and Wales 1981,* Cmnd 8654. London: HMSO

Home Office (1985) *HM Prison Holloway: Report by Chief Inspector of Prisons.* London: Home Office

Home Office (1988a) *Punishment, Custody and the Community,* Cm 424. London: HMSO

Home Office (1988b) *Tackling Offending: An Action Plan.* London: Home Office

Home Office (1990) *Crime, Justice and Protecting the Public.* Cm 965. London: Home Office

Home Office (1992a) *The National Prison Survey: Main Findings,* Home Office Research Study 128. London: HMSO

Home Office (1992b) *Gender and the Criminal Justice System.* London: Home Office

Home Office (1992c) *Race and the Criminal Justice System.* London: Home Office

Home Office (1996) *Protecting the Public: The Government's Strategy on Crime in England and Wales.* London: HMSO

Home Office (2000a) *The Government's Strategy for Women Offenders:* London, Home Office

Home Office (2000b) *Criminal Statistics England and Wales Supplementary Tables 1999,* vols 1 and 2. London: HMSO

Home Office (2000c) *What Works: First Report from the Joint Prison/Probation Accreditation Panel.* www.homeoffice.gov.uk

Home Office (2001a) *Criminal Justice: The Way Ahead.* London: Home Office

Home Office (2001b) *The Government's Strategy for Women Offenders: Consultation Report.* London: Home Office

Home Office (2001c) *Statistics on Women and the Criminal Justice System.* London: HMSO

Home Office (2001d) *Prison Statistics England and Wales,* Cm 5250. London: The Stationery Office

Home Office (2002a) *Statistics on Women and the Criminal Justice System 2001.* London: Home Office

Home Office (2002b) *Statistics on Race and the Criminal Justice System 2001*. London: Home Office

Home Office (2002c) *Probation Statistics England and Wales 2001*. London: Home Office

Home Office (2003a) *Prison Statistics England and Wales 2001*. Cm 5743, London: The Stationery Office

Home Office (2003b) *The Substance Misuse Treatment Needs of Minority Prisoner Groups: Women, Young Offenders and Ethnic Minorities*. Home Office Development and Practice Report 8. London: Home Office

Horn, R. (1995) 'Not real criminals – police perceptions of women offenders', in *Criminal Justice Matters*, 19: 17–18

Horn, R. and Evans, M. (2000) 'The effect of gender on pre-sentence reports', *Howard Journal*, 39(2): 184–204

Hough, M. and Roberts, J. (1999) 'Sentencing trends in Britain: Public knowledge and public opinion', *Punishment and Society*, 1(1): 11–26

Howard League (1997) *Lost Inside – the Imprisonment of Teenage Girls*. London: Howard League for Penal Reform

Howard League (1999) *Do Women Paint Fences Too? Women's Experience of Community Service*. London: Howard League for Penal Reform

Howard League (2000) *A Chance to Break the Cycle: Women and the Drug Treatment and Testing Order*. London: Howard League for Penal Reform

Howe, A. (1994) *Punish and Critique: Towards an Understanding of Feminist Penality*. London: Routledge

Hudson, B. (1987) *Justice Through Punishment: A Critique of the 'Justice' Model of Corrections*. Basingstoke: Macmillan

Hudson, B. (1988) *Content analysis of social enquiry reports written in the Borough of Haringey*, unpublished report, Middlesex Area Probation

Hudson, B. (1993) *Penal Policy and Social Justice*. Basingstoke: Macmillan

Hudson, B. (1995) 'Beyond proportionate punishment: Difficult cases and the 1991 Criminal Justice Act', *Crime, Law and Social Change*, 22: 59–78

Hudson, B. (1996) *Understanding Justice: An Introduction to Ideas, Perspectives and Controversies in Modern Penal Theory*. Buckingham: Open University Press

Hudson, B. (1998) 'Doing justice to difference', in A. Ashworth and M. Wasik, (eds) *Fundamentals of Sentencing Theory*. Oxford: Clarendon Press

Hudson, B. (2002) 'Gender issues in penal policy and penal theory', in P. Carlen (ed.) *Women and Punishment: The Struggle for Justice*. Cullompton: Willan

Inspector of Custodial Services, WA (2003) *Bandyup Prison and the Imprisonment of Women in Western Australia*. Perth: Office of the Inspector of Custodial Services

Jose-Kampfner, C. (1990) 'Coming to terms with existential death: An analysis of women's adaptation to life in prison', *Social Justice*, 17(2): 110–24

Kemshall, H. (1995) *Good Practice in Risk Management*. London: Jessica Kingsley

Kemshall, H. (1998) *Risk in Probation Practice*. Aldershot: Ashgate

Kendall, K. (2000) 'Anger management with women in coercive environments', in R. Horn, and W. Warner (eds) *Positive Directions for Women in Secure Environments*. Leicester: British Psychological Society

Kendall, K. (2002) 'Time to think again about cognitive behavioural progammes', in P. Carlen (ed.) *Women and Punishment: The Struggle for Justice*. Cullompton: Willan

Kennedy, H. (1992) *Eve was Framed*. London: Chatto and Windus

Kershaw, C., Dowdeswell, P. and Goodman, J. (1997) *Life Licensees: Reconvictions and Recalls by the end of 1995 – England and Wales*, Home Office Statistical Bulletin 2/97. London: Home Office

King, R. and Brosnan, F. (1998) 'Psychological group programmes for female prisoners at HMP Holloway', *Prison Research and Development Bulletin* 6: 14–15

Lees, S. (2002) 'Gender, ethnicity and vulnerability in young women in local authority care', *British Journal of Social Work*, 32: 907–22

Lester, A. and Taylor, P. (1989) *'H' Wing HMP, Durham*. London: Women in Prison

Lewis, D. (1997) *Hidden Agendas: Politics, Law and Disorder*. London: Hamish Hamilton.

Liebling, A. (1992) *Suicides in Prison*. London: Routledge

Liebling, A. (1994) 'Suicides amongst women prisoners', *Howard Journal*, 33(1): 1–9

Liebling, A. (1999) 'Prison suicide and prison coping', in M. Tonry and J. Petersilia (eds) *Prisons*, vol. 25 of *Crime and Justice: A Review of Research*. Chicago, IL: University of Chicago Press

Liebling, A., Price, D. and Elliot, C. (1999) 'Appreciative inquiry and relationships in prison', in *Punishment and Society*, 1(1): 71–98

Liebling, A. and Price, D. (2001) *The Prison Officer*. Leyhill: Prison Service Journal

Lloyd, E. (1995) *Prisoners' Children: Research, Policy and Practice*. London: Save the Children

Locke, J. (1967/1690) *Two Treatises of Civil Government*. Cambridge: Cambridge University Press

Lombroso, C. and Ferrero, W. (1895) *The Female Offender*. London: Fisher Unwin

Lowman, J., Menzies, R. and Palys, T. (eds) (1987) *Transcarceration: Essays in the Sociology of Social Control*. Aldershot: Gower

Lowthian, J. (2000) 'Housing needs of women prisoners', *Prison Service Journal*, 132: 59–63

Lowthian, J. (2002) 'Women's prisons in England: Barriers to reform,' in P. Carlen (ed.) *Women and Punishment: The Struggle for Justice*. Cullompton: Willan

Lukacs, G. (1971/1923) trans. R. Livingstone *History and Class Consciousness*. London: Merlin

Lurigio, A.J. and Petersilia, J. (1992) 'The emergence of intensive probation supervision programs in the United States', in J.M. Byrne, A.J. Lurigio and J.

Petersilia (eds) *Smart Sentencing: The Emergence of Intermediate Sanctions.* London: Sage

Lyotard, J. (1984) *The Postmodern Condition.* Manchester: Manchester University Press

MacKinnon, C.A. (1987) *Feminism Unmodified: Discourse on Life and Law.* Massachusetts: Harvard University Press

Maden, A., Swinton, M. and Gunn, J. (1994) 'A criminological and psychological survey of women serving a prison sentence', *British Journal of Criminology*, 34(2): 172–90

Maguire, M., Vagg, J. and Morgan, R. (eds) (1985) *Accountability and Prisons.* London: Tavistock Institute

Mair, G. (1994) 'Evaluating intensive probation', in G. Mair (ed.) *Evaluating the Effectiveness of Community Penalties.* Aldershot: Avebury

Mair, G. (1997) 'Community penalties and probation', in M. Maguire, R. Morgan, and R. Reiner, (eds) *The Oxford Handbook of Criminology*, 2nd edn. Oxford: Oxford University Press

Mair, G. (2000) 'Credible Accreditation?' *Probation Journal*, 47(4): 268–71

Mair, G., Lloyd, C., Nee, C. and Sibbitt, R. (1994) *Intensive Probation in England and Wales: An Evaluation*, Home Office Research Study 133. London: Home Office

Malloch, M.S. (2000) *Women, Drugs and Custody.* Winchester: Waterside Press

Mama, A. (1989) *The Hidden Struggle.* London: Race and Housing Research Unit

Mandaraka-Sheppard, A. (1986) *The Dynamics of Aggression in Women's Prisons in England.* Aldershot: Gower

Mannheim, K. (1960/1936) *Ideology and Utopia.* London: Routledge

Marshall, T.F. (1999) *Restorative Justice: An Overview.* London: Home Office Research Development and Statistics Directorate

Martin, D., MacCrimmon, M., Grant, I. and Boyle, C. (1991) 'A forum on Lavallee v. R: Women and self-defence', *University of British Columbia Law Review*, 23

Martinson, R. (1974) 'What works? Questions and answer about penal reform', *Public Interest*, 35: 22–45

Maruna, S. (2000) *Making Good: How Ex-Convicts Reform and Rebuild their Lives.* Washington, DC: American Psychological Association

Marx, K. (1956/1847) *Wage Labour and Capital*, in T. Bottomore and M. Rubel (eds) *Karl Marx: Selected Writings in Sociology and Social Philosophy.* London: Penguin

Mathiesen, T. (1974) *The Politics of Abolition.* Oxford: Martin Robertson

Mathiesen, T. (2000/1990) *Prison on Trial.* Winchester: Waterside Press

Matthews, R. (1989) 'Alternatives to and in prisons: A realist approach', in P. Carlen and D. Cook (eds) *Paying for Crime.* Buckingham: Open University Press

Matza, D. (1969) *Becoming Deviant.* New Brunswick, NJ: Prentice-Hall

Mauer, M. (1999) *Race to Incarcerate.* New York, NY: New Press

Mawby, R., Worrall, A., Heath, G. and Hope, T. (2002) The Stoke-on-Trent Targeted Policing Initiative Prolific Offender Project evaluation report, unpublished: Keele: Keele University

McGuire, J. (ed.) (1995) *What Works: Reducing Reoffending*. New York, NY: Wiley and Sons

McLaughlin, E. (2001) 'Administrative criminology,' in E. McLaughlin and J. Muncie *Sage Dictionary of Criminology*. London: Sage

McLaughlin, E. and Muncie, J. (2001) *Sage Dictionary of Criminology*. London: Sage

Mead, G.H. (1934) *Mind, Self and Society*. Chicago, IL: Chicago University Press

Melossi, D. (ed.) (1998a) *The Sociology of Punishment*. Aldershot: Ashgate

Melossi, D. (1998b) 'Introduction,' in D. Melossi (ed.) *The Sociology of Punishment*. Aldershot: Ashgate

Melossi, D. and Pavarini, M. (1977) *The Prison and the Factory*. Basingstoke: Macmillan

Messerschmidt, J. (1986) *Capitalism, Patriarchy and Crime*. Totowa, NJ: Rowan and Littlefield

Mills, C. Wright (1970/58) *The Sociological Imagination*. London: Penguin

Mirrlees-Black, C. (1999) *Domestic Violence: Findings from a New British Crime Survey Self-Completion Questionnaire*, Home Office Research Study 191. London: Home Office

Morgan, R. (1997) 'Prisons,' in R. Morgan, M. Maguire and R. Reiner (eds) *The Oxford Handbook of Criminology*. Oxford: Clarendon Press

Morgan, R. and Carlen, P. (1999) 'Regulating crime control,' in P. Carlen and R. Morgan, (eds) *Crime Unlimited?* Basingstoke: Macmillan

Morris, A. Wilkinson, C. Tisi, A. Woodrow, J and Rockley, A. (1995) *Managing the Needs of Female Prisoners*. London: Home Office

Motz, A. (2001) *The Psychology of Female Violence: Crimes Against the Body*. Hove: Brunner-Routledge

Muncer, S., Campbell, A., Jeris, V. and Lewis, R. (2001) ' "Ladettes", social representations and aggression', *Sex Roles*, 44(1/2): 33–44

Murray, C. (1994) *The Emerging British Underclass*. London: Institute of Economic Affairs

Nacro (1991) *A Fresh Start for Women Prisoners*. London: Nacro

Nacro (1993) *Women Leaving Prison*. London: Nacro

Nacro (1996) *Women Prisoners: Towards a New Millennium*. London: Nacro

Nacro (2001) *Women Beyond Bars*. London: Nacro

Naffine, N. (1990) *Law and the Sexes*. London: Allen and Unwin

Naffine, N. (1997) *Feminism and Criminology*. Cambridge: Polity Press

NAPO (1989) *Punishment, Custody and Community: The Response of NAPO*. London: NAPO

Nelkin, D. (1989) 'Discipline and punish: Some notes on the margin'. *Howard Journal* 28(4): 345–54

Nellis, M. (2003) 'Electronic monitoring and the future of the probation service', in W.H. Chui and M. Nellis (eds) *Moving Probation Forward: Evidence, Arguments and Practice.* Harlow: Pearson Longman

O'Dwyer, J. and Carlen, P. (1985) 'Josie: Surviving Holloway and other women's prisons', in P. Carlen, J. Hicks, J. O'Dwyer, D. Christina, and C. Tchaikovsky, (1985) *Criminal Women.* Cambridge: Polity Press
O'Dwyer, J. Wilson, J. and Carlen, P. (1987) 'Women's imprisonment in England, Wales and Scotland: Recurring issues', in P. Carlen and A. Worrall (eds) *Gender, Crime and Justice.* Buckingham: Open University Press
Owen, B. (1998) *In the Mix: Struggle and Survival in a Women's Prison.* Albany, NY: State University of New York Press

Padell, U. and Stevenson, P. (eds) (1988) *Insiders: Women's Experiences of Prison.* London: Virago
Pantazis, C. (1999) 'The criminalization of female poverty', in S. Watson and L. Doyal (eds) *Engendering Social Policy.* Buckingham: Open University Press.
Parent, D. and Snyder, B. (1999) *Police-corrections partnership.* National Institute of Justice Issues and Practices, Washington, DC: US Department of Justice
Peckham, A. (1985) *A Woman in Custody.* London: Fontana
Pellegrini, A. M. (1997) 'Children coping with a father in prison: Psychological tasks', in R. Shaw (ed.) *The Child and the Prison.* Durham: North Eastern Prison After Care Society
Petersilia, J. and Turner, S. (1995) 'Evaluating Intensive Supervision Probation and Parole' in M. Tonry and K. Hamilton (eds) *Intermediate Sanctions in Overcrowded Times.* Boston, MA: Northeastern University Press
Phillips, C. and Brown, D. (1998) *Entry into the Criminal Justice System: A Survey of Police Arrests and their Outcomes.* Home Office Research Study 185. London: Home Office
Phoenix, J. (1999) *Making Sense of Prostitution.* London: Methuen
Pickering, S. and Alder, C. (2000) 'Challenging reforms for feminists and the criminal justice system', in D. Chappell and P. Wilson (eds) *Crime and the Criminal Justice System in Australia: 2000 and Beyond.* Sydney: Butterworths
Player, E. (1994) *Women's Prisons After Woolf.* London: Routledge
Police Executive Research Forum (1990) *Repeat offender programs for law enforcement.* Washington, DC: Police Executive Research Forum
Pollak, O. (1950) *The Criminality of Women.* Philadelphia, PA: University of Pennsylvania Press
Power, M. (1997) *Audit Society.* Oxford: Oxford University Press
Pratt, J. (2000) 'The return of the wheelbarrow men, or the arrival of postmodern penalty?', *British Journal of Criminology*, 40(1): 127–45.
Pratt, J. (2002) *Punishment and Civilisation.* London: Sage
Prison Reform Trust (2000a) *Justice for Women: The Need for Reform*, (The Wedderburn Report). London: Prison Reform Trust

Probation Studies Unit (2000) *Draft report on the retrospective study of the Hereford and Worcester Probation Service Women's Programme.* unpublished report, University of Oxford Centre for Criminological Research

Rafter, N. (1985) *Partial Justice: Women in State Prisons 1800–1935.* Boston, MA: North Eastern University Press

Rafter, N. (1992) *Partial Justice: Women, Prison and Social Control.* New Brunswick, NJ: Transaction Publishers

Rafter, N. and Stanley, D. (1999) *Prisons in America: A Reference Handbook.* Santa Barbara, CA: ABC Clio

Ramsey, M. (2003) *Prisoners' Drug Use and Treatment: Seven Studies,* Findings 186. London: Home Office

Raynor, P. and Vanstone, M. (2002) *Understanding Community Penalties: Probation, Policy and Social Change.* Buckingham: Open University Press

Rex, S. (2000) 'Beyond cognitive behaviouralism? Reflections on the effectiveness literature.' Paper presented at the 24th Cropwood Conference, Future Directions for Community Penalties, University of Cambridge

Roberts, C. (1987) *First Evaluation Report, Young Offender Project.* Department of Social and Administrative Studies, University of Oxford

Roberts, J. and Domurad, F. (1995) 'Re-engineering probation: Lessons from New York City', *Vista,* 1(1): 59–68, Worcester: Association of Chief Officers of Probation

Roberts, J. (2002) 'Women-centred: The West Mercia community-based programme for women offenders,' in P. Carlen (ed.) *Women and Punishment: The Struggle for Justice.* Collumpton: Willan

Roberts, M. (2001) 'Proper punishment, public confidence and community sentences',*Community Safety* 8: 13–15

Robinson, J. (2002) *Pandora's Daughters: The Secret History of Enterprising Women.* London: Constable

Rock, P. (1996) *Reconstructing a Woman's Prison: The Holloway Redevelopment Project, 1968–88.* Oxford: Clarendon Press

Rosenbaum, M. (1983) *Women on Heroin.* New Brunswick, NJ: Rutgers, University Press

Rothman, D. (1980) *Conscience and Convenience: The Asylum and its Alternatives in Progressive America.* Boston, MA: Little Brown

Rutherford, A. (1996) *Transforming Criminal Policy.* Winchester: Waterside Press

Sapsford, R. (1983) *Life Sentence Prisoners: Reaction, Response and Change.* Buckingham: Open University Press

Save the Children Fund (1989) *Prison Visitors' Centres: A Response to the Needs of Prisoners' Families.* London: Save the Children Fund

Schutz, A. (1962) *Collected Papers.* The Hague, NL: Martinus Nijhoff

Seear, N. and Player, E. (1986) *Women in the Penal System.* London: Howard League

Shaw, M. and Hannah-Moffat, K. (2000) 'Gender, diversity and risk assessment in Canadian corrections', *Probation Journal*, 47(3): 163–72

Sim, J. (1990) *Medical Power in Prisons*. Buckingham: Open University Press

Sim, J., Ruggiero, V. and Ryan, M. (1995) 'Punishment in Europe: Perceptions and Commonalities', in V. Ruggiero, M. Ryan and J. Sim (eds) *Western European Penal Systems*. London: Sage

Sim, J. (2001) 'Abolitionism', in E. McLaughlin and J. Muncie *Sage Dictionary of Criminology*. London: Sage

Smart, C. (1976) Women, Crime and Criminology: A Feminist Critique. London: Routledge and Kegan Paul

Smart, C. (1989a) *Feminism and the Power of Law*. London: Routledge

Smart, C. (1989b) Review of 'Women, crime and poverty' *Journal of Law and Society*, 16(4): 521–4

Smart, C. (1990) 'Feminist Approaches to Criminology or Post modern woman meets atavistic man', in L. Gelsthorpe and A. Morris (eds) *Feminist Perspectives in Criminology*. Buckingham: Open University Press

Smart, C. (1992) *Regulating Womanhood*. London: Routledge

Smart, C. (1995) *Law, Crime and Sexuality: Essays in Feminism*. London: Sage

Smartt, U. (1996) 'Prisons in England and Germany – a comparative study of the two systems', in J. Reynolds and U. Smartt (eds) *Prison Policy and Practice*. HMP Leyhill: Prison Service Journal

Smith, A. (1962) *Women in Prison*. London: Stevens

Smith, C. (2000) 'Healthy prisons: A contradiction in terms?', *The Howard Journal*, 39(4): 339–53.

Smith, C. and Wincup, E. (2000) 'Breaking in: Researching criminal justice institutions for women', in R. King and E. Wincup (eds) *Doing Research on Crime and Justice*. Oxford: Oxford University Press

Snider, L. (2003) 'Constituting the punishable woman', *British Journal of Criminology*, 43(2): 354–78

Social Exclusion Unit (2002) *Reducing Re-offending by Ex-prisoners*. London: Cabinet Office

Solicitor General Canada (2001) *Corrections and Conditional Release Overview*. Ottawa: Solicitor General Canada

Sparks, R. Bottoms, A. and Hay, W. (1996) *Prisons and the Problem of Order*. Oxford: Clarendon Press

Stenson, K. and Sullivan, R. (2001) (eds) *Crime, Risk and Justice: The Politics of Crime Control in Liberal Democracies*. Cullompton: Willan

Stern, V. (1998) *A Sin Against the Future: Imprisonment in the World*. London: Penguin

Stewart, C. (2000) 'Responding to the needs of women in prison', *Prison Service Journal*, 132: 41–3

Sudbury, J. (2002) 'Selling black bodies: Black women in the global prison industrial complex', *Feminist Review*, 70(1): 57–74

Sykes, G. (1958/1971) *Society of Captives: A Study of a Maximum Security Prison*. Princeton, NJ: Princeton University Press

Task Force on Federally Sentenced Women (TFFSW) (1990) *Creating Choices – The Report of The Task Force On Federally Sentenced Women.* Ottawa: Solicitor General of Canada

Taylor, I., Walton, P. and Young, J. (1985) *Critical Criminology.* London: Routledge and Kegan Paul

Thomas, D.A. (2002) Case comment, *Crim. L. R. 2002,* April, 331–3

Thomas, W.I. (1923) *The Unadjusted Girl.* Boston, MA: Little Brown and Co.

Turnbull, P.J., McSweeney, T., Webster, R., Edmunds, M. and Hough, M. (2000) *Drug Treatment and Testing Orders: Final Report,* Home Office Research Study 212. London: Home Office

US Department of Justice (1988) *Intensive Supervision Probation and Parole Program Brief.* Washington, DC: Bureau of Justice Assistance

Vanstone, M. (2000) 'Cognitive-behavioural work with offenders in the UK: A history of influential endeavour', *The Howard Journal,* 39(2): 171–83

Van Wormer, K.S. and Bartollas, C. (2000) *Women and the Criminal Justice System.* Boston, MA: Allyn and Bacon

von Hirsch, A. (1986) *Past or Future Crimes: Deservedness and Dangerousness in the Sentencing of Criminals.* Manchester: Manchester University Press

Wacquant, L. (2003) 'Towards a dictatorship over the poor?' *Punishment and Society,* 5(2): 197–206

Walker, S. and Worrall, A. (2000) 'Life as a woman: The gendered pains of indeterminate imprisonment', *Prison Service Journal,* 132: 27–37

Walklate, S. (2001) *Gender, Crime and Criminal Justice.* Cullompton: Willan

Walmsley, R. (2002) *World Prison Population List,* 3rd edn. Research Findings 166. London: Home Office

Walters, R. (2003) *Deviant Knowledge.* Cullompton: Willan

Ward, D. and Kassebaum, G. (1966) *Women's Prison: Sex and Social Structure.* London: Weidenfeld and Nicolson

Weber, M. (ed. Talcott Parsons) (1947) *The Theory of Economic and Social Organization.* New York, NY: Oxford University Press

Whyte, W.F. (1943) *Street Corner Society,* (esp. Appendix). Chicago, IL: University of Chicago Press

Will, R. (1995) 'Intensive supervision probation', in M. Tonry and K. Hamilton (eds) *Intermediate Sanctions in Overcrowded Times.* Boston, MA: Northeastern University Press

Women's National Commission (1991) *Women in Prison.* London: Cabinet Office

Woodrow, J. (1992) 'Mothers inside, children outside', in R. Shaw (ed.) *Prisoners' Children – What are the Issues?* London: Routledge

Woodward, R. (1999) 'Life risk assessment', in E. Cullen and T. Newell *Murderers and Life Imprisonment.* Winchester: Waterside Press

Woolf, Lord (1991) *Prison Disturbances April 1990.* London: HMSO

Woolf, V. (1989/1929) *A Room of One's Own.* London: Grafton

Worrall, A. (1981) 'Out of place: Female offenders in court', *Probation Journal*, 28(3): 90–3

Worrall, A. (1990) *Offending Women: Female Lawbreakers and the Criminal Justice System*. London: Routledge

Worrall, A. (1997) *Punishment in the Community*. Harlow: Longman

Worrall, A. (1998) 'Women in prison: Some international reflections', in *Sister-in-Law*, journal of the Enid Russell Society. Murdoch University, Western Australia, 91–118

Worrall, A. (2000a) 'Failure is the new success', *Prison Service Journal*, 132: 52–4

Worrall, A. (2000b) 'Globalisation, the millenium and the prison, *Theoretical Criminology*. 4(3): 391–97

Worrall, A. (2001) 'Nasty little madams: Changing perceptions of girls' violence', unpublished paper given to 'Still Standing Strong Conference' University of Melbourne: February

Worrall, A. (2002a) 'Rendering them Punishable', in P. Carlen (ed.) *Women and Punishment: The Struggle for Justice*. Cullompton: Willan

Worrall, A. (2002b) 'Missed opportunities? The probation service and women offenders', in D. Ward, J. Scott and M. Lacey (eds) *Probation: Working for Justice* 2nd edn. Oxford: Oxford University Press

Worrall, A. (2003) *Cognitive Skills Programs in Western Australian Prisons – a Discussion Paper*. Perth: Office of the Inspector of Custodial Services

Worrall, A. (2004a) 'Twisted sisters, ladettes and the new penology: The social construction of "violent girls"', in C. Alder, and A. Worrall, *Girls' Violence*. New York, NY: SUNY Press

Worrall, A. (2004b) 'What works and the globalisation of punishment talk', in G. Mair (ed.) *What Matters in Probation*. Cullompton: Willan

Worrall, A., Mawby, R., Heath, G. and Hope, T. (2003) *Intensive Supervision and Monitoring Projects*. Home Office Online Reports 42/03. London: Home Office

Wyner, R. (2003) *From the Inside: Dispatches from a Women's Prison*. London: Aurum Press

Young, J. (1986) ' The failure of radical criminology: The need for a radical realism', in R. Matthews, and J. Young, *Confronting Crime*. London: Sage

Young, J. (2002) 'Critical criminology in the twenty-first century: Critique, irony and the always unfinished', in K. Carrington and R. Hogg *Critical Criminology*. Cullompton: Willan

Zatz, M.S. (2002) 'The convergence of race, ethnicity, gender and class on court decision-making: Looking toward the 21st century', in *Criminal Justice 2000*, vol. 3. Washington, DC: US Department of Justice.

Zedner, L. (1991) *Women, Crime and Custody in Victorian England*. Oxford: Clarendon Press

Index